Ford Anglia 105E Owners Workshop Manual

S. F. Page

Photography by J. H. Haynes

Models covered
All Saloon, Estate and Van models
997 cc and 1198 cc

ISBN 978 0 85733 627 9

®© Haynes Group Limited 1967, 1986

(001-8M1)

THE BOOK

Haynes Group Limited
Haynes North America, Inc

www.haynes.com

The manufacturer's authorised representative in the EU for product safety is:

HaynesPro BV
Stationsstraat 79 F, 3811MH Amersfoort, The Netherlands
gpsr@haynes.co.uk

ACKNOWLEDGEMENTS

It would not have been possible to produce such a detailed work without the generous assistance of Ford of Britain, who, through supplying us with technical data and a number of illustrations, have made a considerable contribution to the accuracy of this publication. However it must be made clear that this manual is not produced by Ford of Britain and that they have no responsibility for it.

Although every care has been taken to ensure all the data in this manual is correct, bearing in mind that manufacturers' current practice is to make small alterations and design changes without reclassifying the model, no liability can be accepted for damage, loss or injury caused by any errors or omissions in the information given.

Thanks are due to Mrs. D. Kean who produced some of the line drawings; to Castrol Ltd. for the lubrications chart; to the Champion Spark Plug Co. Ltd.; to Mr. R. White; Mr. J. Mead; and Mr. G. Fursey.

Special thanks are due to Mr. L. Tooze and Mr. S. Lydford whose ready co-operation, experience, and advice was a great help in the compilation of photographs for this manual.

PHOTOGRAPHIC CAPTIONS & CROSS REFERENCES

For ease of reference this book is divided into numbered chapters, sections and paragraphs. The title of each chapter is self explanatory. The sections comprise the main headings within the chapter. The paragraphs appear within each section.

The captions to the majority of photographs are given within the paragraphs of the relevant section to avoid repitition. These photographs bear the same number as the sections and paragraphs to which they refer. The photograph always appears in the same Chapter as its paragraph. For example if looking through Chapter Ten it is wished to find the caption for photograph 9 . 4 refer to section 9 and then read paragraph 4.

To avoid repitition once a procedure has been described it is not normally repeated. If it is necessary to refer to a procedure already given this is done by quoting the original Chapter, Section and sometimes paragraph number.

The reference is given thus: Chapter No. /Section No. Para. No. For example Chapter 2, Section 6 would be given as : Chapter 2/6. Chapter 2, Section 6, paragraph 5 would be given as Chapter 2/6. 5. If more than one section is involved the reference would be written : Chapter 2/6 to 7 o r where the section is not consecutive 2/6 and 9. To refer to several paragraphs within a section the reference is given thus : Chapter 2/6. 2 to 4.

Fig. 1 THE FORD ANGLIA DE LUXE SALOON IN DUAL TONE FINISH.

Contents

GENERAL INFORMATION

Wheelbase	$90\frac{1}{2}$ ins.	Height	56 ins.
Front Track	46 ins.	Ground Clearance	$6\frac{1}{4}$ ins.
Rear Track	46 ins.	Width	57 ins.
Length	154 ins.	Weight (standard)	1625 lbs.
Weight distribution	56F/44R%	Weight (De Luxe)	1645 lbs.

ROAD TEST AND PERFORMANCE DATA

Maximum speed: 78 m.p.h.   In second gear: 39 m.p.h.

In third gear: 68 m.p.h.   In first gear: 23 m.p.h.

Normal cruising speed: 65 m.p.h.

N. B. The speeds indicated on the car speedometer are likely to be 6% to 9% greater than the true speeds above, due to speedometer error.

ACCELERATION (37 b.h.p. engine)

   0 to 30 m.p.h. ...   7.0 secs.

   0 to 40 m.p.h. ...   11.5 secs.

   0 to 50 m.p.h. ...   18.2 secs.

   0 to 60 m.p.h. ...   30.0 secs.

   0 to 70 m.p.h. ...   49.0 secs.

ACCELERATION (39 b.h.p. engine)

   0 to 30 m.p.h. ...   6.6 secs.

   0 to 40 m.p.h. ...   10.9 secs.

   0 to 50 m.p.h. ...   17.5 secs.

   0 to 60 m.p.h. ...   28.0 secs.

   0 to 70 m.p.h. ...   46.0 secs.

ACCELERATION IN TOP GEAR

   10 to 30 m.p.h. ...   14.0 secs.

   30 to 50 m.p.h. ...   15.5 secs.

   50 to 70 m.p.h. ...   28.0 secs.

ROAD SPEEDS

At 1,000 r.p.m. in top gear 15.7 m.p.h.

At 5,000 r.p.m. in top gear 78.5 m.p.h.

FUEL CONSUMPTION

At steady speed of 30 m.p.h. ...   51 m.p.g.

At steady speed of 50 m.p.h ...   46 m.p.g.

At steady speed of 70 m.p.h. ...   29 m.p.g.

Normal overall fuel consumption: 35 to 40 m.p.g. depending on driving methods.

INTRODUCTION

This is a manual for do-it-yourself minded Ford Anglia enthusiasts. It shows how to maintain these cars in first class condition and how to carry out repairs when components become worn or break. Regular and careful maintenance is essential if maximum reliability and minimum wear are to be achieved.

The step-by-step photographs show how to deal with the major components and in conjunction with the text and exploded illustrations should make all the work quite clear - even to the novice who has never previously attemped the more complex job.

Although Anglias are hardwearing and robust it is inevitable that their reliability and performance will decrease as they become older. Repairs and general reconditioning will become necessary if the car is to remain roadworthy. Early models requiring attention are frequently bought by the more impecunious motorist who can least afford the repair prices charged in garages, even though these prices are usually quite fair bearing in mind overheads and the high cost of capital equipment and skilled labour.

It is in these circumstances that this manual will prove to be of maximum assistance, as it is the ONLY workshop manual written from practical experience specially to help Anglia owners.

Manufacturer's official manuals are usually splendid publications which contain a wealth of technical information. Because they are issued primarily to help the manufacturers, authorised dealers and distributors they tend to be written in very technical language, and tend to skip details of certain jobs which are common knowledge to garage mechanics. Owner's workshop manuals are different as they are intended primarily to help the owner.

Owners who intend to do their own maintenance and repairs should have a reasonably comprehensive tool kit. Some jobs require special service tools, but in many instances it is possible to get round their use with a little care and ingenuity. For example a $3\frac{1}{2}$ in. diameter jubilee clip makes a most efficient and cheap piston ring compressor.

Throughout this manual ingenious ways of avoiding the use of special equipment and tools are shown. In some cases the proper tool must be used. Where this is the case a description of the tool and its correct use is included.

When a component malfunctions repairs are becoming more and more a case of replacing the defective item with an exchange rebuilt unit. This is excellent practice when a component is thoroughly worn out, but it is a waste of good money when overall the component is only half worn, and requires the replacement of but a single small item to effect a complete repair. As an example, a non-functioning dynamo can frequently be repaired quite satisfactorily just by fitting new brushes.

A further function of this manual is to show the owner how to examine malfunctioning parts; determine what is wrong, and then how to make the repair.

Given the time, mechanical do-it-yourself aptitude, and a reasonable collection of tools, this manual will show the enthusiastic owner how to maintain and repair his car really economically.

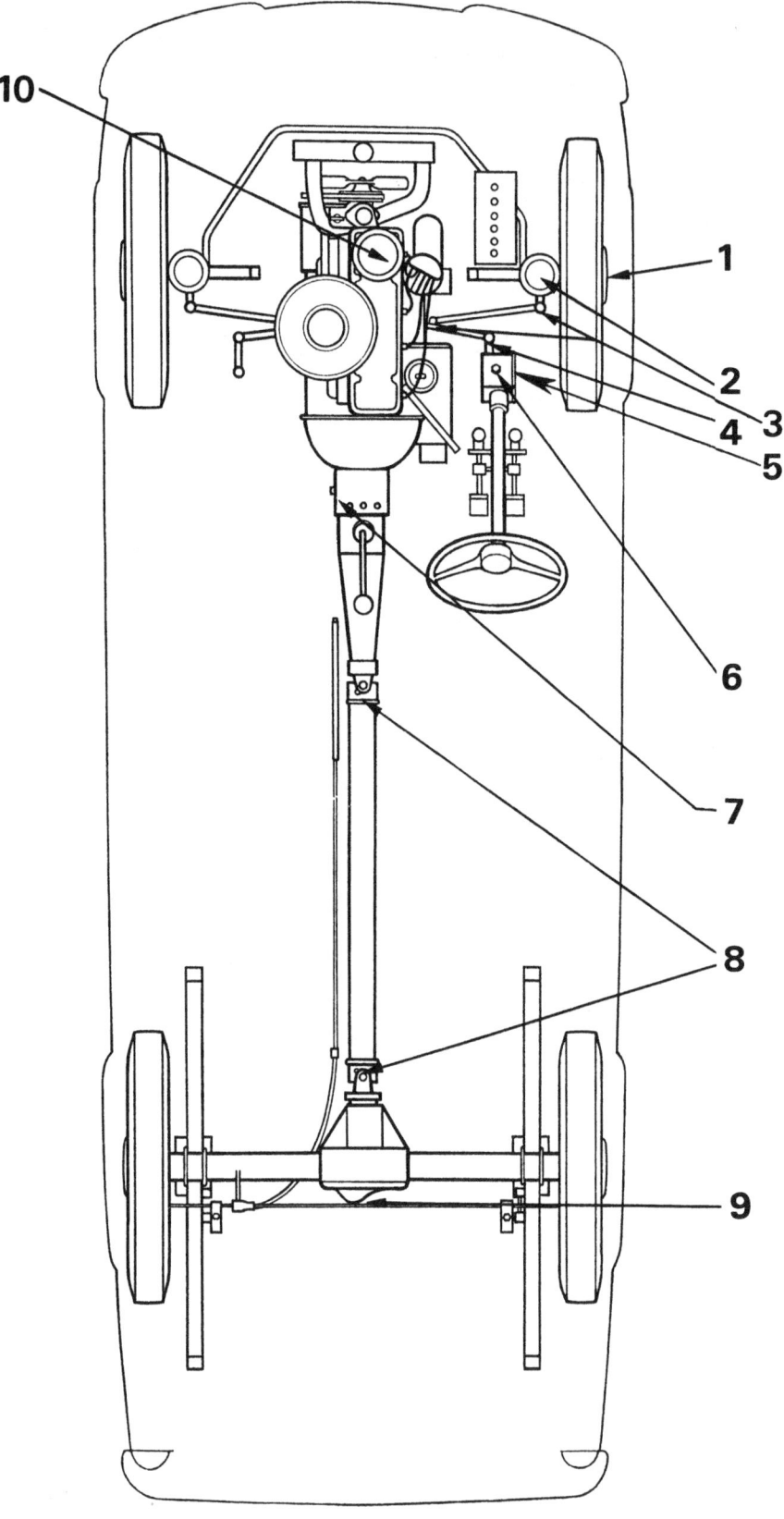

Fig. 2 LUBRICATION CHART FOR THE FORD ANGLIA 105E.

1 Front wheel bearings.   2 Track control arm — 2 nipples.   3 Track rod — 4 nipples.   4 Idler arm — 2 nipples.   5 Steering drop arm — 1 nipple.   6 Steering gear filler.   7 Gearbox filler plug.   8 Universal joint lubricating nipples.   9 Rear axle filler plug.   10 Oil filler.

ROUTINE MAINTENANCE

The maintenance instructions listed below are basically those recommended by the manufacturer. They are supplemented by additional maintenance tasks which, through practical experience, the author recommends should be carried at the intervals suggested.

The additional tasks are indicated by an asterisk, and are primarily of a preventative nature in that they will assist in eliminating the unexpected failure of a component due to fair wear and tear.

The levels of the engine oil, radiator cooling water, windscreen washer water, and the battery electrolyte, should be checked weekly, or more frequently if experience dictates this necessary. If not checked at home it is advantageous to regularly use the same garage for this work.

Every 1,000 miles

1. Fill a grease gun with Castrolease L.M. or a similar recommended multi-purpose grease and thoroughly lubricate the following through the appropriate grease nipple which should first be wiped clean. Give 2-3 strokes of the grease gun to:-
   a) 2 nipples on the track control arm
   b) 4 nipples on the track rod
   c) 2 nipples on the idler arm
   d) 1 nipple on the steering drop arm.
2. Check the level of the hydraulic brake fluid in the clutch and brake master cylinder reservoir and top up as necessary with Castrol Girling Brake and Clutch Fluid (Amber) which conforms to the necessary Ford specification.
3. Lubricate with Castrolite or a good S.A.E. 20 oil the door hinges and locks, bonnet hinges, accelerator linkage bearings, and the handbrake clevises.
4. Remove the distributor cap, pull off the rotor arm and apply two drops of engine oil to the head of the large screw in the centre of the distributor. This lubricates the shaft bearings. Allow three drops of oil past the cam to the automatic timing mechanism. Lubricate the four-sided cam by smearing

a faint trace of grease over it. Apply a tiny spot of oil to the moving contact breaker pivot pin. Any excess might get on the points and create misfiring.
5. Check the clutch clearance at the slave cylinder and adjust as necessary.
6. Remove the plug on the top of the steering box and add Castrol Hypoy Gear Oil until the level reaches the filler plug hole. Then replace the plug.
7. Fill a grease gun with Castrolease L.M. or a similar recommended multi purpose grease and thoroughly lubricate the 2 nipples on the universal joints giving 3-4 strokes of the grease gun. Some later models are fitted with sealed universal joints which do not require lubrication.
8. Check the level of the oil in the gearbox and replenish if necessary by adding Castrol Hypoy light gear oil or similar through the combined level and filler plug. Do not overfill, so allow any surplus oil to drain away before replacing the plug.
9. Check the level of oil in the rear axle and replenish, if necessary, to the bottom of the filler plug orifice with Castrol Hypoy gear oil.

Every 5,000 miles

1. Run the engine until it has reached its normal working temperature. Then remove the oil drain plug and drain the oil into a container with a capacity of at least 4 pints. Renew the oil filter element and refill the sump with 4 pints and the oil filter bowl with $\frac{1}{2}$ pint of Castrolite 10W-30. On older engines it may be advantageous to use a thicker oil such as Castrol GTX 20W - 50.
2. Remove the oil filler cap and clean away any accumulation of foreign matter from the gauze. Wash the gauze-type cap in petrol, thoroughly dry, dip in Castrolite and shake out surplus oil before replacing.
3. Inject 3 drops of Castrolite through the hole in the centre of the rear of the dynamo which gives access to the rear bearing.
4. Remove the filler plug from the rear shock

absorbers and top up as necessary to the level of the filler plug orifice with the approved fluid.

5. With the car unladen and on level ground check the level of the gearbox oil and top up if necessary to the bottom of the plug hole with approved fluid.

6. Spray or brush the rear springs with Castrol Penetrating Oil.

7. Clean the air cleaners as described in Chapter 6/10

8. Attend to the front wheel bearings by removing the hub and dust caps, cleaning out the old grease and repacking with Castrolease LM.

9. If wished the oil in the gearbox and rear axle may be changed but this is no longer essential and later models of the Anglia will be found to have no drain plug on the rear axle.

10. Check the condition of the contact breaker points, clean and regap them, and if necessary, fit a new set and check the timing and advance and retard mechanism. See Chapter 4/3 for further details.

11. Examine the exhaust system for holes and leaks and replace defective components as necessary. *

12. Wax polish the body and also the chromium plating. Force wax polish into any joins in the bodywork to help prevent rust formation. *

13. Balance the front wheels to eliminate steering vibration as necessary. *

14. Check and adjust the steering 'toe-in' of the front wheels.

15. Examine the fan belt and adjust as necessary.

16. Check the battery cell specific gravity readings and clean the terminals.

17. Check the condition of the heater and cooling system hoses and replace as necessary. *

18. Check the fuel lines and the union joints for leaks and replace defective parts as necessary. *

19. Remove and clean the filter in the fuel pump and clean and regap the sparking plugs.

20. Check and adjust the brakes. See Chapter 9/3 and 4 for further details.

21. Check and if necessary tighten the 'U' bolts on the rear suspension.

Every 10,000 miles

1. In addition to the maintenance tasks previously listed carry out the following operations:-

2. Remove the carburettor float chamber, empty any sediment present, check the condition of the needle valve, clean and refit.

3. Remove the speedometer cable, clean, and lightly lubricate the inner cable with Castrolease LM. or similar. When reassembling the inner cable should be withdrawn approximately 8 in. and the surface grease wiped off. This is so none will work its way into the speedometer head.

4. Steam clean the underside of the body and clean the engine and engine compartment. *

5. Remove the sparking plugs, and fit new ones, correctly gapped.

6. Inspect the ignition leads for cracks and perishing and replace as necessary. *

7. Remove the brake drums, blow out the dust, and inspect the linings for wear.

8. Examine the dynamo brushes, replace them if worn, and clean the commutator. See page 146 for further details.

9. Renew the windscreen wiper blades. *

10. Check the headlamp bulbs and renew them if slightly blackened or if the element sags.

Every 20,000 miles

1. In addition to the maintenance tasks listed previously carry out the following operations:-

2. Check and adjust any loose play in the steering gear.

3. Examine the ball joints and hub bearings for wear and replace as necessary.

4. Check the tightness of the battery earth lead on the bodywork. *

5. Renew the condenser in the distributor.

6. Remove the starter motor, examine the brushes replace as necessary and clean the commutator and starter drive.

7. Test the cylinder compressions, and if necessary remove the cylinder head, decarbonise, grind the valves and fit new valve springs. *

CHAPTER ONE

ENGINE

CONTENTS

SPECIFICATIONS

The engine originally fitted to the 105E Anglia introduced in September 1959 was of 997 c.c. capacity. Production continued until January 1968 when the Anglia was superceded by the Ford Escort. In July 1962 the 123E 1198 c.c. engine was introduced and was made available as an alternative to the 105E engine in all the models being produced including the vans. Both the 105E and 123E engines are virtually identical, the increase in capacity of the latter being obtained by lengthening the stroke.

ENGINE

ENGINE SPECIFICATION & DATA - 997 c.c. TYPE 105E

Engine:

Type	4 cylinder-in-line with O.H.V. pushrod operated
Bore	3.1875 ins. (80.96 mm.)
Stroke	1.906 ins. (48.41 mm.)
Cubic Capacity	60.84 cu. ins. (996.6 c.c.)
Compression Ratio: High	8.9 : 1 (standard)
Low	7.5 : 1 (optional)
Oversize bore	1st. .020 ins. (.508 mm.)
	2nd. .030 ins. (.762 mm.)
Maximum Torque	52.5 lbs/ft. at 2,700 r.p.m. (standard C.R.)
	50.0 lbs/ft. at 2,700 r.p.m. (optional C.R.)
Maximum B.H.P.	39.0 at 5,000 r.p.m. (standard C.R.)
	37.0 at 5,000 r.p.m. (optional C.R.)
Firing Order	1, 2, 4, 3.
Location of No.1 cylinder	Next to radiator
Engine Mountings	3 point suspension on rubber mountings

Camshaft & Camshaft Bearings

Material	Special Ford cast alloy iron
Bearings	3 steel backed white metal
Camshaft endfloat	0.002 to 0.007 ins. (0.051 to 0.178 mm.)
Journal diameter	1.56 ins. (36.92 mm.)
Bearing Lengths - Front	0.79 ins. (20.07 mm.)
Centre	0.68 ins. (17.27 mm.)
Rear	0.79 ins. (20.07 mm.)
Camshaft thrust plate thickness ...	0.176 to 0.178 ins. (4.47 to 4.52 mm.)

Connecting Rods, Small & Big-end Bearings

Length between centres	4.611 to 4.612 ins. (117.12 to 117.14 mm.)
Big-end Bearings	4 steel backed copper lead or copper bronze with lead overlay
Side clearance	0.0005 to 0.0022 ins. (0.0127 to 0.057 mm.)
Small-end Bearings	Steel backed bronze bush
Diameter	0.812 ins. (20.62 mm.)

Crankshaft & Main Bearings

Main bearings	3 steel backed white metal liners
Main bearing clearance	0.0005 to 0.002 ins. (0.0127 to 0.051 mm.)
Main bearing length	1.00 ins. (2.54 cm.)
Crankshaft endfloat	0.003 to 0.011 ins. (0.076 to 0.279 mm.)
Side Thrust	Taken by thrust washers located on either side of the centre main bearing.
Undersizes available	-.010 ins. (-.254 mm.) -.020 ins. (-.508 mm.)
	-.030 ins. (-.762 mm.) -.040 ins. (-1.02 mm.)

Cylinder Block

Type	Cast integral with top half of crankcase
Water Jackets	Full length

Cylinder Head

Type	Cast iron with vertical valves. Separate inlet and exhaust ports.
Combustion chamber	Fully machined

Gudgeon Pin

Type	Fully floating. Held by circlips.
Fit to piston	Hand push fit
Fit in connecting rod	Hand push fit

ENGINE

Lubrication System ... ...

    Type ... ...   Pressure feed. Pressure fed bearings-Main, cam-shaft and connecting rods. Reduced pressure to rocker shaft. Piston pin and cylinder wall lubrication - splash.

    Oil Filter ... ...   Full flow

    Capacity of oil filter   ... ... $\frac{1}{2}$ pint

    Crankcase ventilation   ... ...   Directed flow via road draught tube on right hand side of engine.

    Grade of oil: Summer   ... ...   S.A.E. 20 or 20W

                Winter   ... ...   S.A.E. 20 or 20W

    Sump capacity ... ...   4 pints

    Oil pump: Type ... ...   Eccentric bi-rotor

    Oil pump relief pressure ... ...   35 to 40 lbs/sq.in. (2.46 to 2.81 Kg/sq.cm.)

    Oil pressure warning light comes on at   5 to 7 lbs/sq.in. or lower

    Normal oil pressure... ... ...   25 to 40 lbs/sq.in.

Pistons

    Type ... ...   Solid skirt, autothermic aluminium alloy

    No. of rings   ... ...   Three

    Piston fit ... ...   8 to 11 lbs. (3.63 to 4.99 kg.) pull on a 0.0015 in. (0.038 mm.) feeler blade 0.5 in. (12.7mm.) wide.

    Piston oversizes available   ... ...   +.010 ins. (+.254 mm.)., +.020 ins. (+.508 mm.) +.030 ins. (+.762 mm.)

Piston Rings

    Top compression ring gap   ... ...   0.009 to 0.014 ins. (0.229 to 0.356mm.)

    2nd compression ring gap   ... ...   0.009 to 0.014 ins. (0.229 to 0.356 mm.)

    Oil control ring gap ... ...   0.009 to 0.014 ins. (0.229 to 0.356 mm.)

    Top compression ring to wall pressure   6.4 to 8.3lbs. (2.900 to 3.765 kg.)

    2nd compression ring to wall pressure   6.0 to 8.0 lbs. (2.427 to 3.629 kg.)

    Oil control ring to wall pressure   ...   5.35 to 6.90 lbs. (2.272 to 3.130 kg.)

Tappets

    Type ... ...   Mushroom

Valves

    Head diameter : Inlet   ... ...   1.262 to 1.272 ins. (32.05 to 32.31 mm.)

                 Exhaust ... ...   1.183 to 1.193 ins. (30.04 to 30.30 mm.)

    Valve lift : Inlet   ... ...   0.289 ins. (7.347 mm.)

             Exhaust ... ...   0.290 ins. (7.380 mm.)

    Seat Angle ... ... 45° Inlet & exhaust

    Valve clearance : Inlet   ... ...   0.008 ins. (0.203mm.)Cold. 0.010in. (0.254mm.) hot.

                Exhaust   ... ...   0.018 ins. (0.457mm.)Cold. 0.017in. (0.432mm.)hot.

    Stem diameter : Inlet   ... ...   0.3095 to 0.3105 ins. (7.861 to 7.882mm.)

                Exhaust ... ...   0.3086 to 0.3096 ins. (7.838 to 7.864 mm.)

    Valve stem to guide clearance : Inlet   0.0008 to 0.003 ins. (0.021 to 0.076 mm.)

                          Exhaust   0.0017 to 0.0039 ins. (0.043 to 0.099mm.)

Valve Timing

    Inlet valve opens 10° B.T.D.C.   Exhaust valve opens 44° B.B.D.C.

          closes 50° A.B.D.C.   closes 10° A.T.D.C.

    Valve timing marks   Lines on crankshaft and camshaft sprockets. Notch on crankshaft pulley.

Valve Springs

    Type ... ...   Single valve springs

    Free length   ... ...   1.48 ins. (45.70 mm.)

    Load at fitted length ... ...   45 lbs. (20.41 kg.)

CHAPTER ONE

TORQUE WRENCH SETTINGS

Big end bearing bolts	20 to 25 lbs.ft.
Cylinder head bolts	65 to 70 lbs.ft.
Main bearing bolts	55 to 60 lbs.ft.
Flywheel retaining bolts	45 to 50 lbs.ft.

ENGINE SPECIFICATION & DATA 1198 c.c. TYPE 123

The 1198 cc engine is mechanically similar to the 997 cc and the major differences are listed below:

Stroke	2.29 ins. (58.17 mm.)
Cubic Capacity	73.09 cu.ins. (1,198 c.c.)
Compression Ratio: High	8.7 : 1 (standard) 9.0 : 1 post Oct. 1964
Low	7.3 : 1 (optional)
Maximum Torque	66 lbs.ft. at 2,700 r.p.m. (8.7 : 1 C.R.)
	69 lbs.ft. at 2,700 r.p.m. (9.0 : 1 C.R.)
	62 lbs.ft. at 2,700 r.p.m. (7.3 : 1 C.R.)
Maximum B.H.P.	48.5 at 4,800 r.p.m. (8.7 : 1 C.R.)
	50.0 at 4,900 r.p.m. (9.0 : 1 C.R.)
	46.0 at 4,800 r.p.m. (7.3 : 1 C.R.)

1. GENERAL DESCRIPTION

The Anglia engine is a four-cylinder overhead valve type of either 997 or 1198 c.c. depending on the model and its year of manufacture. It is supported by rubber mountings to reduce noise and vibrations.

Two valves per cylinder are mounted vertically in the cast iron cylinder head and run in cast in valve guides. They are operated by rocker arms and pushrods from the camshaft which is located at the base of the cylinder bores in the right-hand side of the engine (viewed from the clutch end.)

The cylinder head has all eight inlet and exhaust ports on the left-hand side.

The cylinder block and the upper half of the crankcase are cast together. The bottom half of the crankcase consists of a pressed steel sump.

The four pistons are of the autothermic solid skirt type, having fully floating gudgeon pins which are retained by means of end circlips in the piston bosses. Two compression rings and an oil control ring are fitted to all models above the gudgeon pin. Renewable steel backed copper lead, or copper/bronze lead big end bearings are fitted.

At the front of the engine a single row chain drives the camshaft via the camshaft and crankshaft chain wheels. On all models the chain is automatically tensioned by a special tensioner held in place by two bolts.

The camshaft runs in three steel backed white metal bearings, as does also the statically and dynamically balanced crankshaft. Crankshaft end float is controlled by two semicircular thrust washers fitted either side of the centre main bearing.

The centrifugal water pump and radiator cooling fan are driven together with the dynamo from the crankshaft pulley wheel by a rubber/fabric belt. The distributor is mounted towards the front of the right-hand side of the cylinder block and advances and retards the ignition timing by mechanical and vacuum means. The distributor is driven at half crankshaft speed by a short shaft and skew gear from a skew gear on the camshaft. The oil pump is driven from the same skew gear on the camshaft.

2. MAJOR OPERATIONS WITH ENGINE IN PLACE

The following major operations can be carried out to the engine with it in place in the bodyframe:-
1. Removal and replacement of the cylinder head assembly.
2. Removal and replacement of the sump.
3. Removal and replacement of the big end bearings.
4. Removal and replacement of the pistons and connecting rods.
5. Removal and replacement of the timing chain and gears.
6. Removal and replacement of the camshaft.
7. Removal and replacement of the oil pump.

MAJOR OPERATIONS WITH ENGINE REMOVED.

The following major operations can be carried out with the engine out of the bodyframe and on the bench or floor:-
1. Removal and replacement of the main bearings.
2. Removal and replacement of the crankshaft.
3. Removal and replacement of the flywheel.

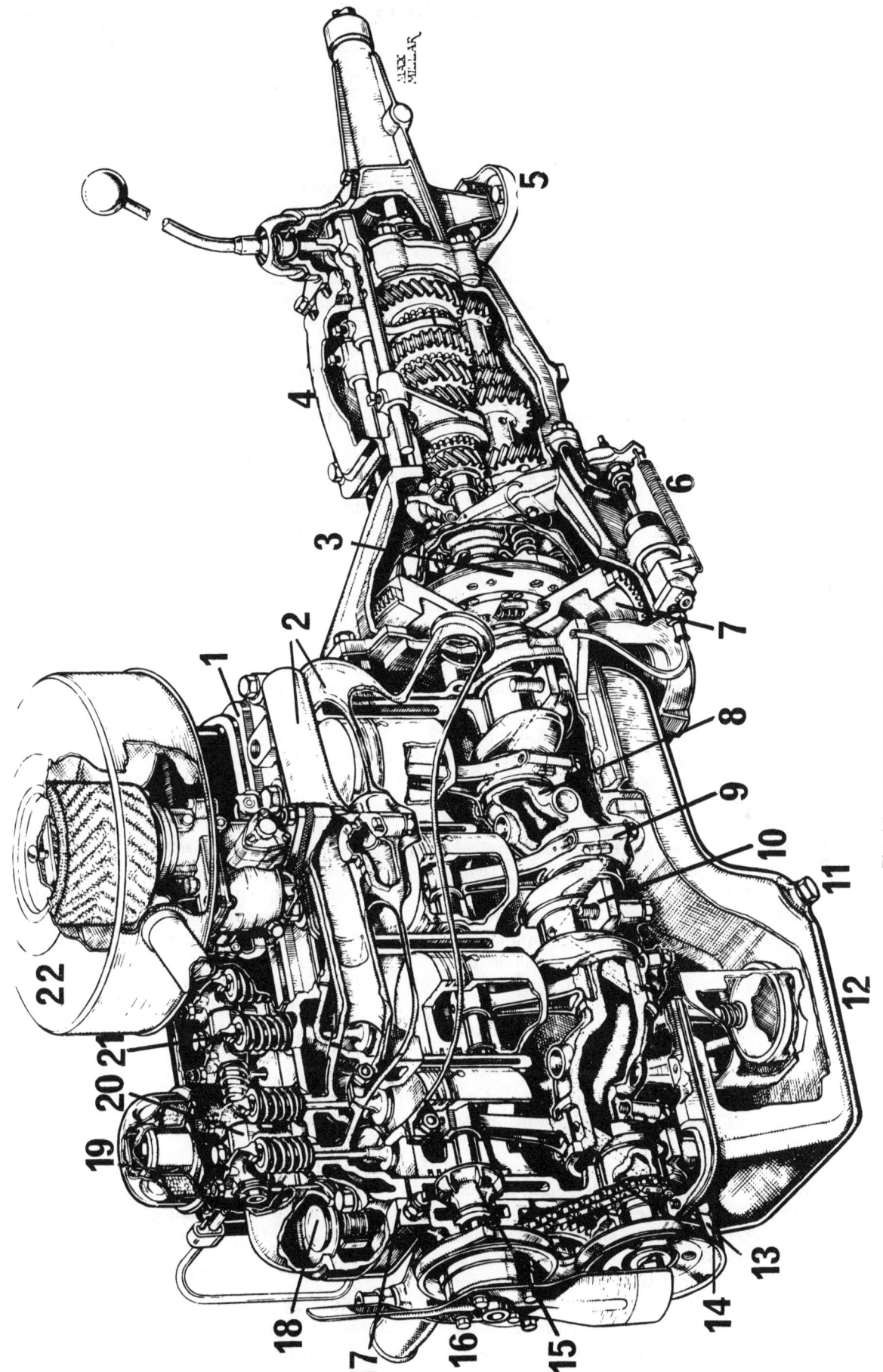

Fig. 1:1 SECTIONED VIEW OF THE ANGLIA 105E ENGINE.

1 Cylinder head. 2 Inlet & exhaust manifolds. 3 Clutch disc. 4 Gearbox. 5 Gearbox support. 6 Slave cylinder return spring. 7 Flywheel. 8 Crankshaft. 9 Big end. 10 Main bearing. 11 Sump plug. 12 Sump. 13 Fan belt. 14 Timing chain. 15 Water pump impellor. 16 Fan. 17 Temperature sender unit. 18 Thermostat. 19 Oil filler/breather cap. 20 Rocker shaft. 21 Valve spring. 22 Air cleaner.

CHAPTER ONE

3. METHODS OF ENGINE REMOVAL

There are two methods of engine removal. The engine can either be removed complete with gearbox, or the engine can be removed without the gearbox by separation at the gearbox bell-housing. Both methods are described below.

4. ENGINE REMOVAL WITHOUT GEARBOX

The engines on all 105E and 123E Anglia models can be removed by the system detailed below. Where slight variations occur between one model and another these are described fully.

On all models the engine is lifted out of the engine compartment. Apart from the normal spanners and other tools required for general mechanical work, lifting tackle is necessary (we recommend the Haltrec unit which costs about £3) and also a jack, preferably of the quick acting hydraulic type.

It is also necessary to raise and support the front of the car for a time so it can be worked on from underneath. Two special support stands or supports such as strong metal beer crates should therefore be to hand.

Practical experience has proved that the engine can be removed easily and quickly in about two hours by adhering to the following sequence of operations:-

1. Turn on the water drain taps found at the bottom of the radiator and on the left-hand side of the cylinder block. Do not drain the water in your garage or the place where you will remove the engine if receptacles are not available to catch the water.

2. Disconnect the battery by removing the earth lead. For safety from electrical shocks it is best to remove the battery from the engine compartment.

3. With a suitable container in position unscrew the drain plug at the bottom right-hand corner of the sump and drain off the engine oil. When the oil is drained screw the plug back in tightly to ensure it is not mislaid. If the engine is to be stripped right down remove the oil filter and empty away the oil.

4. Disconnect the bonnet support, unscrew the pivot bolt, lockwasher and flat washers on each side of the front hinged bonnet and lift the bonnet off.

5. Remove the engine splash shield, and the air cleaner from the carburettor.

6. Unscrew the clip on the lower radiator hose, at the radiator pipe outlet, and remove the hose off the pipe. Unscrew the clip on the upper radiator hose at the thermostat housing outlet pipe, and remove the hose off the pipe. Also disconnect the heater unit inlet

and outlet hoses, (On models fitted with heater units), by releasing the securing clips on the control valve and heater return pipe.

7. Remove the four bolts (two on each side of the radiator) which secures the radiator to the body and lift the radiator out. Close the drain tap.

8. Disconnect the throttle linkage and the choke control cable from the carburettor.

9. Unscrew the two exhaust pipe clamp bolts at the joint between the exhaust manifold and the exhaust pipe. Pull the exhaust pipe away from the manifold.

10. Undo the screws from the flange which hold the heater motor to the heater motor box and remove the heater motor together with the multi-bladed fan from inside the box.

11. Disconnect the cable to the starter motor, unscrew the two retaining bolts and withdraw the motor.

12. Unscrew the single bolt securing the engine breather pipe to the clutch housing and lift off the pipe together with its rubber connector.

13. Unscrew the fuel pipe union and lift away from the fuel pump.

14. Remove the ignition distributor cap, disconnect the high tension lead from the coil centre terminal and the low tension lead from the contact breaker terminal.

15. Remove the splash shield secured to the front of the clutch housing, and undo the bolts securing the clutch housing to the rear of the engine.

16. Leave the clutch operating cylinder connected to its flexible pipe, but remove it from its mounting clamp by unhooking the spring, removing the circlip from the cylinder body and pushing the cylinder out of its location.

17. Position a rope sling around the engine and support the weight on suitable lifting tackle.

18. Remove the two bolts securing each engine mounting at the cross tube, pull the engine forward to free it from the main drive gear and lift the unit upwards from the engine compartment.

5. ENGINE REMOVAL WITH GEARBOX

1. Follow the instructions given in 1/4. 1 to 10, 1/4. 12 to 14 and 1/4. 16 to 17.

2. Follow the instructions given in 6/3. 3 to 6.

3. Place the gearlever in neutral, remove the gaiter, unscrew the gear lever cap, and lift out the lever.

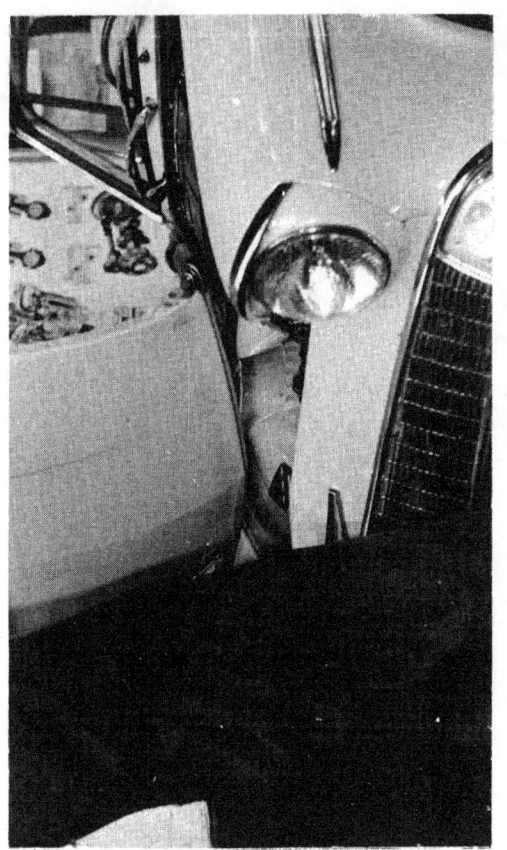

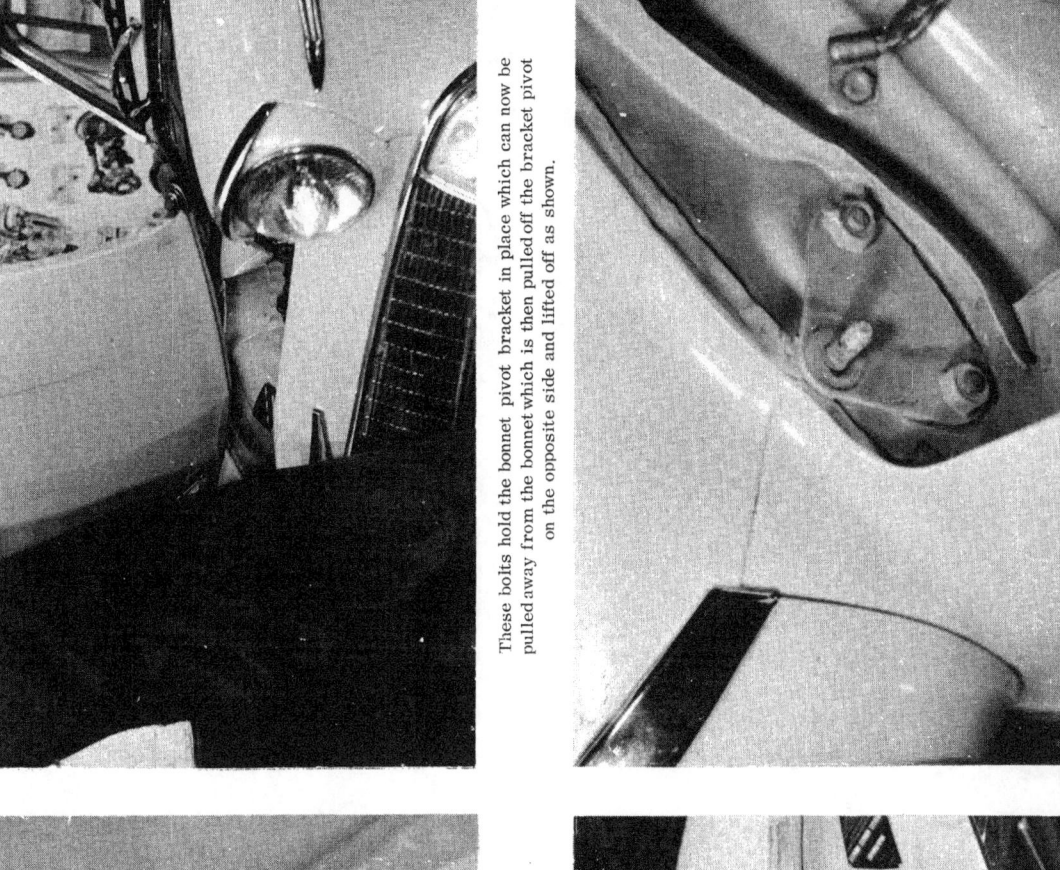

These bolts hold the bonnet pivot bracket in place which can now be pulled away from the bonnet which is then pulled off the bracket pivot on the opposite side and lifted off as shown.

Shown above is the left hand bonnet pivot bracket. This is identical to the right hand bracket. The position of the securing bolts are clearly shown.

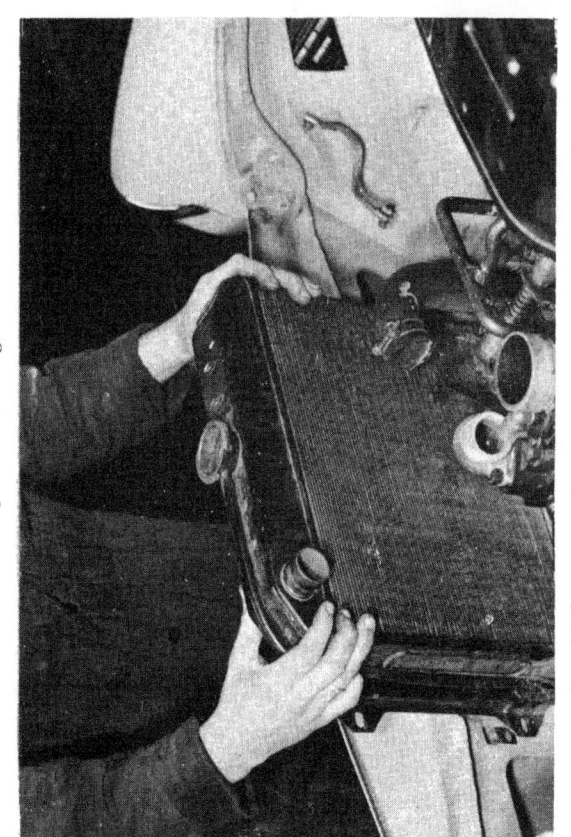

To remove the bonnet first remove the support securing nut and then undo the two bolts – one is hidden by the open bonnet – from inside the right hand front wing.

Undo the clips securing the radiator hoses to the radiator and the four bolts holding the radiator in place. Lift out the radiator.

When lifting the engine it is necessary to turn it slightly to clear obstructions in the engine compartment.

Shown above is the empty engine compartment. The battery shelf fouls the oil pump very easily during engine removal - watch this point.

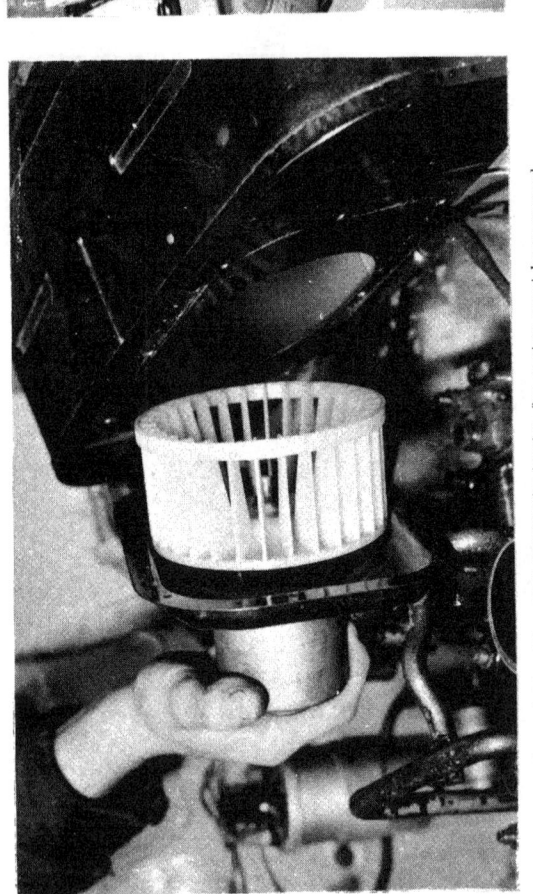

A special point to watch is that the heater fan motor must be removed from the heater box or it will foul the engine when it is tried to remove the latter.

Before separating the engine from the bellhousing — the engine has been removed for photographic clarity — place a jack under the front of the bellhousing.

4. Support the rear end of the engine, remove the four bolts with their locking washers from the engine rear support crossmember to the floorpan, and then remove the crossmember from the gearbox, by undoing the two bolts which hold the gearbox mounting to the extension housing.

5. Remove the two bolts securing each mounting at the cross tube, pull the engine forward and lift the unit together with the gearbox up out of the engine compartment.

6. DISMANTLING THE ENGINE - GENERAL

1. It is best to mount the engine on a dismantling stand, but as this is frequently not available, then stand the engine on a strong bench so as to be at a comfortable working height. Failing this, it can be stripped down on the floor. During the dismantling process the greatest care should be taken to keep the exposed parts free of dirt. As an aid to achieving this aim, it is a very sound scheme to thoroughly clean down the outside of the engine, removing all traces of oil and congealed dirt. A good grease solvent such as 'Gunk' will make the job much easier, as, after the solvent has been applied and allowed to stand for a time, a vigorous jet of water will wash off the solvent and all the grease and dirt. If the dirt is thick and deeply embedded, work the solvent into it with a wire brush.

2. Finally wipe down the exterior of the engine with a clean rag and only then, when it is finally quite free from dirt, should the dismantling process begin. As the engine is stripped, clean each part in a bath of paraffin or petrol. Never immerse parts with oilways in paraffin, i.e. the crankshaft, but to clean wipe down carefully with a petrol dampened rag. Oilways can be cleaned out with pipe cleaners. If an air line is present all parts can be blown dry and the oilways blown through as an added precaution.

3. Re-use of old engine gaskets is a false economy and can give rise to oil and water leaks, if nothing worse. To avoid the possibility of trouble after the engine has been reassembled always use new gaskets throughout. Do not throw old gaskets away as it sometimes happens that an immediate replacement cannot be found and the old gasket is then very useful as a template. Hang up the old gaskets as they are removed on a suitable hook or nail.

4. To strip the engine it is best to work from the top down. The sump provides a firm base on which the engine can be supported in an upright position. When the stage where the sump must be removed is reached, the engine can be turned on its side and all other work carried out with it in this position.

5. Wherever possible, replace nuts and bolts and washers finger-tight from wherever they were removed. This helps avoid later loss and muddle. If they cannot be replaced then lay them out in such a fashion that it is clear from where they came.

7. DISMANTLING PROCEDURE - ENGINE ANCILLARIES

1. Remove the dynamo.

2. Remove the distributor by disconnecting the vacuum pipe, unscrew the single bolt at the clamp plate and lift out the distributor.

3. Remove the oil pump and filter assembly by unscrewing the three securing bolts with their lockwashers.

4. Unscrew the two bolts securing the fuel pump.

5. Unscrew the oil pressure gauge unit.

6. Remove the inlet and exhaust manifolds together with the carburettor as a unit by unscrewing the two bolts and also the nuts on a stud at either end. NOTE that there is a gasket between the manifolds and the cylinder block so care should be taken not to damage the contact faces.

7. Unbolt the securing bolts of the water elbow, and lift out the water thermostat.

8. CYLINDER HEAD REMOVAL & DISMANTLING

1. To remove the cylinder head the same procedure is employed when the engine is in the car.

2. First unscrew the rocker cover bolts which have flat washers, and lift away the cover from its gasket.

3. Slacken the four rocker shaft support bolts evenly so that no strain is put on the supports, remove these bolts and lift away the rocker shaft as a unit.

4. Withdraw the valve rocker push rods from their positions, taking care to note their correct order.

5. Unscrew the cylinder head bolts evenly and in the order shown in the drawing. Lift off the cylinder head and the gasket.

6. The valves can be removed from the cylinder head by extracting the split tapered collets from the recess in the top of each valve stem with the aid of a valve spring

CHAPTER ONE

compressing tool, and then lifting out each valve. An umbrella type of rubber seal is fitted on each valve stem and this must be removed before the valve will slide out.

7. Keep the valves in their correct sequence as they are removed by placing them in a container having eight holes numbered from 1 to 8.

9. SUMP REMOVAL - ENGINE IN CAR

1. The sump may be removed from the engine when it is in position in the car, in order to inspect the crankshaft and big end bearings.
2. Remove the engine splash shield.
3. Unbolt the starter motor. (Make certain that the battery has been disconnected.)
4. Support the weight of the engine with lifting tackle, and remove the bolts securing the forward engine mountings to the front crossmember, and then lift the engine about two inches.
5. This will allow the set screws securing the sump flange to the bottom of the cylinder block to be extracted and the sump removed.

10. STRIPPING THE ENGINE

1. Starting at the rear of the engine first remove the clutch assembly. Unscrew the pressure plate bolts evenly and remove the pressure plate and clutch disc, noting that the pressure plate is located in its correct position by three dowels projecting from the face of the flywheel.
2. The flywheel is secured to the end of the crankshaft by four bolts and a locking plate, and is located in its correct position by a sleeve and dowel in the crankshaft flange.
3. After removing the engine rear plate the engine can be stripped down by first unscrewing the bolt retaining the crankshaft pulley so that the pulley can be drawn off. Next unscrew the bolts securing the timing cover and withdraw the cover. Note that two of these bolts are dowel bolts.
4. To dismantle the timing chain tensioner unscrew the two bolts securing the tensioner cylinder to the cylinder block. Detach the tensioner arm from the pivot pin on the front main bearing cap.
5. The camshaft sprocket and chain are removed by first bending back the locking tabs, unscrewing the two retaining bolts and then removing the locking plate; the camshaft sprocket is then pulled from its locating dowel on the camshaft, and the timing chain can then be removed.

6. The crankshaft sprocket is pulled away with the aid of an ordinary puller. If not available then ease the sprocket wheel forward a little at a time by levering behind it with two large screwdrivers at 180° to each other. The crankshaft key should then be carefully removed.
7. To remove the camshaft and thrust plate from the engine, bend back the thrust plate bolt locking tabs, unscrew the two bolts and withdraw the plate from its groove behind the camshaft flange. With the engine set vertical rotate the camshaft to lift the tappets so that they will clear the cams, and the shaft can then be withdrawn. Lift away the tappets making certain that they are kept in their correct positions.
8. To withdraw a piston and its connecting rod release the locking tabs on the big end bolts, unscrew the bolts three threads and then tap them in order to release the connecting rod from its cap, since these are located by dowel pins. Remove the two bolts and detach the big end caps. The piston together with the connecting rod is then pushed along the cylinder bore for withdrawal.
9. To remove the crankshaft from the engine first note that each main bearing cap is correctly marked for its location in relation to the cylinder block, and then unscrew each cap bolt evenly and lift off each cap.
10. As the crankshaft is lifted out note that there are two half thrust washers one on either side of the centre main bearing journal, and these can be withdrawn. To remove the crankshaft rear bearing oil seal unscrew the four bolts which secure this seal housing to the block, noting that the two lower bolts are dowelled to ensure correct alignment.

11. LUBRICATION SYSTEM

1. A forced feed system of lubrication is fitted with oil circulated round the engine from the sump below the block. The level of engine oil in the sump is indicated on the dipstick which is fitted on the right hand side of the engine. It is marked to indicate the optimum level which is the maximum mark. The level of oil in the sump, ideally, should not be above or below this line. Oil is replenished via the filler cap on the front of the rocker cover.
2. The oil pump is mounted on the side of the engine and is driven by a skew gear off the camshaft. The eccentric bi-rotor type

Fig. 1:2 View of the engine compartment. 1 Heater box. 2 Air cleaner. 3 Bonnet support. 4 Heater motor unit. 5 Top radiator hose. 6 Thermostat elbow. 7 Dipstick. 8 Rocker cover breather and oil filler cap. 9 Rocker cover. 10 Heater return hose. 11 Clutch master cylinder and reservoir. 12 Fuel pump. 13 Suspension strut mounting. 14 Coil. 15 Bottom radiator hose. 16 Radiator. 17 Earth lead — Positive terminal.

pump incorporates the oil pressure relief valve and also acts as the mounting head for the oil filter.

3. Oil is drawn from the sump through a gauze screen in the oil strainer and is sucked up the pick-up pipe into the oil pump. From the oil pump it is forced under pressure along a gallery on the side of the engine, and through drillings to the big end, main and camshaft bearings. A small hole in each connecting rod allows a jet of oil to lubricate the cylinder wall with each revolution.

4. From the camshaft front bearing oil is fed through drilled passages in the cylinder block and head to the front rocker pedestal where it enters the hollow rocker shaft. Holes drilled in the shaft allow for the lubrication of the rocker arms, and the valve stems and push rod ends. This oil is at a reduced pressure to the oil delivered to the crankshaft bearings. Oil from the front camshaft bearing also lubricates the timing gears and the timing chain. Oil returns to the sump by various passages, the tappets being lubricated by oil returning via the push rod drillings in the block.

5. On all models a full flow oil filter is fitted, and all oil passes through this filter before it reaches the main oil gallery. The oil is passed directly from the oil pump which feeds into the filter head.

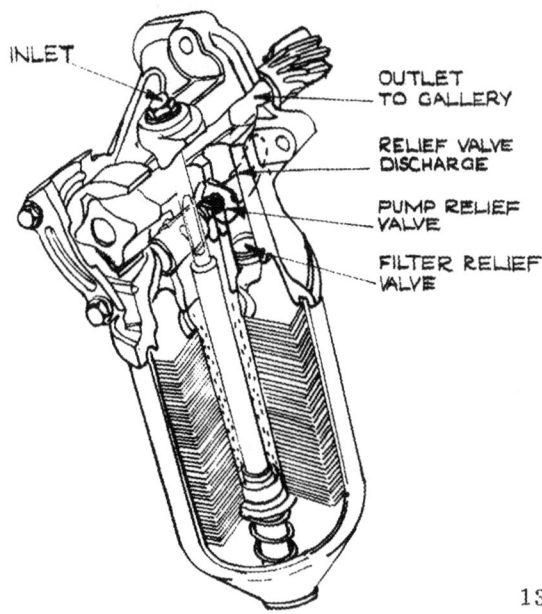

INLET

OUTLET TO GALLERY

RELIEF VALVE DISCHARGE

PUMP RELIEF VALVE

FILTER RELIEF VALVE

Fig. 1:3 A sectioned view of the oil pump and filter unit.

12. OIL FILTER - REMOVAL & REPLACEMENT

1. The full flow oil filter fitted to all engines is located three quarters of the way down the right-hand side of the engine towards the front. It is removed by unscrewing the long centre bolt which holds the filter bowl to the filter head. With the bolt released carefully lift away the filter bowl which contains the filter and will also be full of oil. It is helpful to have a large basin under the filter body to catch the amount which is bound to spill.

2. Throw the old filter element away and thoroughly clean down the filter bowl, the bolt and associated parts with petrol and when perfectly clean wipe dry with a non-fluffy rag.

3. A rubber sealing ring is located in a groove round the head of the oil filter and forms an effective leak-proof joint between the filter head and the filter bowl. A new rubber sealing ring is supplied with each new filter element.

4. Carefully prise out the old sealing ring from the locating groove. If the ring has become hard and is difficult to move take great care not to damage the sides of the sealing ring groove.

5. With the old ring removed, fit the new ring in the groove at four equidistant points and press it home a segment at a time. Do not insert the ring at just one point and work round the groove pressing it home as, using this method, it is easy to stretch the ring and be left with a small loop of rubber which will not fit into the locating groove.

6. Offer up the bowl to the rubber sealing ring and before finally tightening down the centre bolt, check that the lip of the filter bowl is resting squarely on the rubber sealing ring and is not offset and off the ring. If the bowl is not seating properly, rotate it until it is. Run the engine and check the bowl for leaks.

7. Reassemble the oil filter assembly by first passing up the bolt through the hole in the bottom of the bowl, with a steel washer under the bolts head and a rubber or felt washer on top of the steel washer and next to the filter bowl.

13. OIL PUMP OVERHAUL

1. To overhaul the oil pump, detach the pump and filter unit from the cylinder block, and remove the filter body and element.

2. Remove the four bolts and lockwashers securing the end plate and remove the plate.

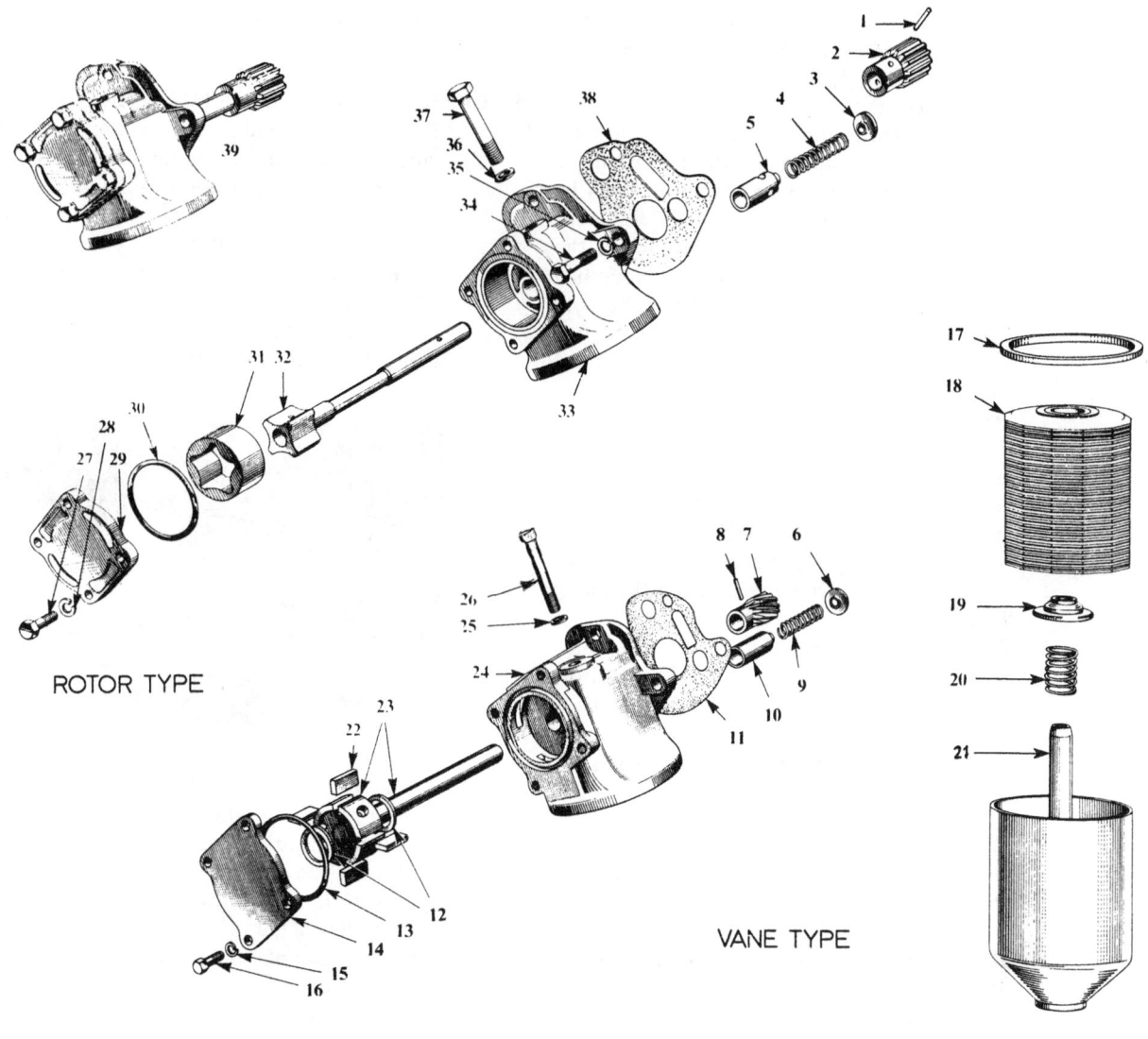

ROTOR TYPE

VANE TYPE

Fig. 1:4 EXPLODED VIEWS OF THE ROTOR AND VANE OIL PUMPS AND THE OIL FILTER.

1 Locking pin.   2 Oil pump drive gear.   3 Oil pressure relief valve retainer.   4 Relief valve spring.   5 Relief valve plunger. 6 Oil pressure relief valve retainer.   7 Oil pump drive gear.   8 Locking pin.   9 Relief valve spring.   10 Relief valve plunger. 11 Gasket.   12 Spacer.   13 Oil pump cover sealing ring.   14 Cover.   15 Spring washer.   16 Bolt.   17 Filter sealing ring. 18 Oil filter element.   19 Seat.   20 Spring.   21 Oil filter bowl.   22 Rotor blade.   23 Rotor and shaft assembly.   24 Pump assembly.   25 Spring washer.   26 Bolt.   27 Bolt.   28 Spring washer.   29 Cover.   30 Sealing ring.   31 Rotor.   32 Rotor shaft.   33 Pump body.   34 Bolt.   35 Spring washer.   36 Spring washer.   37 Securing bolt.   38 Gasket.   39 Complete pump assembly.

Lift away the 'O' ring from the sealing groove in the body.

3. Check the clearance between the lobes of the inner and outer rotors in the positions shown in Fig. 1.5 parts 2 and 3, and the clearance must not exceed 0.006 ins.

4. Replacement rotors are only supplied as a matched pair, so that if the clearance is excessive a new rotor assembly must be fitted.

5. Lay a straight edge across the face of the pump in order to check the clearance between the faces of the rotors and the bottom of the straight edge. This clearance should not exceed 0.005 in. If the clearance is excessive the face of the pump body can be carefully lapped on a flat surface.

6. When it is necessary to renew the rotors, drive out the pin securing the skew gear and pull the gear from the shaft. Remove the inner rotor and drive shaft and withdraw the outer rotor. Install the outer rotor with the chamfered end towards the pump body.

7. Fit the inner rotor and drive shaft assembly, position the skew gear and install the pin. Tap over each end of the pin to prevent it loosening in service. Position a new 'O' ring in the groove in the pump body, fit the end plate in position and secure with the four bolts and lockwashers.

8. Refit the oil pump assembly together with a new gasket and secure in place with three bolts and lockwashers.

14. EXAMINATION & RENOVATION-GENERAL

With the engine stripped down and all parts thoroughly cleaned, it is now time to examine everything for wear. The following items should be checked and where necessary renewed or renovated as shown below:-

15. CRANKSHAFT EXAMINATION & RENOVATION

1. Examine the crankpin and main journal surfaces for signs of scoring or scratches. Check the ovality of the crankpins at different positions with a micrometer, as shown. If more than 0.001 in. out of round, the crankpins will have to be reground. It will also have to be reground if there are any scores or scratches present. Also check the journals in the same fashion.

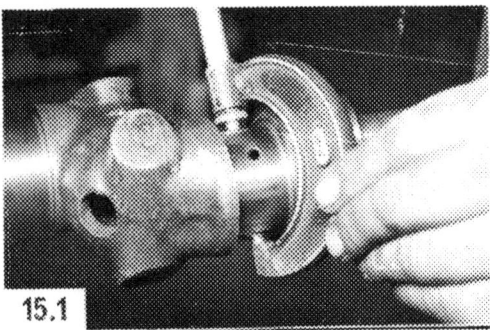

Photograph 15 : 1

2. If one journal is marked lightly and it is therefore not wished to have the whole crank reground an attempt can be made to eliminate the trouble. Mount the flange of the crank in the jaws of a vice. (See Photo).

3. With a strip of glass paper polish all round the journal checking frequently with the micrometer to ensure concentricity - as shown in the photograph.

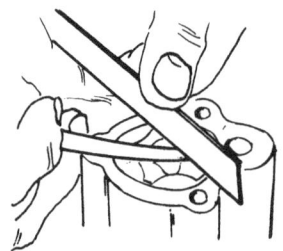 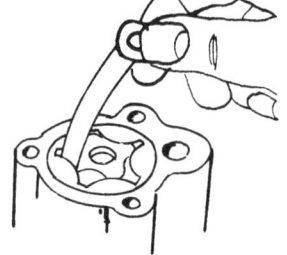 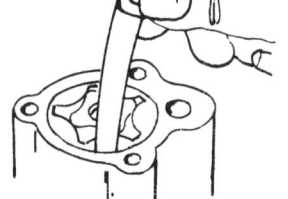

Fig. 1:5 MEASURING THE OIL PUMP CLEARANCES.

1 Measuring the rotor end float.   2 Measuring clearance between inner and outer rotors.   3 Measuring clearance between outer rotor and pump body.

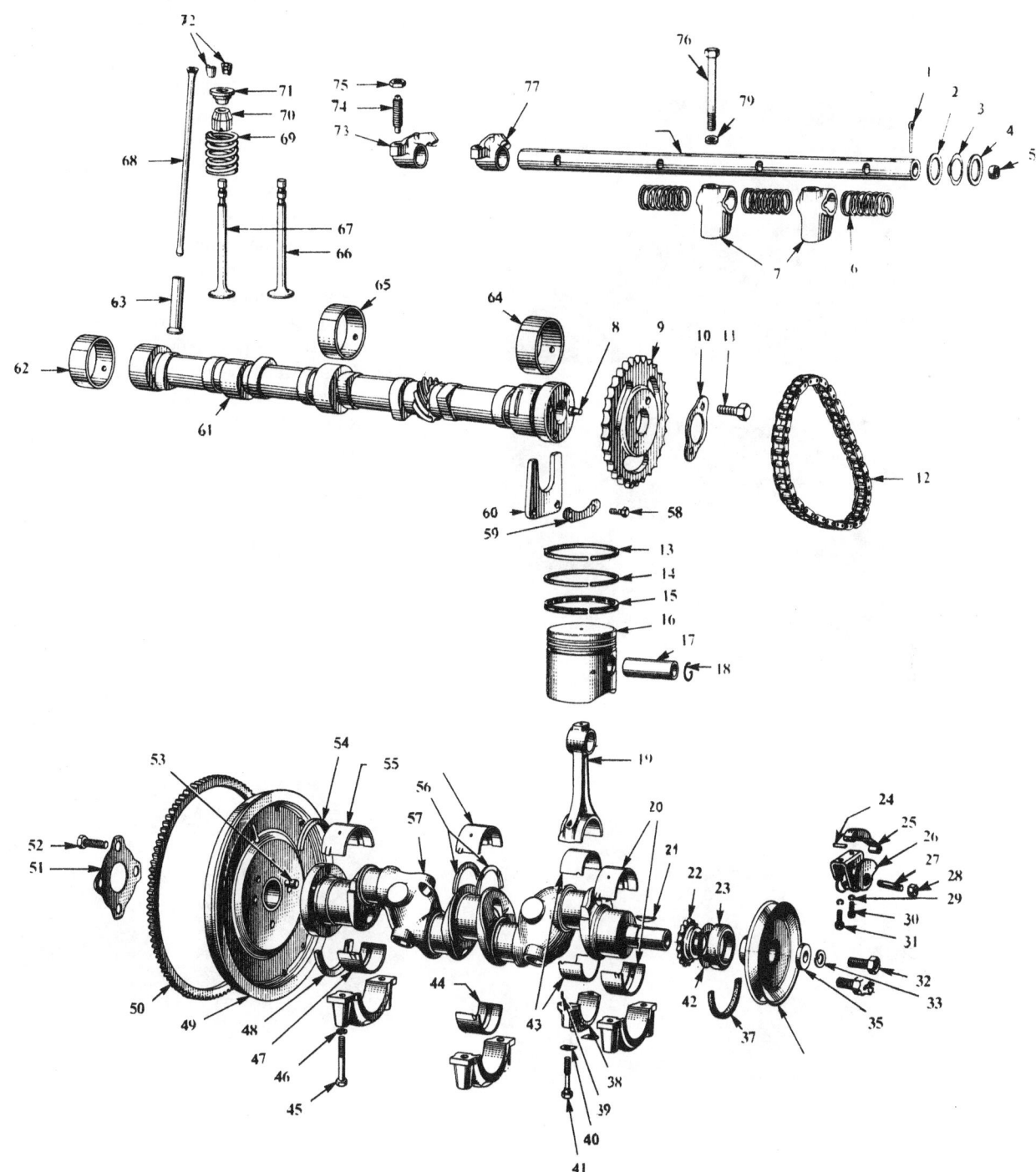

Fig. 1:6 EXPLODED VIEW OF INTERNAL ENGINE COMPONENTS.

1 Split pin. 2 Spring washer. 3 Flat washer. 4 Spring washer. 5 Plug. 6 Rocker arm locating spring. 7 Rocker shaft support bracket. 8 Dowel. 9 Camshaft timing gearwheel. 10 Retaining plate. 11 Bolt. 12 Timing chain. 13 Compression ring. 14 Second compression ring. 15 Oil control ring. 16 Piston. 17 Gudgeon pin. 18 Circlip. 19 Connecting rod. 20 Main bearing. 21 Dowel. 22 Crankshaft timing gearwheel. 23 Crankshaft main bearing oil seal. 24 Timing chain tensioner arm pin. 25 Tensioner arm. 26 Tensioner. 27 Stud. 28 Nut. 29 Spring washer. 30 Bolt. 31 Bolt. 32 Pulley wheel bolt. 33 Spring washer. 34 Bolt with dog for starting handle — alternative to 32. 35 Flat washer. 36 Crankshaft pulley wheel. 37 Crankshaft oil seal. 38 Connecting rod cap. 39 Dowel. 40 Locking tab. 41 Bolt. 42 Oil slinger. 43 Big end bearings. 44 Centre main bearing — lower half. 45 Main bearing cap bolt. 46 Spring washer. 47 Rear main bearing — lower half. 48 Rear bearing oil seal. 49 Flywheel. 50 Starter ring. 51 Plate. 52 Bolt. 53 Dowel — crankshaft flange to flywheel. 54 Oil seal. 55 Centre and rear bearings — upper halves. 56 Thrust washers. 57 Crankshaft. 58 Bolt. 59 Tab washer. 60 Camshaft thrust plate. 61 Camshaft. 62 Camshaft rear bearing. 63 Cam follower. 64 Camshaft front bearing. 65 Camshaft centre bearing. 66 Inlet valve. 67 Exhaust valve. 68 Pushrod. 69 Valve spring. 70 Valve stem seal. 71 Valve spring retainer. 72 Split collets. 73 Valve rocker arm. 74 Valve adjusting screw. 75 Locknut. 76 Bolt. 77 Valve rocker arm. 78 Rocker shaft. 79 Double coil lockwasher.

15.2

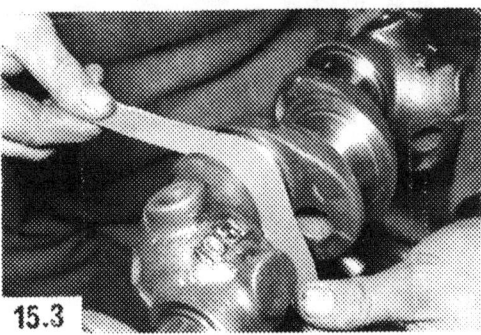

15.3

4. When the mark has been eliminated smear the journal with engineer's blue and fit the connecting rod with shell bearings as shown.

15.4

5. Check for high spots and for even spread of the blue. If all is well the crank can be replaced in the engine after it has been

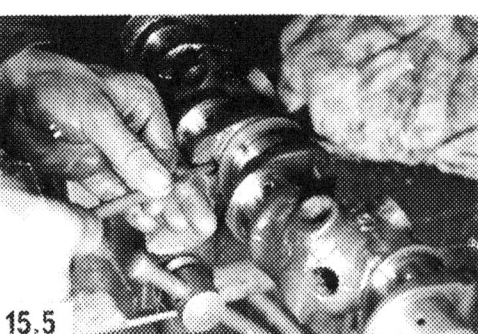

15.5

thoroughly cleaned. In particular take great care to clean out the hollow portions of the crank as shown.

16. BIG END & MAIN BEARINGS - EXAMINATION AND RENOVATION

1. Big end bearing failure is accompanied by a noisy knocking from the crankcase, and a slight drop in oil pressure. Main bearing failure is accompanied by vibration which can be quite severe as the engine speed rises and falls and a drop in oil pressure.

2. Bearings which have not broken up, but are badly worn will give rise to low oil pressure and some vibration. Inspect the big ends, main bearings, and thrust washers for signs of general wear, scoring, pitting, and scratches. The bearings should be mat grey in colour. With lead-indium bearings should a trace of copper colour be noticed the bearings are badly worn as the lead bearing material has worn away to expose the indium underlay. Renew the bearings if they are in this condition or if there is any sign of scoring or pitting. The difference between the old bearing on the right and the new one on the left is clearly seen.

16.2

3. The undersizes available are designed to correspond with the regrind sizes, i.e. -.010 bearings are correct for a crankshaft reground -.010 undersize. The bearings are in fact, slightly more than the stated undersize as running clearances have been allowed for during their manufacture.

4. Very long engine life can be achieved by changing big end bearings at intervals of 30,000 miles and main bearings at intervals of 50,000 miles, irrespective of bearing wear. Normally, crankshaft wear is infinitesimal and regular changes of bearings will ensure mileages of between 100,000 to 125,000 miles before crankshaft regrinding becomes necessary. Crankshafts normally have to be reground because of scoring due to bearing failure.

17. CYLINDER BORES - EXAMINATION & REN-
OVATION

1. The cylinder bores must be examined for
taper, ovality, scoring and scratches. Start
by carefully examining the top of the cylinder
bores. If they are at all worn a very slight
ridge will be found on the thrust side. This
marks the top of the piston ring travel. The
owner will have a good indication of the bore
wear prior to dismantling the engine, or
removing the cylinder head. Excessive oil
consumption accompanied by blue smoke
from the exhaust is a sure sign of worn
cylinder bores and piston rings.

2. Measure the bore diameter just under the
ridge with a micrometer, as shown in the
photograph, and compare it with the diameter at the bottom of the bore, which is
not subject to wear. If the difference between the two measurements is more than
.006 in. then it will be necessary to fit
special piston rings or to have the cylinders rebored and fit oversize pistons and
rings. If no micrometer is available remove the rings from a piston and place the
piston in each bore in turn about $\frac{3}{4}$in. below
the top of the bore. If an 0.015 feeler gauge
can be slid between the piston and the cylinder wall on the thrust side of the bore
then the engine should be rebored and new
pistons fitted. Also shown in the photograph is a typical reboring machine in position.

17.2

3. When the bores have been attended to put a
fine chamfer on the top circumference of
each cylinder with the aid of a fine file.

18. PISTON & PISTON RINGS - EXAMINATION &
RENOVATION

1. If the old pistons are to be refitted, carefully remove the piston rings and then thoroughly clean them. Take particular care
to clean out the piston ring grooves. At the
same time do not scratch the aluminium in
any way. If new rings are to be fitted to

17.3

the old pistons then the top ring should be
stepped so as to clear the ridge left above
the previous top ring. If a normal but oversize new ring is fitted, it will hit the ridge
and break, because the new ring will not
have worn in the same way as the old, which
will have worn in unison with the ridge.

2. Before fitting the rings on the pistons each
should be inserted approximately 3in. down
the cylinder bore and the gap measured with
a feeler gauge. This should be between
.009 in. and .014 in. It is essential that
the gap should be measured at the bottom
of the ring travel, as if it is measured at
the top of a worn bore and gives a perfect
fit, it could easily sieze at the bottom.

19. CAMSHAFT & CAMSHAFT BEARINGS - EXAM-
INATION & RENOVATION

1. Carefully examine the camshaft bearings
for wear. NOTE On early engines that
only the front camshaft bearing is renewable. If the bearings are obviously worn
or pitted or the metal underlay is showing
through, then they must be renewed. This
is an operation for your local Ford dealer
or the local engineering works as it
demands the use of specialised equipment.
The bearings are removed with a special
drift after which new bearings are pressed
in, care being taken to ensure the oil holes
in the bearings line up with those in the
block. With a special tool the bearings are
then reamed in position.

2. The camshaft itself should show no sign of
wear, but, if very slight scoring on the
cams is noticed, the score marks can be
removed by very gentle rubbing down with
very fine emery cloth. The greatest care
should be taken to keep the cam profiles
smooth.

VALVES & VALVE SEATS - EXAMINATION &
RENOVATION

1. Examine the heads of the valves for pitting

and burning, especially the heads of the exhaust valves. The valve seatings should be examined at the same time. If the pitting on valve and seat is very slight the marks can be removed by grinding the seats and valves together with coarse, and then fine, valve grinding paste.

2. Where bad pitting has ocurred to the valve seats it will be necessary to recut them and fit new valves.

3. If the valve seats are so worn that they cannot be recut, then it will be necessary to fit new valve seat inserts. These latter two jobs should be entrusted to the local Ford agent or engineering works.

4. In practice it is very seldom that the seats are so badly worn that they require renewal. Normally, it is the valve that is too badly worn for replacement, and the owner can easily purchase a new set of valves and match them to the seats by valve grinding.

5. Valve grinding is carried out as follows:- Place the cylinder head upside down on a bench, with a block of wood at each end to give clearance for the valve stems. Alternatively place the head at 45° to a wall with the combustion chambers facing away from the wall.

6. Smear a trace of coarse carborundum paste on the seat face and apply a suction grinder tool to the valve head. With a semi-rotary motion, grind the valve head to its seat, lifting the valve occasionally to redistribute the grinding paste. When a dull matt even surface finish is produced on both the valve seat and the valve, then wipe off the paste and repeat the process with fine carborundum paste, lifting and turning the valve to redistribute the paste as before. A light spring placed under the valve head will greatly ease this operation. When a smooth unbroken ring of light grey matt finish is produced, on both valve and valve seat faces, the grinding operation is completed.

7. Scrape away all carbon from the valve head and the valve stem. Carefully clean away every trace of grinding compound, taking great care to leave none in the ports or in the valve guides. Clean the valves and valve seats with a paraffin soaked rag then with a clean rag, and finally, if an air line is available, blow the valves, valve guides and valve ports clean.

Fig. 1:7 EXPLODED VIEW OF STATIC ENGINE COMPONENTS.
1 Rocker breather/oil filler cap.
2 Rocker cover.
3 Rocker cover gasket.
4 Water temperature thermostat.
5 Blanking plug — ommitted if temperature gauge fitted.
6 Cylinder head gasket.
7 Exhaust valve seat.
8 Dipstick.
9 Bolt.
10 Dipstick tube.
11 Spring washer.
12 Bolt.
13 Timing chain cover.
14 Crankshaft main bearing oil seal.
15 Spring.
16 Bolt.
17 Spring washer.
18 Bolt.
19 Washer.
20
21 Bolt and washer.
22 Oil pump pick up.
23 Sump plug.
24 Sump washer.
25 Spring washer.
26 Nut.
27 Pick up pipe.
28 Pick up point.
29 Nut.
30 Spring washer.
31 Undertray.
32 Bracket.
33 Support clip.
34 Sump.
35 Sump bolt.
36 Spring washer.
37 Washer.
38 Sump gasket.
39 Bolt.
40 Breather extension.
41 Breather tube.
42 Starter motor drive cover.
43 Dowel.
44 Bolt.
45 Spring washer.
46 Rear main oil seal bearing retainer.
47 Gasket.
48 Flywheel housing cover.
49 Nut.
50 Spring washer.
51 Breather tube elbow.
52 Tube.
53 Cylinder block.
54 Cylinder liner — if required.
55 Engine mounting bracket.
56 Oil gallery drain plug.
57 Tab washer.
58 Bolt.
59 Gasket.
60 Oil gallery plug.
61 Spring washer.
62 Bolt.

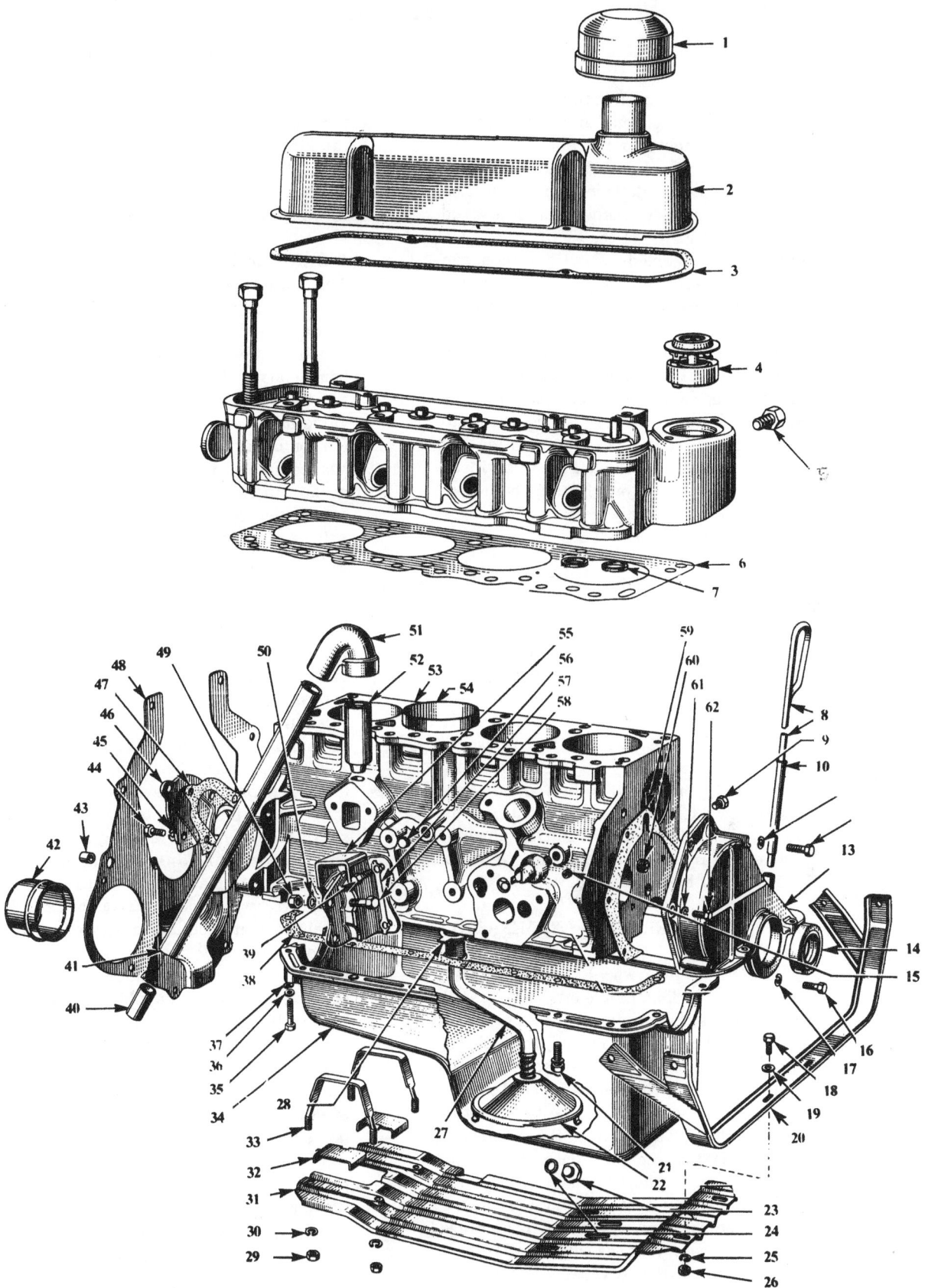

29

21. TIMING GEARS & CHAIN - EXAMINATION & RENOVATION

1. Examine the teeth on both the crankshaft gear wheel and the camshaft gearwheel for wear. Each tooth forms an inverted 'V' with the gearwheel periphery, and if worn the side of each tooth under tension will be slightly concave in shape when compared with the other side of the tooth, i.e., one side of the inverted 'V' will be concave when compared with the other. If any sign of wear is present the gearwheels must be renewed.

2. Examine the links of the chain for side slackness and renew the chain if any slackness is noticeable when compared with a new chain. It is a sensible precaution to renew the chain at about 30,000 miles and at a lower mileage if the engine is stripped down for a major overhaul. The actual rollers on a very badly worn chain may be slightly grooved.

22. TAPPETS-EXAMINATION & RENOVATION

1. Examine the bearing surface of the tappets which lie on the camshaft. Any indentation in this surface or any cracks indicate serious wear and the tappets should be renewed. Thoroughly clean them out, removing all traces of sludge. It is most unlikely that the sides of the tappets will prove worn, but, if they are a very loose fit in their bores and can readily be rocked, they should be exchanged for new units. It is very unusual to find any wear in the tappets, and any wear present is likely to occur only at very high mileages.

23. FLYWHEEL STARTER RING - EXAMINATION & RENOVATION

1. If the teeth on the flywheel starter ring are badly worn, or if some are missing, then it will be necessary to remove the ring. This is achieved by hacksawing through the bottom of one of the 'V's between the teeth and then splitting the ring with a cold chisel. The greatest care should be taken not to damage the flywheel during this process.

2. To fit a new ring, heat it gently and evenly with an oxyacetylene flame until a temperature of approximately 205°C is reached. This is indicated by a light metallic yellow surface colour. With the ring at this temperature, fit it to the flywheel with the front of the teeth facing the flywheel register.

3. The ring should be tapped gently down onto its register and left to cool naturally when the contraction of the metal on cooling will ensure that it is a secure and permanent fit.

4. Great care must be taken not to overheat the ring, as if this happens the temper of the ring will be lost.

5. Alternatively, your local Ford agent or engineering works may have a suitable oven in which the flywheel can be heated.

24. CYLINDER HEAD - DECARBONISATION

1. This can be carried out with the engine either in or out of the car. With the cylinder head off carefully remove with a wire brush and blunt scraper all traces of carbon deposits from the combustion spaces and the ports. The valve head stems and valve guides should also be freed from any carbon deposits. Wash the combustion spaces and ports down with petrol and scrape the cylinder head surface free of any foreign matter with the side of a steel rule, or a similar article.

2. Clean the pistons and top of the cylinder bores. If the pistons are still in the block then it is essential that great care is taken to ensure that no carbon gets into the cylinder bores as this could scratch the cylinder walls or cause damage to the pistons and rings. To ensure this does not happen, first turn the crankshaft so that two of the pistons are at the top of their bores. Stuff rag into the other two bores or seal them off with paper and masking tape. The waterways should also be covered with small pieces of masking tape to prevent particles of carbon entering the cooling system and damaging the water pump.

3. There are two schools of thought as to how much carbon should be removed from the piston crown. One school recommends that a ring of carbon should be left round the edge of the piston and on the cylinder bore wall as an aid to low oil consumption. Although this is probably true for early engines with worn bores, on later engines the second school recommends that for effective decarbonisation all traces of carbon should be removed.

4. If all traces of carbon are to be removed press a little grease into the gap between the cylinder walls and the two pistons which are to be worked on. With a blunt scraper carefully scrape away the carbon from the piston crown, taking great care not to scratch the aluminium. Also scrape away the carbon from the surrounding lip of the cylinder wall. When all carbon has been removed, scrape away the grease

which will now be contaminated with carbon particles, taking care not to press any into the bores. To assist prevention of carbon build-up the piston crown can be polished with a metal polish such as Brasso. Remove the rags or masking tape from the other two cylinders and turn the crankshaft so that the two pistons which were at the bottom are now at the top. Place rag or masking tape in the cylinders which have been decarbonised and proceed as before.

5. If a ring of carbon is going to be left round the piston then this can be helped by inserting an old piston ring into the top of the bore to rest on the piston and ensure that carbon is not accidently removed. Check that there are no particles of carbon in the cylinder bores. Decarbonising is now complete.

25. VALVE GUIDES - EXAMINATION & RENOVATION

1. Examine the valve guides internally for wear. If the valves are a very loose fit in the guides and there is the slightest suspicion of lateral rocking, then new valves will have to be fitted.

2. The valve guide bores are machined direct in the cylinder head, and to compensate for wear valves with stems 0.003 in and 0.015 in. oversize are available, the oversize figure being marked on the valve stem.

3. Where it is necessary to ream out the bore of the guide to accept the oversize stems a reamer 0.015 oversize and with a standard pilot is available. The reamer should be used with a small tap wrench, care being taken to ensure that the operation of reaming is in line with existing bore. After reaming, recut the valve seats in line with the guide bores, lightly grind in each valve taking care to ensure that every particle of grinding paste is cleaned away.

26. ENGINE REASSEMBLY - GENERAL

To ensure maximum life with minimum trouble from a rebuilt engine, not only must everything be correctly assembled, but everything must be spotlessly clean, all the oilways must be clear, locking washers and spring washers must always be fitted where indicated and all bearing and other working surfaces must be thoroughly lubricated during assembly. Before assembly begins renew any bolts or studs the threads of which are in any way damaged, and whenever possible use new spring washers. Apart from your normal tools, a supply of clean rag, an oil can filled with engine oil (an empty plastic detergent bottle thoroughly cleaned and washed out, will invariably do just as well), a new supply of assorted ring washers, a set of new gaskets, and preferably a torque spanner, should be collected altogether.

27. ASSEMBLING THE ENGINE

1. Thoroughly clean the block and ensure all traces of old gaskets etc. are removed as

2. Fit a new rear main oil seal bearing retainer gasket to the rear end of the cylinder block. (See Photograph).

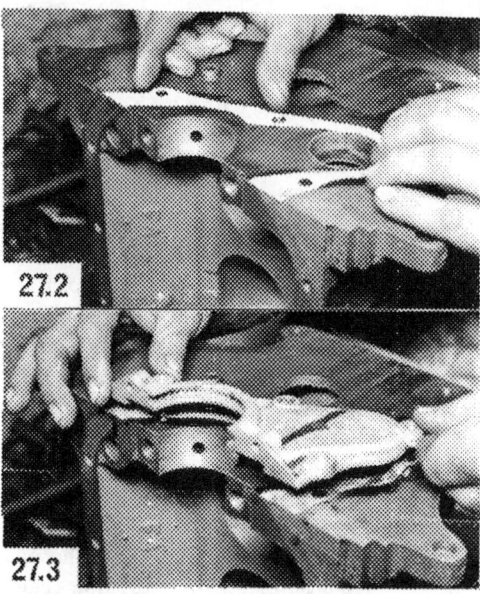

27.2

27.3

3. Then fit the rear main oil seal bearing retainer housing. (See Photograph).

27.4

4. Do up the four retaining bolts with spring washers under their heads noting that the two bolts (arrowed), nearest the edge of the crankcase are dowelled to ensure correct alignment, and should be tightened first.

5. Turn the block upside down and fit the crankshaft rear bearing oil seal (arrowed) to its housing and make sure that the ends of the seal do not project more than 1/32 in. above the face of the housing. Oil the seal generously. Position the upper halves of

the main bearing liners in their correct positions so that the tabs of the liners engage in the machined key-ways in the sides of the bearing locations. Oil the main bearing liners after they have been fitted in position.

6. Thoroughly clean out the oilways in the crankshaft with the aid of a thin wire brush or pipe cleaners. (See Photograph).

7. Carefully lower the crankshaft into place. (See Photograph).

8. Fit new end float thrust washers. These locate in recesses on either side of the centre main bearing in the cylinder block and must be fitted with the oil grooves facing the crankshaft flange. With the crankshaft in position check for float which should be between 0.003 and 0.011 in. (0.076 to 0.279 mm). If the end float is incorrect remove the thrust washers and select suitable washers to give the correct end float. (See Photograph).

9. Position the lower halves of the main bearing liners in their correct caps making sure that the locking tabs fit into the machined grooves. Refit the main bearing caps in accordance with the mating marks and with the arrows pointing to the front of the engine. Tighten the cap bolts to a torque of 55 to 60 lbs. ft. (7.604 to 8.295 kg. m). (See Photograph). Spin the crankshaft to make certain it is turning freely.

10. Check that the piston ring grooves and oilways are thoroughly clean and unblocked. Piston rings must always be fitted over the head of the piston and never from the bottom. The easiest method to use when fitting rings is to wrap a .020 feeler gauge round the top of the piston and place the rings one at a time, starting with the bottom oil control ring, over the feeler gauge.

   The feeler gauge, complete with ring, can then be slid down the piston over the other piston ring grooves until the correct groove is reached. The piston ring in then slid gently off the feeler gauge into the groove.

11. An alternative method is to fit the rings by holding them slightly open with the thumbs and both of your index fingers. This method requires a steady hand and great care as it is easy to open the ring too much and break it. (See Photograph).
   When assembling the rings note that the compression rings are marked 'top' and that the upper ring is chromium plated. The ring gaps should be spaced equally round the piston.

12. If the same pistons are being used, then they must be mated to the same connecting rod with the same gudgeon pin. If new pistons are being fitted it does not matter which connecting rod they are used with. Note that the word FRONT is stamped on one side of each of the rods. (See Photograph). On reassembly the side marked 'FRONT' must be towards the front of the engine.

13. Fit a gudgeon pin circlip in position at one end of the gudgeon pin hole in the piston and fit the piston to the connecting rod by sliding in the gudgeon pin as shown. The arrow on the crown of each piston must be on the same side as the word 'FRONT' on the connecting rod.

14. Fit the second circlip in position. Repeat this procedure for the remaining three pistons and connecting rods. (See Photograph).

15. Fit the connecting rod in position and check that the oil hole (arrowed) in the upper half of each bearing aligns with the oil squirt hole in the connecting rod.

16. With a wad of clean rag wipe the cylinder bores clean, and then oil them generously. The pistons complete with connecting rods, are fitted to their bores from above. (See Photograph). As each piston is inserted into its bore ensure that it is the correct piston/connecting rod assembly for that particular bore and that the connecting rod is the right way round, and that the front of the piston is towards the front of the bore, i.e., towards the front of the engine.

17. The piston will only slide into the bore as far as the oil control ring. It is then necessary to compress the piston rings in a clamp. (See Photograph).

18. Gently tap the piston into the cylinder bore with a wooden or plastic hammer. If a proper piston ring clamp is not available then a suitable jubilee clip does the job very well. (See Photograph).

19. Fit the shell bearings to the big end caps so the tongue on the back of each bearing (arrowed) lies in the machined recess.

20. Generously oil the crankshaft connecting rod journals. (See Photograph).

21. Then replace each big end cap on the same connecting rod from which it was removed. (See Photograph).

22. Fit the locking plates under the head of the big end bolts, tap the caps right home on the dowels and then tighten the bolts to a torque of 20 to 25 lbs. ft. (See Photograph).

23. Lock the bolts in position by knocking up

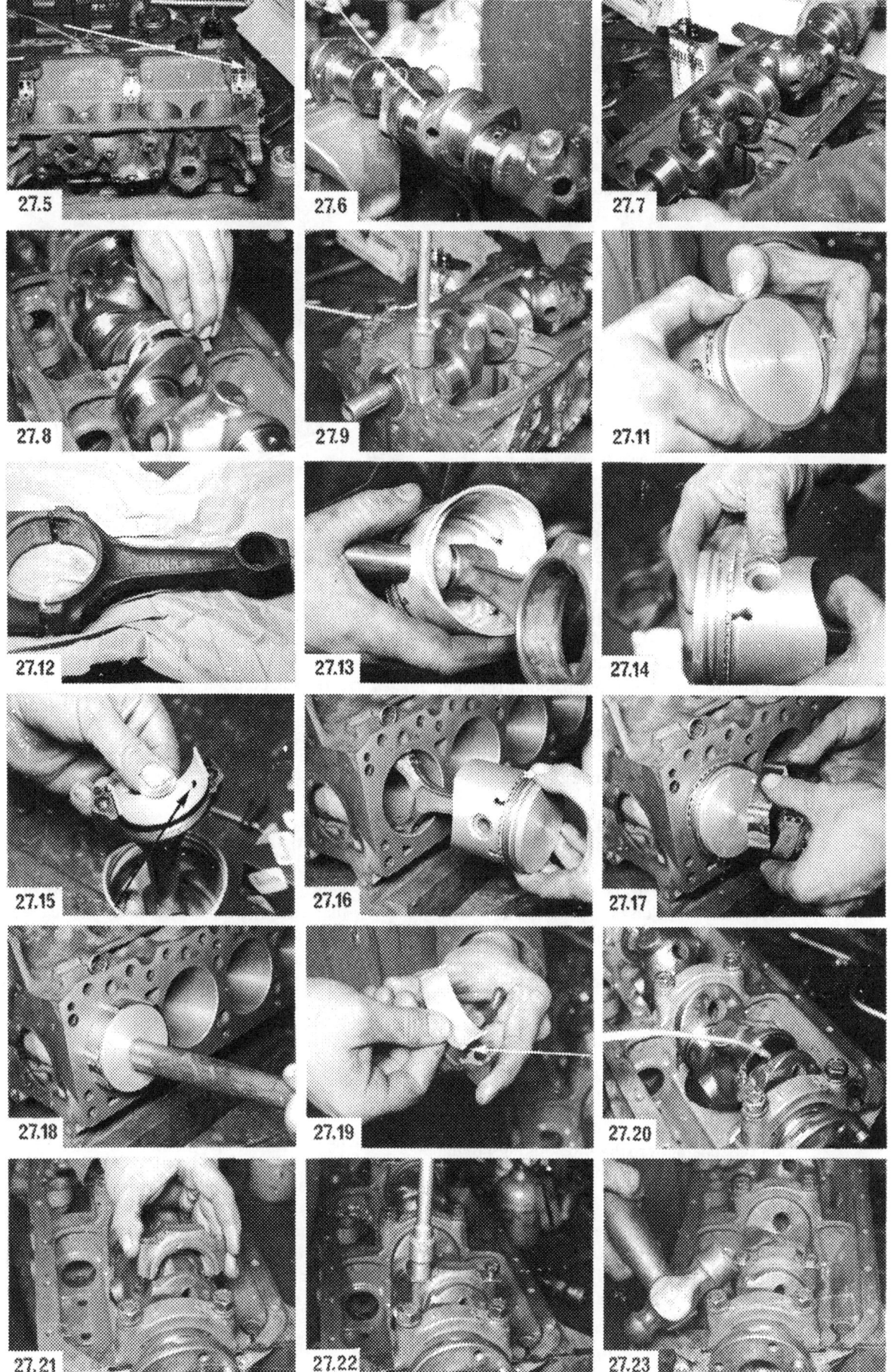

the tabs on the locking washers. (See Photograph).

24. Fit the eight cam followers into the same holes in the block from which each was removed. Two of the eight holes are arrowed. The cam followers can only be fitted with the block upside down.

25. Fit the woodruff key in its slot on the front of the crankshaft and then press the timing sprocket into place so the timing mark faces forward. Oil the camshaft shell bearings and insert the camshaft into the block (which should still be upside down). (See Photograph).

26. Make sure the camshaft turns freely and then fit the thrust plate behind the camshaft flange as shown. Measure the endfloat with a feeler gauge - it should be between 0.002 and 0.007 in. If this is not so then renew the plate.

27. Fit the two camshaft flange bolts into their joint washer and screw down the bolts securely. (See Photograph).

28. Turn up the tab (arrowed) under the head of each bolt to lock it in place.

29. When refitting the timing chain round the gearwheels and to the engine, the two timing lines (arrowed) must be adjacent to each other on an imaginary line passing through each gearwheel centre.

30. With the timing marks correctly aligned turn the camshaft until the protruding dowel locates in the hole (arrowed) in the camshaft sprocket wheel.

31. Tighten the two retaining bolts and bend up the tabs on the lockwasher. (See Photograph).

32. Fit the oil slinger to the nose of the crankshaft, cancave side facing outwards. The cut out (arrowed) locates over the woodruff key.

33. Then slide the timing chain tensioner arm over its hinge pin on the front of the block. (See Photograph).

34. Turn the tensioner back from its free position so it will apply pressure to the tensioner arm and replace the tensioner on the block sump flange. (See Photograph).

35. Bolt the tensioner to the block using spring washers under the heads of the two bolts (arrowed).

36. Remove the front oil seal from the timing chain cover and with the aid of a vice carefully press a new seal into position. (See Photograph). Lightly lubricate the face of the seal which will bear against the crankshaft.

37. Using jointing compound fit a new gasket in place. (See Photograph).

38. Fit the timing chain cover replacing and tightening the two dowel bolts first. These fit in the holes nearest the sump flange and serve to align the timing cover correctly. Ensure spring washers are used and then tighten the bolts evenly.

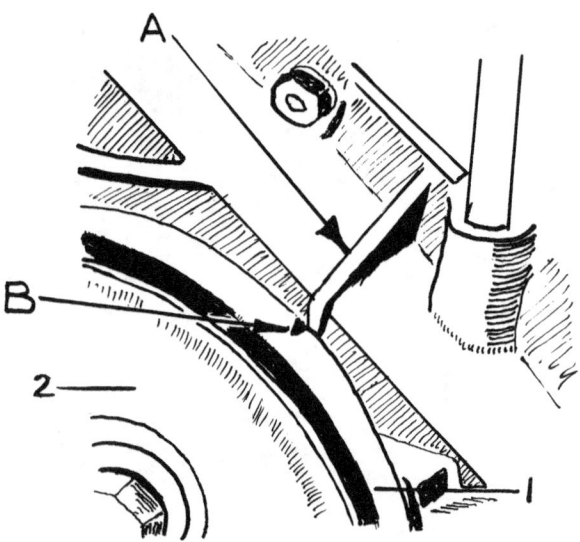

Fig. 1:8 The external marks indicating when Nos. 1 and 4 pistons are at T.D.C. A Timing mark. B Notch in crankshaft pulley wheel.

39. Refit the tube to its recess in the top of the petrol pump housing on the block tapping it gently into place. (See Photograph). Replace the oil pump suction pipe using a new tab washer and position the gauze head so it clears the crankshaft throw and the oil return pipe (where fitted). Tighten the nut and bend back the tab of the lockwasher.

40. Clean the flanges of the sump and push home a new crankshaft rear oil seal in the groove at the rear of the sump. Cut off any excess so the ends stand not more than 1/32 in. proud. (See Photograph). Oil the seal generously.

41. Place two half gaskets on the block flanges and use jointing compound to get a good seal. Press a new cork seal into the groove on the front of the sump and carefully fit the sump to the block. (See Photograph).

42. Replace the sump bolts and tighten them down evenly. NOTE the washers under the heads of the bolts and that the two longer sump bolts are fitted at the rear as shown.

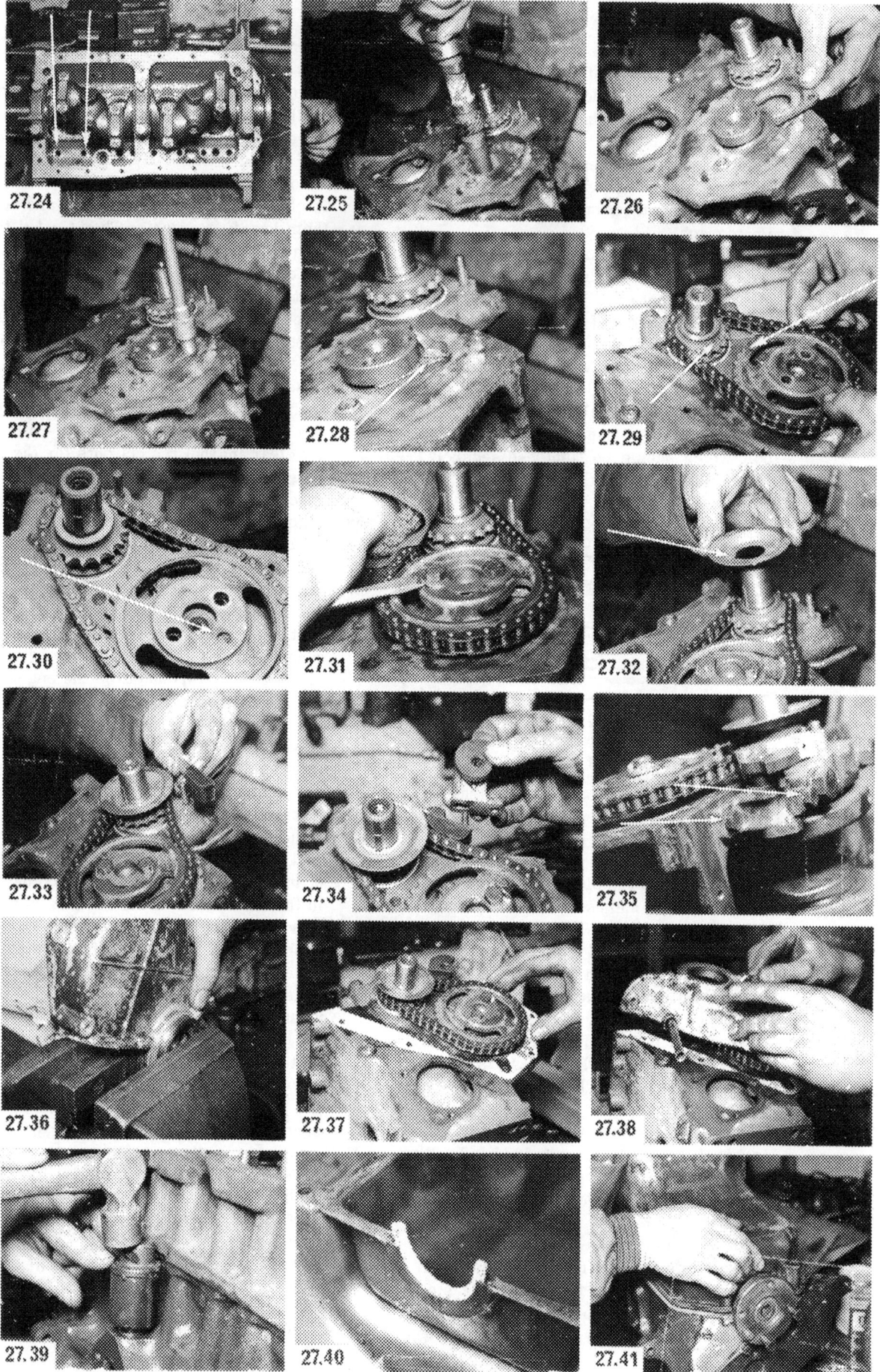

27.24

27.25

27.26

27.27

27.28

27.29

27.30

27.31

27.32

27.33

27.34

27.35

27.36

27.37

27.38

27.39

27.40

27.41

43. The engine can now be turned over so it is the right way up. Coat the oil pump flanges with jointing compound. (See Photograph).

44. Fit a new gasket in place on the oil pump. (See Photograph).

45. Position the oil pump against the block ensuring the skew gear teeth on the drive shaft mate with those on the camshaft. (See Photograph).

46. Replace the three securing bolts and spring washers and tighten them down evenly. (See Photograph).

47. Moving to the front of the engine align the slot in the crankshaft pulley wheel with the key on the crankshaft and gently tap the pulley wheel home. (See Photograph).

48. Secure the pulley wheel by fitting the large flat washer, the spring washer and then the bolt which should be tightened securely. (See Photograph).

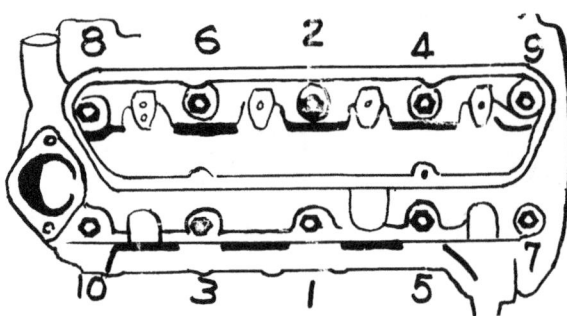

Fig. 1 : 9

49. Moving to the rear of the engine clean and lightly grease the bush (arrowed) in the crankshaft flange and refit the flywheel so the hole mates with the dowel on the flange.

50. With the flywheel in place replace the four retaining bolts and use a new lockwasher. (See Photograph).

51. Prevent the flywheel from turning by refitting two of the clutch securing bolts placing a strong screwdriver between them and the bench as shown. Tighten the bolts to 45 to 50 lbs. ft. (See Photograph).

52. Knock up the tabs on the lockwasher to firmly secure the bolts in place. (See Photograph).

53. The next step is to thoroughly clean the faces of the block and cylinder head. Fit a new cylinder head gasket with the side marked top facing upwards. (See Photograph).

54. With the cylinder head on its side lubricate the valve stems and refit them to their correct guides. Then fit the valve stem umbrella oil seals, open ends down, valve springs and spring retainer. Compress

the valve spring with a compressor. Fit the split collets. A trace of grease will help hold them to the valve stem recess until the spring compressor is slackened off and the collets are wedged in place by the spring. Carefully lower the cylinder head onto the block as shown.

55. Replace the cylinder head bolts and screw them down finger tight. Then tighten them with a torque wrench to 65 to 70 lbs. ft. in the order shown in Fig. 1. 9.

56. Fit the pushrods into the same holes in the block from which they were removed. Make sure the pushrods seat properly in the cam followers. (See Photograph).

57. Reassemble the rocker gear into the rocker shaft and fit the shaft to the cylinder head. (See Photograph). Ensure that the oil holes are clear and that the cut outs for the securing bolts lie facing the holes in the brackets.

58. Tighten down the four rocker bracket washers and bolts to a torque of 17 - 22 lbs. ft. (See Photograph).

59. The valve adjustments should be made with the engine cold. The importance of correct rocker arm/valve stem clearances cannot be overstressed as they vitally affect the performance of the engine. If the clearances are set too open, the efficiency of the engine is reduced as the valves open late and close earlier than was intended. If, on the other hand the clearances are set too close there is a danger that the stems will expand upon heating and not allow the valves to close properly which will cause burning of the valve head and seat and possible warping. If the engine is in the car access to the rockers is by removing the two holding down studs from the rocker cover, and then lifting the rocker cover and gasket away.

60. It is important that the clearance is set when the tappet of the valve being adjusted is on the heel of the cam, (i.e., opposite the peak). This can be ensured by carrying out the adjustments in the following order (which also avoids turning the crankshaft more than necessary).

Valve fully open	Check & adjust	Clearance
Valve No. 8 ...	Valve No. 1 ...	0.018 in.
" " 6 ...	" " 3 ...	0.008 in.
" " 4 ...	" " 5 ...	0.018 in.
" " 7 ...	" " 2 ...	0.008 in.
" " 1 ...	" " 8 ...	0.018 in.
" " 3 ...	" " 6 ...	0.008 in.
" " 5 ...	" " 4 ...	0.018 in.
" " 2 ...	" " 7 ...	0.008 in.

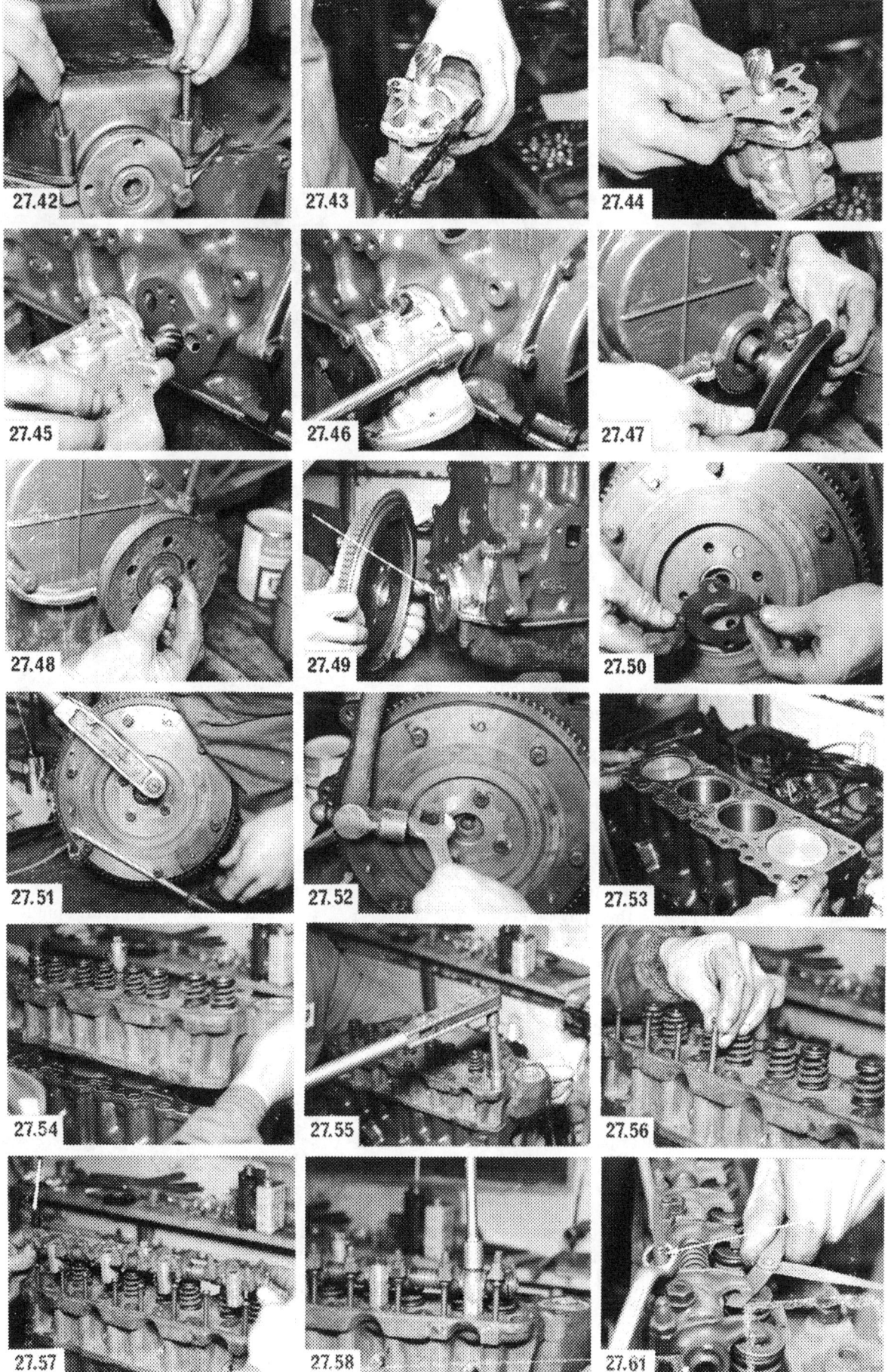

37

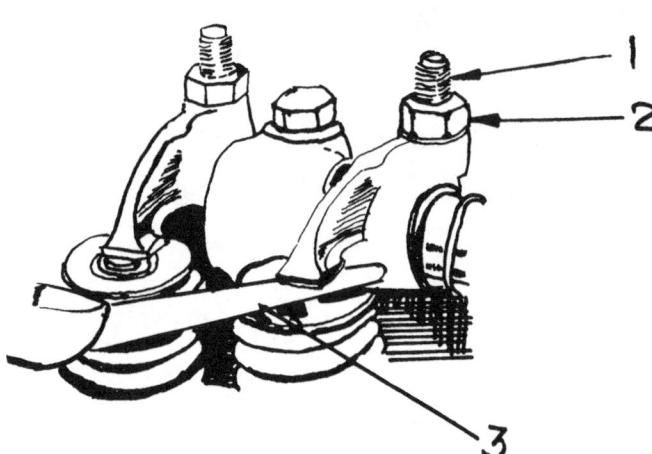

Fig. 1:10 Setting the rocker pad to valve stem gap.
1 Adjusting screw. 2 Locknut. 3 Feeler blade.

61. The correct feeler gauge clearances between the valve stem and the rocker arm pad with the engine cold is 0.008 in. for the inlet valves and 0.018 in. for the exhausts. Working from the front of the engine (No. 1 valve) the correct clearance is obtained by slackening the hexagon locknut with a spanner while holding the ball pin (arrowed) against rotation with the screwdriver. Then, still pressing down with the screwdriver, insert a feeler gauge in the gap between the valve stem head and the rocker arm and adjust the ball pin until the feeler gauge will just move in and out without nipping. (See Photograph). Then, still holding the ball pin in the correct position, tighten the locknut. An alternative method is to set the gaps with the engine running, and although this may be faster it is no more reliable.

62. It is important to set the distributor drive correctly as otherwise the ignition timing will be totally incorrect. It is possible to set the distributor drive in apparently the right position, but, in fact, 180° out, by omitting to select the correct cylinder which must not only be at T.D.C. but must also be on its firing stroke with both valves closed. The distributor drive should therefore not be fitted until the cylinder head is in position and the valves can be observed. Alternatively, if the timing cover has not been replaced, the distributor drive can be replaced when the lines on the timing wheels are adjacent to each other.

63. Rotate the crankshaft so that No. 1 piston is at T.D.C. and on its firing stroke (the lines in the timing gears will be adjacent

to each other). When No. 1 piston is at T.D.C. both valves will be closed and both rocker arms will 'rock' slightly because of the stem to arm pad clearance. (See Photograph).

27.63

27.64

64. Note the two timing marks on the timing case (arrowed) and the notch on the crankshaft pulley wheel periphery. Turn the crankshaft until the bottom of the notch lies midway between the two marks.

65. Position the distributor so that the tip of the rotor arm is adjacent to the low tension terminal and the vacuum unit spindle parallel to the cylinder block as shown.

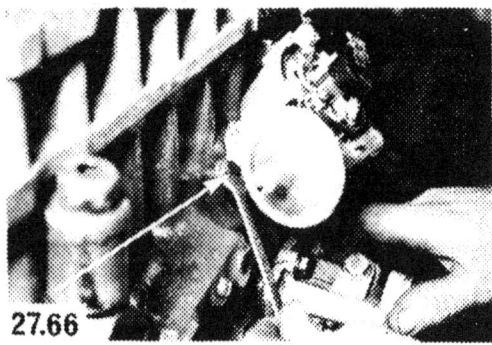

27.66

66. As the gear on the end of the drive meshes with the skew gear on the camshaft the rotor arm will turn slightly so it points to No. 1 segment in the distributor cap and the points are just opening. This is its correct

position. Secure the distributor to the cylinder block with one bolt (arrowed) and lockwasher through the clamp plate.

27.67

67. Then loosen the clamp plate bolt and nut (arrowed) and adjust the distributor body so that the contact breaker points are just opening. For a full description of how to do this see Chapter 4/11. If the clamp bolt on the clamping plate was not previously loosened and the distributor body was not turned in the clamping plate, then the ignition timing will be as previously.

27.68

68. Fit a new gasket to the water pump and attach it to the front of the cylinder block. (See Photograph).

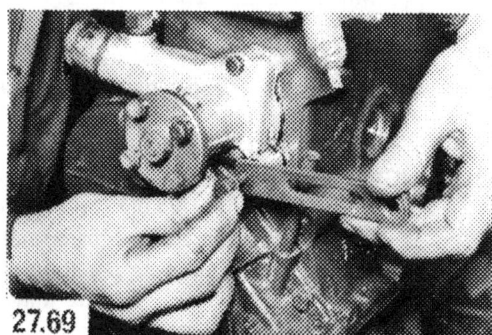
27.69

69. Note that the dynamo support strap fits under the head of the lower bolt on the water pump as shown.

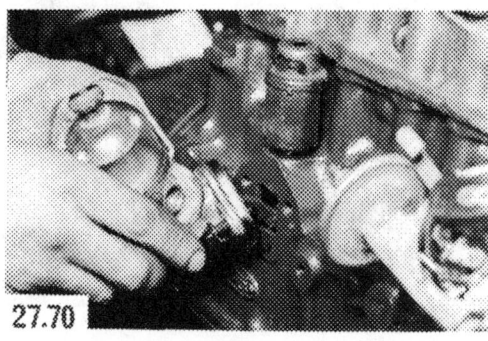
27.70

70. Replace the fuel pump using a new gasket and tighten up the two securing bolts. (See Photograph).

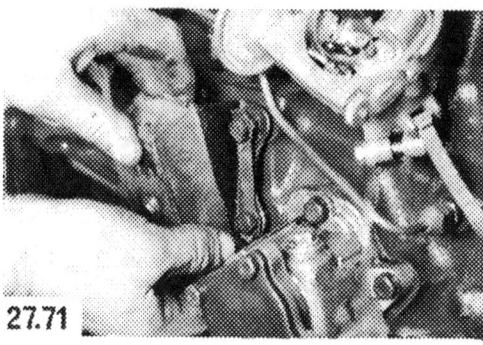
27.71

71. Refit the engine mounting rubber on the right hand side remembering to fit a new lockwasher under the heads of the bolts. Knock up the lock tabs on the washers. (See Photograph).

27.72

72. Fit the thermostat and thermostat gasket to the cylinder head outlet as shown.
73. Then fit the thermostat elbow and tighten up the two securing bolts and lockwashers. (See Photograph).
74. Replace the sparking plugs; refit the rocker cover using a new gasket; fit the dynamo so there is $\frac{1}{2}$ in. play in the fan belt between the water pump and dynamo pulleys; refit the vacuum advance pipe to the distributor; and refit the oil pressure sender unit.

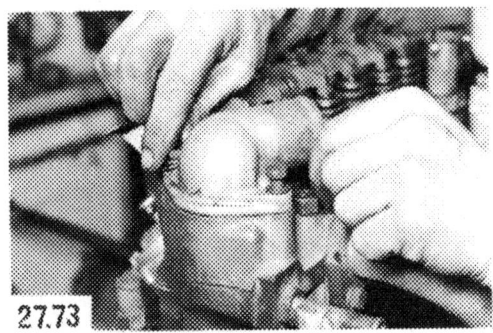

27.73

28. FINAL ASSEMBLY

1. Reconnect the ancilliary components to the engine in the reverse order to which they were removed.
2. It should be noted that in all cases it is best to reassemble the engine as far as possible before refitting it to the car. This means that the inlet and exhaust manifolds, carburettor, dynamo, water thermostat, oil filter, distributor and engine mounting brackets, should all be in position. Ensure that the oil filter is filled with engine oil, as otherwise there will be a delay in the oil reaching the bearings while the oil filter refills.

29. ENGINE REPLACEMENT - GENERAL

Although the engine can be replaced with one man and a suitable winch, it is easier if two are present. One to lower the engine into the engine compartment and the other to guide the engine into position and to ensure it does not foul anything. Generally speaking, engine replacement is a reversal of the procedure used when removing the engine. There are several points however which if noted will make replacement much easier. These are given below.

30. ENGINE REPLACEMENT WITHOUT GEARBOX

1. Position a sling around the engine and support its weight on suitable lifting tackle. If using a fixed hoist raise the engine and then roll the car under it. Place a jack under the gearbox.
2. Lower the engine into the engine compartment ensuring that nothing is fouling. Line up the engine and gearbox raising the height of the gearbox if necessary with the jack until the splines on the gearbox input shaft mate with the splined grooves in the clutch disc centre.
3. To line up the mounting bracket holes it may be necessary to move the engine about slightly and this will be found to be much

easier if the lifting slings are still in position and taking most of the weight.
4. Replace the two bolts and spring washers holding the engine mountings to the cross tube.
5. Remove the slings from the engine, and jack up the front of the car securely so it can be worked on from underneath.
6. Working underneath the car replace the splash shield secured to the front of the clutch housing and do up the bolts holding the clutch housing to the rear of the engine. Replace the clutch slave cylinder and secure it with its circlip.
7. Refit the starter motor, replace the two retaining bolts, and the starter cable which is held in place with a nut and washer.
8. Replace the engine breather pipe on the clutch housing, and reconnect the fuel lines.
9. Reconnect the high tension lead to the coil centre terminal and the low tension lead to the terminal on the side of the distributor. Refit the ignition distributor cap and connect the H.T. leads to the plugs (if not already done).
10. Refit the heater motor to the heater motor box; reconnect the exhaust downpipe to the exhaust manifold; and secure the throttle linkage and choke control to the carburettor.
11. Replace the radiator and reconnect the top and bottom hoses and the heater hoses (on models fitted with a heater unit.)
12. Replace the engine splash shield; the air cleaner; the bonnet; and reconnect the two leads to the rear of the dynamo.
13. Reconnect the battery.
14. Check that the drain taps are closed and refill the cooling system with water and the engine with the correct grade of oil. Start the engine and carefully check for oil or water leaks. There should be no oil or water leaks if the engine has been reassembled carefully, all nuts and bolts tightened down correctly, and new gaskets and joints used throughout.

31. ENGINE REPLACEMENT WITH GEARBOX

1. Position a sling roung the engine/gearbox unit and support its weight on suitable lifting tackle. If using a fixed hoist raise the power unit and roll the car under it so the power unit will easily drop into the engine compartment.
2. Lower the power unit into position moving the car forward at the same time. When the engine is $\frac{3}{4}$ in it will be found helpful to place a trolley jack under the gearbox.

3. Follow the instructions in Chapter 1/30, paras. 3 to 5.

4. Reposition the jack under the rear of the engine and replace the rear support cross-member tightening down the four bolts and locking washers. Refit the gearlever and gaiter. Refit the propeller shaft.

5. Replace the clutch slave cylinder and then follow the instructions given in Chapter 1/30, paragraphs 7 to 14.

ENGINE

Cause	Trouble	Remedy
SYMPTOM:	EXCESSIVE OIL CONSUMPTION	
Oil being burnt by engine	Badly worn, perished or missing valve stem oil seals	Remove, fit new oil seals to valve stems.
	Excessively worn valve stems and valve guides	Remove cylinder head and fit new valves and valve guides.
	Worn piston rings	Fit oil control rings to existing pistons or purchase new pistons.
	Worn pistons and cylinder bores	Fit new pistons and rings, rebore cylinders.
	Excessive piston ring gap allowing blow-by	Fit new piston rings and set gap correctly.
	Piston oil return holes choked	Decarbonise engine and pistons.
Oil being lost due to leaks	Leaking oil filter gasket	Inspect and fit new gasket as necessary.
	Leaking rocker cover gasket	" " " " " " "
	Leaking tappet chest gasket	" " " " " " "
	Leaking timing case gasket	" " " " " " "
	Leaking sump gasket	" " " " " " "
	Loose sump plug	Tighten, fit new gasket if necessary.
SYMPTOM:	UNUSUAL NOISES FROM ENGINE	
Excessive clearances due to mechanical wear	Worn valve gear (Noisy tapping from rocker box)	Inspect and renew rocker shaft, rocker arms, and ball pins as necessary.
	Worn big end bearing (Regular heavy knocking)	Drop sump, if bearings broken up clean out oil pump and oilways, fit new bearings. If bearings not broken but worn fit bearing shells.
	Worn timing chain and gears (Rattling from front of engine)	Remove timing cover, fit new timing wheels and timing chain.
	Worn main bearings (Rumbling and vibration)	Drop sump, remove crankshaft, if bearings worn but not broken up, renew. If broken up strip oil pump and clean out oilways.
	Worn crankshaft (Knocking, rumbling and vibration)	Regrind crankshaft, fit new main and big end bearings.

FAULT FINDING CHART

Cause	Trouble	Remedy
SYMPTOM:	**ENGINE FAILS TO TURN OVER WHEN STARTER BUTTON PULLED**	
No current at starter motor	Flat or defective battery Loose battery leads Defective starter solenoid or switch or broken wiring Engine earth strap disconnected	Charge or replace battery. Push-start car. Tighten both terminals and earth ends of earth lead. Run a wire direct from the battery to the starter motor or by-pass the solenoid. Check and retighten strap.
Current at starter motor	Jammed starter motor drive pinion Defective starter motor	Place car in gear and rock from side to side. Alternatively, free exposed square end of shaft with spanner. Remove and recondition.
SYMPTOM:	**ENGINE TURNS OVER BUT WILL NOT START**	
No spark at sparking plug	Ignition damp or wet Ignition leads to spark plugs loose Shorted or disconnected low tension leads Dirty, incorrectly set, or pitted contact breaker points Faulty condenser Defective ignition switch Ignition leads connected wrong way round Faulty coil Contact breaker point spring earthed or broken	Wipe dry the distributor cap and ignition leads. Check and tighten at both spark plug and distributor cap ends. Check the wiring on the CB and SW terminals of the coil and to the distributor. Clean, file smooth, and adjust. Check contact breaker points for arcing, remove and fit new. By-pass switch with wire. Remove and replace leads to spark plugs in correct order. Remove and fit new coil. Check spring is not touching metal part of distributor. Check insulator washers are correctly placed. Renew points if the spring is broken.
No fuel at carburettor float chamber or at jets	No petrol in petrol tank Vapour lock in fuel line (In hot conditions or at high altitude) Blocked float chamber needle valve Fuel pump filter blocked Choked or blocked carburettor jets Faulty fuel pump	Refill tank! Blow into petrol tank, allow engine to cool, or apply a cold wet rag to the fuel line. Remove, clean, and replace. Remove, clean, and replace. Dismantle and clean. Remove, overhaul, and replace.
Excess of petrol in cylinder or carburettor flooding	Too much choke allowing too rich a mixture to wet plugs Float damaged or leaking or needle not seating Float lever incorrectly adjusted	Remove and dry sparking plugs or with wide open throttle, push-start the car. Remove, examine, clean and replace float and needle valve as necessary. Remove and adjust correctly.
SYMPTOM:	**ENGINE STALLS & WILL NOT START**	
No spark at sparking plug	Ignition failure - Sudden Ignition failure - Misfiring precludes total stoppage Ignition failure - In severe rain or after traversing water splash	Check over low and high tension circuits for breaks in wiring Check contact breaker points, clean and adjust. Renew condenser if faulty. Dry out ignition leads and distributor cap.
No fuel at jets	No petrol in petrol tank Petrol tank breather choked Sudden obstruction in carburettor Water in fuel system	Refill tank. Remove petrol cap and clean out breather hole or pipe. Check jets, filter, and needle valve in float chamber for blockage Drain tank and blow out fuel lines

ENGINE FAULT FINDING CHART

Cause	Trouble	Remedy
SYMPTOM:	ENGINE MISFIRES OR IDLES UNEVENLY	
Intermittent sparking at sparking plug	Ignition leads loose	Check and tighten as necessary at spark plug and distributor cap ends.
	Battery leads loose on terminals	Check and tighten terminal leads.
	Battery earth strap loose on body attachment point	Check and tighten earth lead to body attachment point.
	Engine earth lead loose	Tighten lead.
	Low tension leads to SW and CB terminals on coil loose	Check and tighten leads if found loose.
	Low tension lead from CB terminal side to distributor loose	Check and tighten if found loose.
	Dirty, or incorrectly gapped plugs	Remove, clean, and regap.
	Dirty, incorrectly set, or pitted contact breaker points	Clean, file smooth, and adjust.
	Tracking across inside of distributor cover	Remove and fit new cover.
	Ignition too retarded	Check and adjust ignition timing.
	Faulty coil	Remove and fit new coil.
Fuel shortage at engine	Mixture too weak	Check jets, float chamber needle valve, and filters for obstruction. Clean as necessary. Carburettor(s) incorrectly adjusted.
	Air leak in carburettor(s)	Remove and overhaul carburettor.
	Air leak at inlet manifold to cylinder head, or inlet manifold to carburettor	Test by pouring oil along joints. Bubbles indicate leak. Renew manifold gasket as appropriate.
Mechanical wear	Incorrect valve clearances	Adjust rocker arms to take up wear.
	Burnt out exhaust valves	Remove cylinder head and renew defective valves.
	Sticking or leaking valves	Remove cylinder head, clean, check and renew valves as necessary.
	Weak or broken valve springs	Check and renew as necessary.
	Worn valve guides or stems	Renew valve guides and valves.
	Worn pistons and piston rings	Dismantle engine, renew pistons and rings.
SYMPTOM:	LACK OF POWER & POOR COMPRESSION	
Fuel/air mixture leaking from cylinder	Burnt out exhaust valves	Remove cylinder head, renew defective valves.
	Sticking or leaking valves	Remove cylinder head, clean, check, and renew valves as necessary.
	Worn valve guides and stems	Remove cylinder head and renew valves and valve guides.
	Weak or broken valve springs	Remove cylinder head, renew defective springs.
	Blown cylinder head gasket (Accompanied by increase in noise)	Remove cylinder head and fit new gasket.
	Worn pistons and piston rings	Dismantle engine, renew pistons and rings.
	Worn or scored cylinder bores	Dismantle engine, rebore, renew pistons & rings.
Incorrect Adjustments	Ignition timing wrongly set. Too advanced or retarded	Check and reset ignition timing.
	Contact breaker points incorrectly gapped	Check and reset contact breaker points.
	Incorrect valve clearances	Check and reset rocker arm to valve stem gap.
	Incorrectly set sparking plugs	Remove, clean and regap.
	Carburation too rich or too weak	Tune carburettor(s) for optimum performance.
Carburation and ignition faults	Dirty contact breaker points	Remove, clean, and replace.
	Fuel filters blocked causing top end fuel starvation	Dismantle, inspect, clean, and replace all fuel filters.
	Distributor automatic balance weights or vacuum advance and retard mechanisms not functioning correctly	Overhaul distributor.
	Faulty fuel pump giving top end fuel starvation	Remove, overhaul, or fit exchange reconditioned fuel pump.

CHAPTER TWO

COOLING SYSTEM

CONTENTS

SPECIFICATION

Type:	Pressurised radiator. Thermo-syphon, pump assisted, and fan cooled.
Thermostat Settings: Opens	170° to 179°F.
Fully Open	199°F.
Blow-off pressure of radiator cap	7 lb/sq. in (0.49 kg./cm^2).
Correct belt tension	1/2 in. free movement.
Cooling system capacity	11.4 pints (6.48 litres) with heater. 10.25 pints (5.8 litres) without heater.
Antifreeze Mixture: Not exceeding 15°F of frost	1.25 pints.
Not exceeding 25°F of frost	1.75 pints.
(ME1167-B or equivalent) Not exceeding 35°F of frost	2.25 pints.

GENERAL DESCRIPTION

The engine cooling water is circulated by a thermo-syphon, water pump assisted system, and the coolant is pressurised. This is to both prevent the loss of water down the overflow pipe with the radiator cap in position and to prevent premature boiling in adverse conditions. The radiator cap is pressurised to 7 lb/sq. in. and increases the boiling point to 225°F. If the water temperature exceeds this figure and the water boils, the pressure in the system forces the internal part of the cap off its seat, thus exposing the overflow pipe down which the steam from the boiling water escapes thus relieving the pressure. It is, therefore, important to check that the radiator cap is in good condition and that the spring behind the sealing washer is not weakened. Most garages have a special machine in which radiator caps can be tested.

The cooling system comprises the radiator, top and bottom water hoses, heater hoses (if heater/demister fitted), the impeller water pump, (mounted on the front of the engine it carries the fan blades and is driven by the fan belt), the thermostat and the two drain taps.

The system functions in the following fashion. Cold water in the bottom of the radiator circulates up the lower radiator hose to the water pump where it is pushed round the water passages in the cylinder block, helping to keep the cylinder bores and pistons cool.

The water then travels up into the cylinder head and circulates round the combustion spaces and valve seats absorbing more heat, and then, when the engine is at its proper operating temperature, travels out of the cylinder head, past the open thermostat into the upper radiator hose, and so into the radiator header tank. The water travels down the radiator where it is rapidly cooled by the in-rush of cold air through the radiator core, which is created by both the fan and the motion of the car. The water, now cold, reaches the bottom of the radiator, when the cycle is repeated.

When the engine is cold the thermostat (which is a valve which opens and closes according to the temperature of the water) prevents the cold water from flowing into the radiator, thus enabling the engine to warm up quickly. Only when the correct minimum operating temperature has been reached, as shown in the specification, does the thermostat begin to open, allowing water to return to the radiator.

2. COOLING SYSTEM - DRAINING

With the car on level ground drain the system as follows:

1.   If the engine is cold remove the filler cap from the radiator by turning the cap anti-clockwise. If the engine is hot having just been run, then turn the filler cap very slightly until the pressure in the system had had time to disperse. Use a rag over the cap to protect your hand from escaping steam. If, with the engine very hot, the cap is released suddenly the drop in pressure can result in the water boiling. With the pressure released the cap can be removed.

2.   If anti-freeze is in the radiator drain it into a clean bucket or bowl for re-use.

3.   Open the two drain taps. When viewed from the front the radiator drain tap or plug is on the bottom right-hand side of the radiator, and the engine drain tap is halfway down the rear right-hand side of the cylinder block. A short length of rubber tubing over the radiator drain tap nozzle will assist draining the coolant into a container without splashing.

4.   When the water has finished running, probe the drain tap orifices with a short piece of wire to dislodge any particles of rust or sediment which may be blocking the taps and preventing all the water draining out.

3. COOLING SYSTEM - FLUSHING

With time the cooling system will gradually lose its efficiency as the radiator becomes choked with rust scales, deposits from the water, and other sediment. To clean the system out, remove the radiator cap and the drain tap and leave a hose running in the radiator cap orifice for ten to fifteen minutes.

In very bad cases the radiator should be reverse flushed. This can be done with the radiator in position. The cylinder block tap is closed and a hose placed over the open radiator drain tap. Water, under pressure, is then forced up through the radiator and out of the header tank filler orifice.

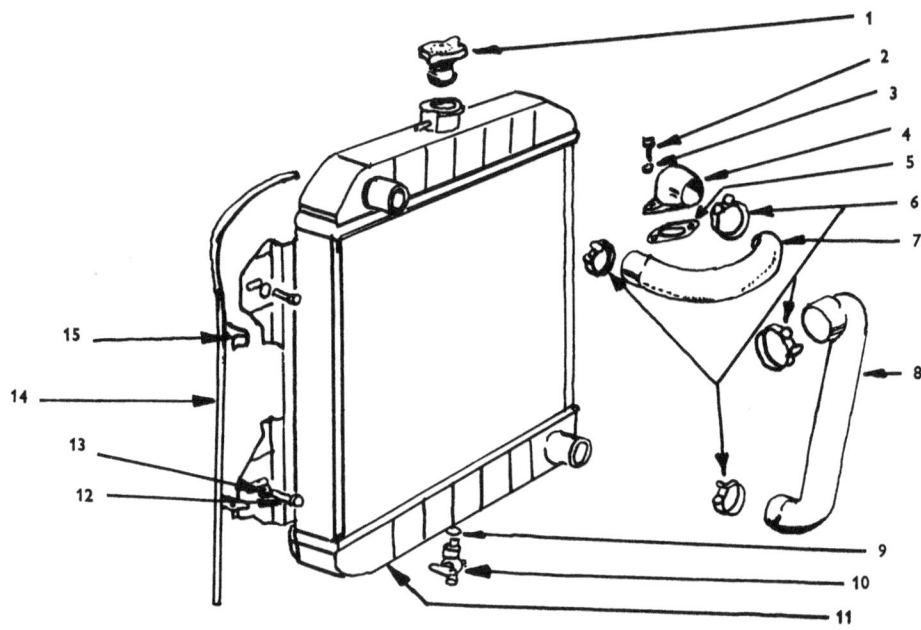

Fig. 2:1 EXPLODED VIEW OF THE RADIATOR AND ANCILLIARY COMPONENTS. 1 Radiator cap. 2 Bolt. 3 Spring washer. 4 Take off pipe. 5 Gasket. 6 Clips. 7 Top pipe. 8 Bottom pipe. 9 Washer. 10 Drain tap. 11 Radiator. 12 Bracket. 13 Spring washer & bolt. 14 overflow pipe. 15 Clip.

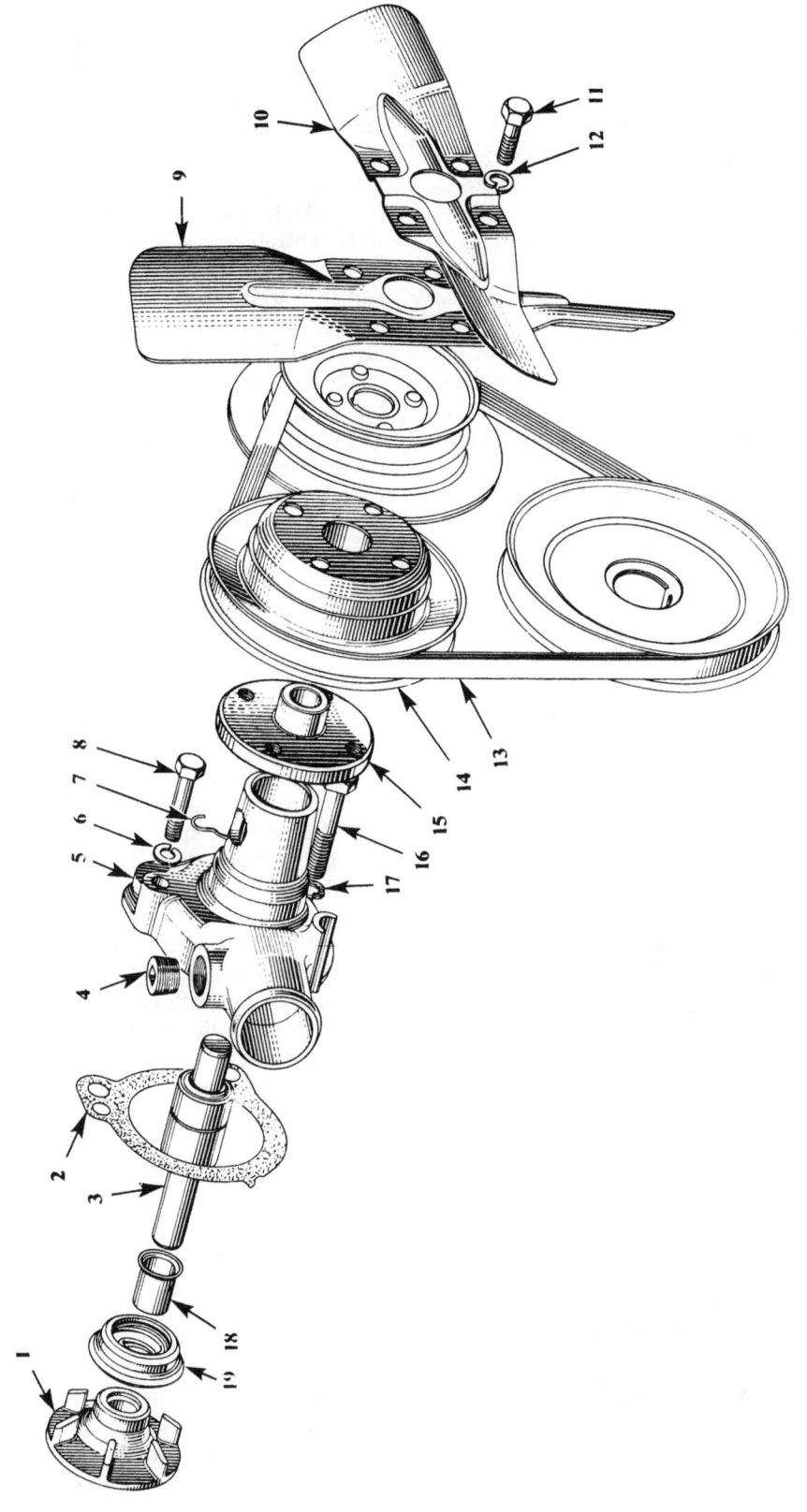

Fig. 2:2 EXPLODED VIEW OF THE WATER PUMP.

1 Impellor. 2 Gasket. 3 Spindle & bearing. 4 Plug. 5 Water pump body. 6 Spring washer. 7 Bearing securing wire. 8 Bolt. 9 Fan blade. 10 Additional fan blade — export only. 11 Bolt. 12 Spring washer. 13 Fan belt. 14 Fan & water pump pulley. 15 Hub pulley. 16 Bolt. 17 Spring washer. 18 Slinger. 19 Seal.

The hose is then removed and placed in the filler orifice and the radiator washed out in the usual fashion.

4. COOLING SYSTEM - FILLING

1. Close the two drain taps.
2. Fill the system slowly to ensure that no air locks develop. If a heater unit is fitted, check that the valve to the heater unit is open, otherwise an air lock may form in the heater. The best type of water to use in the cooling system is rain water, so use this whenever possible.
3. Do not fill the system higher than within 1/2 in. of the filler orifice. Overfilling will merely result in wastage which is especially to be avoided when anti-freeze is in use.
4. Only use anti-freeze mixture with a glycerine or ethylene base.
5. Replace the filler cap and turn it firmly clockwise to lock it into position.

Fig. 2:3 The bottom thermostat should be discarded since the large valve is permanently jammed open.

5. RADIATOR REMOVAL - INSPECTION & CLEANING

The radiator is removed by the procedure described in Chapter 1/4. 6 and 7.

With the radiator out of the car any leaks can be soldered up or repaired with a substance such as 'Cataloy'. Clean out the inside of the radiator by flushing as detailed in the section before last. When the radiator is out of the car it is advantageous to turn it upside down for reverse flushing. Clean the exterior of the radiator by hosing down the radiator matrix with a strong jet of water to clear away road dirt, dead flies, etc.

Inspect the radiator hoses for cracks, internal or external perishing, and damage caused by over-tightening of the securing clips. Replace the hoses as necessary. Examine the radiator hose securing clips and renew them if they are rusted or distorted. The drain taps should be renewed if leaking, but ensure the leak is not because of a faulty washer behind the tap. If the tap is suspected try a new washer to see if this clears the trouble first.

6. RADIATOR REPLACEMENT

1. Fit the radiator bottom hose to the water pump but do not tighten the clip completely. Fit the top hose in position on the top radiator pipe and again do not completely tighten the clip.
2. Replace the radiator in the bodyshell.
3. Screw in the four bolts and spring washers which hold the radiator in place.
4. Fit the top radiator hose to the thermostat outlet pipe and the bottom hose to the outlet pipe on the bottom of the radiator.
5. Tighten up the radiator hose clips. Fill the system with 11.4 pints of water; replace the radiator cap; run the engine; and check for leaks.

7. THERMOSTAT REMOVAL, TESTING & REPLACEMENT

1. To remove the thermostat partially drain the cooling system (4 pints is enough), loosen the upper radiator hose at the thermostat elbow end and pull it off the elbow. Unscrew the two set bolts and spring washers from the thermostat housing and lift the housing and paper gasket away. Take out the thermostat.
2. Test the thermostat for correct functioning, by immersing it in a saucepan of cold water together with a thermometer. Heat the water and note when the thermostat begins to open. Discard the thermostat if it opens too early. Continue heating the water until

the thermostat is fully open. Then let it cool down naturally. If the thermostat will not open fully in boiling water, or does not close down as the water cools, then it must be exchanged for a new one. If the thermostat is stuck open when cold this will be apparent when removing it from the housing.

3. Replacing the thermostat is a reversal of the removal procedure. Remember to use a new paper gasket between the thermostat housing elbow and the thermostat. Renew the thermostat elbow if it is badly eaten away.

8. WATER PUMP REMOVAL

1. Drain the cooling system and then remove the hose from the bottom of the radiator at the pump inlet. Also remove the heater hose if this is fitted from the top of the pump. Numerical references in this section refer to Fig. 2:1.

2. Loosen the dynamo securing bolts and swing the dynamo in towards the block so the fan belt can be removed.

3. Undo the four bolts 11 which hold the fan blades 9, 10 and the pulley wheel 14 in place. (Most models have only a two bladed fan).

4. Remove the fan blades and the pulley wheel and undo the three bolts which hold the water pump 5 to the block.

5. Take off the pump together with its gasket. A worn out pump can be exchanged as a unit, or dismantled and repaired using the special repair kit supplied.

9. WATER PUMP DISMANTLING & REASSEMBLY

1. Remove the hub 15 from the water pump shaft and heating assembly 3 either by judicious levering or by using a suitable hub puller, such as Ford tools CPT8000 and P8000-4.

2. Carefully pull out the bearing retainer wire 7 and then with the aid of two blocks (a small mandrel and a large vice, if the proper tools are not available) press out the shaft and bearing assembly 3 together with the impeller 1, and seal from the water pump body 5.

3. The impeller vane is removed from the spindle by judicious tapping and levering, or preferably, to ensure no damage and for ease of operation, with an extractor.

4. Remove the seal 19 and the slinger 18 by splitting the latter with the aid of a sharp cold chisel.

5. The repair kit comprises a new shaft and bearing assembly, a slinger, seal, bush, clip and gasket.

To reassemble the water pump press the shaft and bearing assembly into the housing with the short end of the shaft to the front until the groove in the shaft is in line with the groove inside the housing. The retainer clip can then be inserted.

6. Press the pulley hub on to the front end of the shaft until the end of the shaft is half an inch from the outer face of the hubs.

7. Fit the new slinger bush with the flanged end first on to the rear of the shaft, and refit the pump seal on to the bush with the carbon thrust face towards the impeller.

8. Press the impeller on to the shaft until a clearance of 0.030 in. is obtained between the impeller blades and the housing face. This gap is checked with the aid of a feeler gauge. Check that the pump turns freely.

9. Replacement of the pump on the front of the block is a reversal of the sequence in Chapter 2:8.

10. The fan belt tension must be correct when all is reassembled. If the belt is too tight undue strain will be placed on the water pump and dynamo bearings, and if the belt is too loose it will slip and wear rapidly as well as giving rise to low electrical output from the dynamo. Finally check carefully for leaks.

10. FAN BELT ADJUSTMENT

1. The fan belt tension is correct when there is 1/2 in. of lateral movement at the mid-point position of the belt between the dynamo pulley wheel and the water pump pulley wheel.

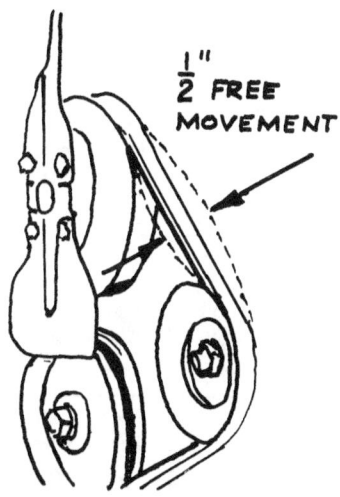

Fig. 2:4 The correct fan belt tension is set midway between the water pump and dynamo pulley wheels.

2. To adjust the fan belt, slacken the dynamo securing bolts and move the dynamo either in or out until the correct tension is obtained. It is easier if the dynamo bolts are only slackened a little so it requires some force to move the dynamo. In this way the tension of the belt can be arrived at more quickly than by making frequent adjustments. If difficulty is experienced in moving the dynamo away from the engine a long spanner placed behind the dynamo and resting against the block serves as a very good lever and can be held in this position while the dynamo bolts are tightened.

11. TEMPERATURE GAUGE

Fitted in the instrument panel is a temperature gauge which is controlled electrically by a sender unit located in the cylinder head.

After the engine has warmed up the gauge needle should normally rest in the top of the sector of the gauge marked N or the bottom half of the sector marked H. If the gauge malfunctions then check the connections to it and to the sender unit.

If a loose connection is not found then test the sender unit and the gauge by substitution. Unfortunately, neither are repairable. The gauge is removed from the rear of the instrument panel after undoing a small screw. See Fig. 10.7

The higher the temperature of the cooling water the more efficient the engine becomes, so, providing the water does not boil and so escape, there is nothing to worry about if the gauge needle normally rests in the sector marked H.

FAULT FINDING CHART

Cause	Trouble	Remedy
SYMPTOM: OVERHEATING		
Heat generated in cylinder not being successfully disposed of by radiator	Insufficient water in cooling system	Top up radiator
	Fan belt slipping (Accompanied by a shrieking noise on rapid engine - acceleration	Tighten fan belt to recommended tension or replace if worn.
	Radiator core blocked or radiator grill restricted	Reverse flush radiator, remove obstructions.
	Bottom water hose collapsed, impeding flow	Remove and fit new hose.
	Thermostat not opening properly	Remove and fit new thermostat.
	Ignition advance and retard incorrectly set (Accompanied by loss of power, and perhaps, misfiring)	Check and reset ignition timing.
	Carburettor(s) incorrectly adjusted (mixture too weak)	Tune carburettor(s).
	Exhaust system partially blocked	Check exhaust pipe for constrictive dents and blockages.
	Oil level in sump too low	Top up sump to full mark on dipstick.
	Blown cylinder head gasket (Water/ steam being forced down the radiator overflow pipe under pressure)	Remove cylinder head, fit new gasket.
	Engine not yet run-in	Run-in slowly and carefully.
	Brakes binding	Check and adjust brakes if necessary.
SYMPTOM: UNDERHEATING		
Too much heat being dispersed by radiator	Thermostat jammed open	Remove and renew thermostat.
	Incorrect grade of thermostat fitted allowing premature opening of valve	Remove and replace with new thermostat which opens at a higher temperature.
	Thermostat missing	Check and fit correct thermostat.
SYMPTOM LOSS OF COOLING WATER		
Leaks in system	Loose clips on water hoses	Check and tighten clips if necessary.
	Top, bottom, or by-pass water hoses perished and leaking	Check and replace any faulty hoses.
	Radiator core leaking	Remove radiator and repair.
	Thermostat gasket leaking	Inspect and renew gasket.
	Radiator pressure cap spring worn or seal ineffective	Renew radiator pressure cap.

CHAPTER THREE

FUEL SYSTEM AND CARBURATION

CONTENTS

SPECIFICATIONS

At the time of writing no information was available concerning overhaul of the Ford Motorcraft carburettor fitted to 1966 on models.

Fuel pump
    Type ... ... Mechanical
    Delivery pressure ... ... 1.25 to 2 lb/sq in (0.09 to 0.14 kg/sq cm)
    Diaphragm spring test length ... ... 0.47 in (11.88 mm)
    Diaphragm spring test pressure ... ... 3.25 to 3.50 lb (1.48 to 1.59 kg/sq cm)
    Rocker arm spring test length ... ... 0.44 in (11.18 mm)
    Rocker arm spring test pressure ... ... 5 to 5.50 lb (2.27 to 2.50 kg)

Fuel tank capacity
    Saloon ... ... 31.82 litres (7 UK gals)
    Van ... ... 27.24 litres (6 UK gals)

Carburettor
    Type ... ... Solex or Ford downdraught
Specifications
    997 cc engine:

Solex 30 ZIC-3	Prior to Jan 1960	Jan 1960 to May 1962
Main jet	115	115
Main air correction jet	175	175
Economiser jet	140	140
Economiser air correction jet	195	195
Idling jet	50	40
Idling air correction jet	120	150

Starter jet 125	125
Venturi diameter (mm) 22	22

997 and 1200 cc engines (May 1962 to 1965):

Solex B 30 PSE ... ...997 cc	1200 cc
Main jet 97.5	110
Main air correction jet 160	200
Accelerator pump jet 45	40
Idling jet. 50	50
Idling air bleed (fixed) 0.85	60
Venturi diameter (mm) 21.5	23
Needle valve 1.3	1.6

997 and 1200 cc engines (1966 on):

Ford Motorcraft

Venturi diameter (mm) 21.6

Main jet:

Saloon... ... ...1.15

Van 1.12

Idling speed ... ...600 rpm

Fast idle speed ... ...1000 to 1100 rpm

Fast idle setting:

Saloon .. ..0.032 in (0.8 mm) No. 68 drill

Van ... ...0.035 in (0.9 mm) No. 64 drill

Choke plate pull-down . ...0.156 in (3.97 mm)

Accelerator pump stroke ... ...0.078 in (1.98 mm)

Float setting:

Inverted ... ...1.13 in (28.7 mm)

Upright ... ...1.38 to 1.40 in (35.1 to 35.6 mm)

1. GENERAL DESCRIPTION

The fuel system of all models consists of a fuel tank, a mechanically operated fuel pump and a downdraught carburettor.

The type of carburettor fitted differed slightly on models from May 1962 onwards and is dealt with later in this Chapter.

The fuel line between the rear mounted fuel tank and the fuel pump is clipped to the underside of the body floor pan and normally only requires occasional checking to ensure that it is not rubbing on the floor at any point.

The fuel tank is located at the rear beneath the luggage boot, and is retained by two straps and clamps. Anti-squeak pads are attached to the tank in the area of the straps, and a drain-plug is fitted to the tank.

2. FUEL TANK - MAINTENANCE

1. In the course of time rust sediment and droplets of water collect in the fuel tank and these may be drawn into the glass bowl of the pump filter.

2. If any quantity of water is suspected in the tank it will be helpful to allow the level of fuel in the tank to drop to a minimum and then the pipe connection from the tank is unscrewed and the fuel with its water and sediment content allowed to drain into a clean receptacle. In addition to indicating the condition of the fuel lines it will empty away any sediment before it reaches and blocks the carburettor jets.

3. Any appreciable amount of water or sediment in the tank will require that the tank drain plug be removed and the contents allowed to drain, but this may not clear unwanted matter from the actual fuel pipe. To clean unwanted matter from the fuel pipe it should be blown out under pressure by an air compressor

3. FUEL TANK - REMOVAL & REPLACEMENT

1. To remove the tank, first disconnect the battery and then remove the fuel pipe from the front face of the tank, draining any fuel into a container.

2. Remove the filler cap, unscrew the two filler neck hoses, remove the rubber hose and filler neck from inside the boot.

3. Support the tank while unscrewing the nuts from the threaded clamps, and then unhook the clamps from their brackets.

4. Lower the tank to a point permitted by the fuel tank contents gauge and disconnect the yellow-green covered wire from the tank unit. The tank may then be lowered and removed.

5. Replacement is a straightforward reversal of the removal sequence.

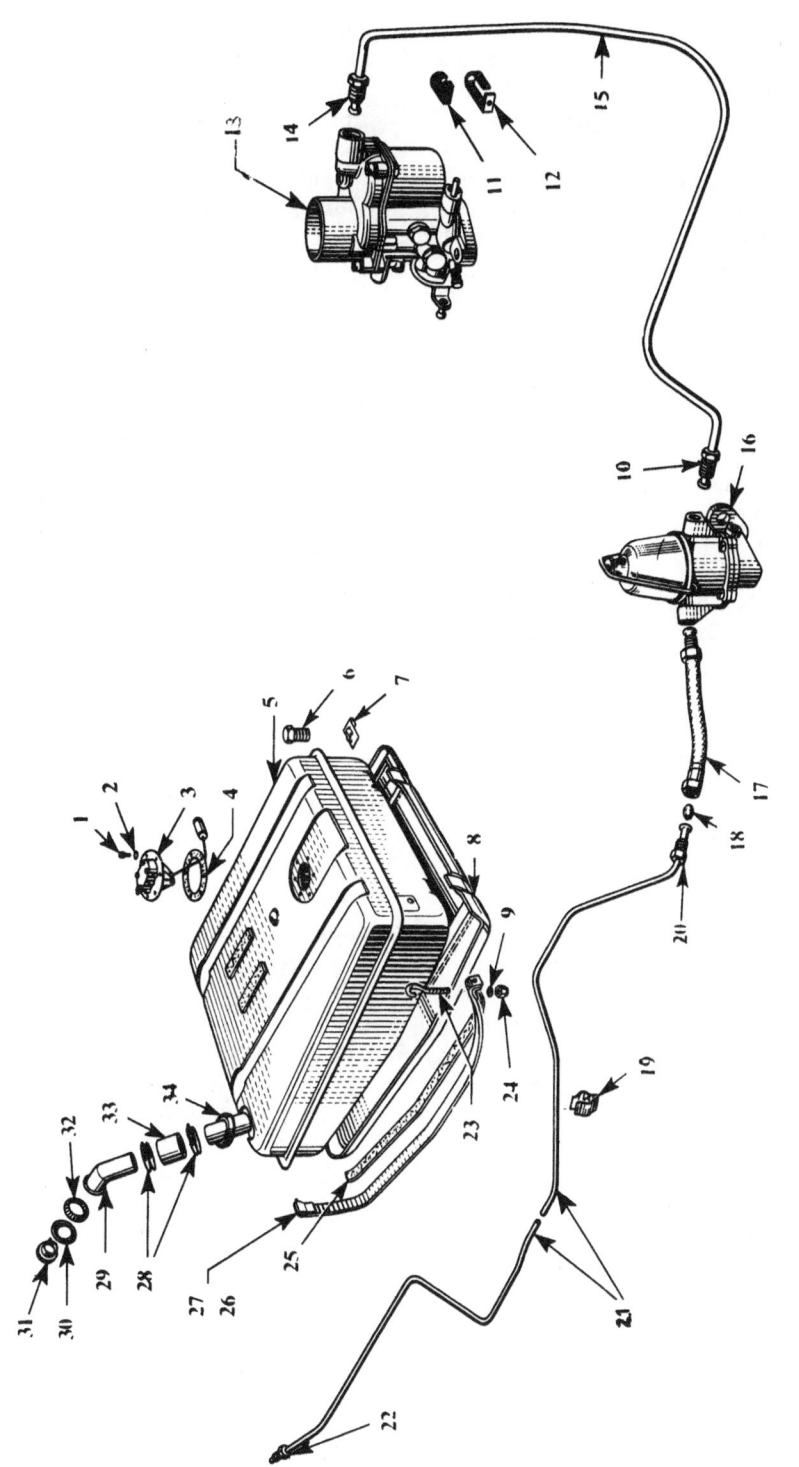

Fig. 3:1 EXPLODED VIEW OF THE ANGLIA FUEL SYSTEM.

1 Screw. 2 Washer. 3 Fuel gauge sender unit. 4 Seal. 5 Fuel tank. 6 Bolt. 7 Clip. 8 Tray. 9 Washer. 10 Petrol pipe union. 11 Bush. 12 Clip. 13 Carburettor. 14 Petrol pipe union. 15 Petrol pipe. 16 Fuel pump. 17 Flexible pipe. 18 Ferrule. 19 Clip. 20 Fuel pipe union nut. 21 Fuelpipe. 22 Fuel pipe union nut. 23 Support hook. 24 Nut. 25 Felt strip. 26 Right hand support bracket. 27 Left hand support bracket. 28 Fuel tank filler hose clamps. 29 Fuel tank filler pipe. 30 Fuel tank cap gasket. 31 Fuel cap. 32 Grommet. 33 Filler hose. 34 Grommet.

4. FUEL TANK CONTENTS GAUGE UNIT - REMOVAL, REPAIR & REPLACEMENT
   1. Mounted on top of the tank is the gauge unit. This consists of a float hinged and provided with a wiper contact so that when the float rises and falls a rheostat controls the electrical current voltage which is reflected at the fuel tank gauge on the dashboard.
   2. The float may be sluggish in operation, or may not work at all, and to obtain access the tank should be removed and then the six screws holding the unit to the tank are removed and the unit lifted out, taking care not to bend the float arm.
   3. Examine the tank unit to ensure that the rheostat is not damaged and that the wiper contact is bearing against the coil. Check the float for any accumulation of dirt which will give it additional weight and the pivot of the arm for easy movement, without excessive side play.
   4. When replacing the float, note that the float arm must make an angle of about 30° with the float towards the left-hand rear corner of the tank on the saloon cars. On the estate versions the float arm is vertical as the tank is in the side of the body.
   5. Use a new sealing ring between the gauge unit and the tank during reassembly.

5. FUEL PUMP - GENERAL DESCRIPTION
   1. The mechanically operated fuel pump is actuated through a spring loaded rocker arm. One arm of the rocker (8) bears against an eccentric on the camshaft and the other arm operates a diaphragm pull rod NOTE all numerical references in brackets should be co-related with Fig. No. 3:1.
   2. As the engine camshaft rotates, the eccentric moves the pivoted rocker arm outwards which in turn pulls the diaphragm pull rod and the diaphragm (5) down against the pressure of the diaphragm spring.
   3. This creates sufficient vacuum in the pump chamber to draw in fuel from the tank through the fuel filter gauze and non-return inlet valve (21).
   4. The rocker arm is held in constant contact with the eccentric by an anti-rattle spring (6), and as the engine camshaft continues to rotate the eccentric allows the rocker arm to move inwards. The diaphragm spring (20) is thus free to push the diaphragm (5) upwards forcing the fuel in the pump chamber out to the carburettor through the non-return outlet valve (21). NOTE that on some models a metal dome cover is used instead of the transparent bowl (24) illustrated. The metal dome is held in place by a centre bolt, the layout of the fuel pump being otherwise identical.
   5. When the float chamber in the carburettor is full the float chamber needle valve will close so preventing further flow from the fuel pump.
   6. The pressure in the delivery line will hold the diaphragm downwards against the pressure of the diaphragm spring, and it will remain in this position until the needle valve in the float chamber opens to admit more petrol.

6. FUEL PUMP - REMOVAL & REPLACEMENT
   1. The fuel pump is mounted on the right-hand side of the engine on a level with the camshaft.
   2. Remove the fuel inlet and outlet pipes by unscrewing the union nuts.
   3. Unscrew the two set bolts and spring washers which hold the pump to the crankcase.
   4. Lift the pump together with the gasket away from the crankcase.
   5. Replacement of the pump is a reversal of the above process. Remember to use a new crankcase to fuel pump gasket to ensure no oil leaks, ensure that both faces of the flange are perfectly clean, and check that the rocker arm lies on top of the camshaft eccentric and not underneath it.

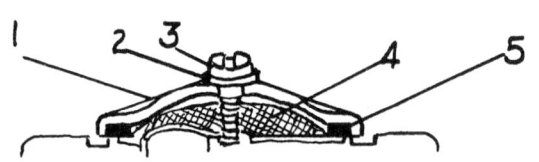

Fig. 3:2 Section through the top of the fuel pump fitted on earlier models. 1 Pressed cover. 2 Fibre washer. 3 Centre securing screw. 4 Mesh filter. 5 Gasket.

7. FUEL PUMP - TESTING
   1. Presuming that the fuel lines and unions are in good condition and that there are no leaks anywhere, check the performance of the fuel pump in the following manner.
   2. Disconnect the fuel pump at the carburettor inlet union, and the high tension lead to the coil, and with a jar or a large rag in position to catch the ejected fuel, turn the engine over on the starter motor solenoid.
   3. A good spurt of petrol should emerge from the end of the pipe every second revolution.

8. FUEL PUMP - MAINTENANCE

1. On the earlier models up to May 1962, the pump employed a wire gauze filter on the top of the unit, while later models have a glass bowl in which sediment is collected.

2. To clean the filter screen type, remove the central cover screw and fibre washer, lift off the dished cover, carefully remove the gasket and then lift away the filter screen together with the sediment which will have collected.

3. When replacing the top, take great care not to over-tighten the centre screw, otherwise the thread inside the body of the pump will be stripped. If this does happen the pump will have to be removed from the engine, the hole drilled out and re-threaded with a larger tap, and a larger bolt provided. It should be noted that the screw should only be tightened just enough to press the new gasket down to form an air-tight seal.

4. On later models the filter and glass sediment bowl can be cleaned after unscrewing the bowl retainer clamp. At the same time clean the filter screen.

9. FUEL PUMP - DISMANTLING, OVERHAUL & REASSEMBLY.

1. To overhaul the fuel pump, disconnect the pipe to the carburettor, unscrew the union nut on the fuel line from the tank and withdraw the pipe, plugging the end to prevent loss of fuel.

2. Unscrew the two bolts and spring washers holding the body of the pump to the cylinder block and by lifting the operating lever clear of the eccentric withdraw the pump.

3. To dismantle the pump, unscrew the top cover centre bolt, remove the cover and filter, and then mark the two parts of the body with a file to assist in re-assembly.

4. Remove the five screws and spring washers which secure the two halves of the pump body together, and separate taking care not to damage the diaphragm which is clamped between the two flanges.

5. The diaphragm will stand up, and can be removed by turning a quarter turn in either direction in order to free the centre rod from the operating lever. Remove the spring, oil seal retaining washer and rubber seal.

6. Inlet and outlet valves are retained by a spring steel plate, when the two valve assemblies together with a special gasket can be lifted from the body. To dismantle the lower body, remove the circlip from one end of the pivot pin on which the rocker

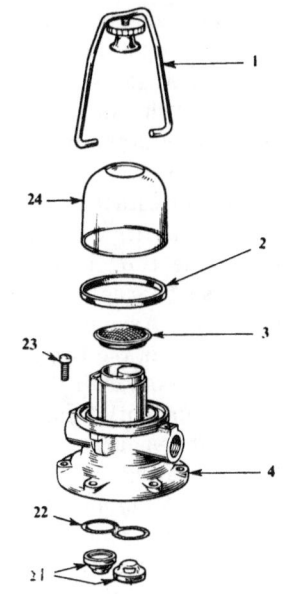

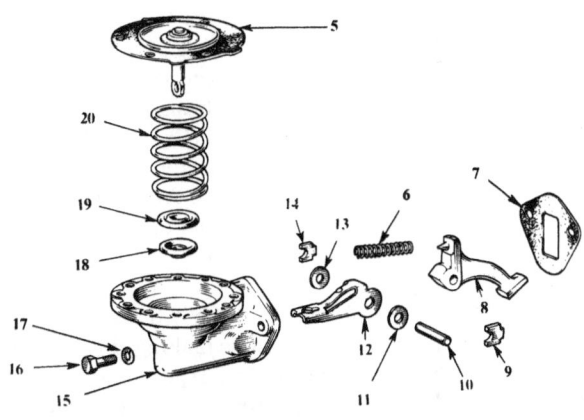

Fig. 3:3 EXPLODED VIEW OF THE MECHANICAL FUEL PUMP.
1 Clamp. 2 Gasket. 3 Filter. 4 Upper pump body. 5 Diaphragm. 6 Rocker arm spring. 7 Gasket. 8 Rocker arm. 9 Rocker arm pin retainer. 10 Rocker arm pin. 11 Washer. 12 Rocker arm link. 13 Washer. 14 Rocker arm pin retainer. 15 Lower pump body. 16 Bolt. 17 Spring washer. 18 Fuel pump oil seal. 19 Oil seal retainer. 20 Diaphragm spring. 21 Inlet and outlet valves. 22 Gasket. 23 Screw. 24 Sediment bowl.

arm operates and press out the pin. The rocker arm, spring, link and two washers can then be removed.

7. The general trouble with this type of pump relates to the diaphragm which breaks down in service and sometimes tears or develops a series of holes. This means that fuel is not drawn and pumped.

8. To reassemble the pump after a new diaphragm has been obtained, assemble the spring oil seal washer and seal to the pull rod of the new diaphragm. Insert the end of the rod in the slotted end of the link

(assuming the lower body has not been dismantled, or has been reassembled), engaging the grooves in the pull rod by turning a quarter of a turn against the pressure of the spring so that the smaller tabs on the diaphragm align with the mating mark on the lower body flange.

9. Hold the upper body with the valve locations uppermost and fit the figure 8 gasket in the body, then fit the two valve assemblies which will only seat correctly in their respective locations. Assemble the retainer plate and secure with the two screws.

10. Position the upper body over the diaphragm so that the inlet and outlet unions are directly opposite the mounting flange, and ensure that the mating mark on the lower body is in line with the smaller tab of the diaphragm. Press down the rocker arm until the diaphragm is level with the flange, put the five screws and their spring washers into position and screw them up finger tight. Work the rocker arm several times in order to centralise the diaphragm and make the final tightening of the screws with the rocker in the down position.

11. Complete the assembling by replacing the filter screen with the reinforcement upwards, fit a new gasket to the cover, fit the cover, making sure that there is a fibre washer under the head of the centre bolt. It is essential that the cover joint be airtight.

12. To refit the pump onto the engine, clean the mounting flanges making sure that none of the old gasket is left, otherwise oil may leak out of the joint. Fit a new gasket and then insert the rocker arm through the slot in the crankcase so that it lays on the camshaft eccentric, and secure with the two bolts and spring washers, drawing these tight evenly to prevent possible fracture of either of the flanges. Refit the inlet and outlet pipes and then run the engine and check for possible leaks at the unions.

10. AIR CLEANERS - MAINTENANCE

1. Early 997 c.c. models use either a paper element or oil bath type of air cleaner. Later models including the 1200 use either an oil wetted gauze or paper element cleaner. At intervals of 5,000 miles service the air cleaners in the following manner.

2. Detach the top cover by undoing the centre screw. This exposes the air cleaner element. If of the disposable type, remove and renew the element.

3. If an oil bath cleaner is fitted remove the complete cleaner from the car by undoing the clamp bolt and empty the dirty oil out of the cleaner body. Wash out the cleaner and the element with petrol. Replace the cleaner and fill it with engine oil to the arrow mark found on the side of the body. Shake off excess petrol from the element and replace in the cleaner. Refit the top cover.

4. If the cleaner comprises the dry gauze oil wetted type, after the gauze element has been removed it is washed in petrol. When clean dip the element in fresh engine oil, shake off the surplus, clean the inside of the cleaner body and replace the oil wetted element in the cleaner body. Refit the top cover and tighten the securing screw.

11. SOLEX 30 ZIC CARBURETTOR - REMOVAL, DISMANTLING & REPLACEMENT

1. The carburettor fitted to models between 1959 and 1962 (May) is of the single venturi down-draught type, having a separate two-stage starter device which progressively weakens the fuel mixture as the choke control is pushed in from the intermediate to the fully off positions.

2. The starter device is dustproof, all combustion air being drawn in from above the choke tube.

3. Unscrew the clamp securing the air cleaner to the carburettor and lift away the cleaner. Disconnect the fuel feed pipe and the vacuum pipe to the ignition distributor.

4. Detach the throttle control link from the throttle lever by springing it off at the ball joint against the spring pressure.

5. Slacken the choke cable and outer casing bolts and disconnect the cable control from the starter device.

6. Unscrew the nuts on the two carburettor flange studs and lift the carburettor away taking care of the two lockwashers.

7. Unscrew the four screws with their spring washers which secure the float chamber cover to the body and lift off the cover and gasket.

8. Lift out the float arm and hinge pin and remove the float. Remove the nut and flat washer securing the operating lever to the starter device spindle, pull off the lever and extract the locking ball and spring.

9. Unscrew the four bolts holding the starter device to the body and remove. The disc valves are removed as an assembly after removal of the circlip which secures the inner cover to the shaft.

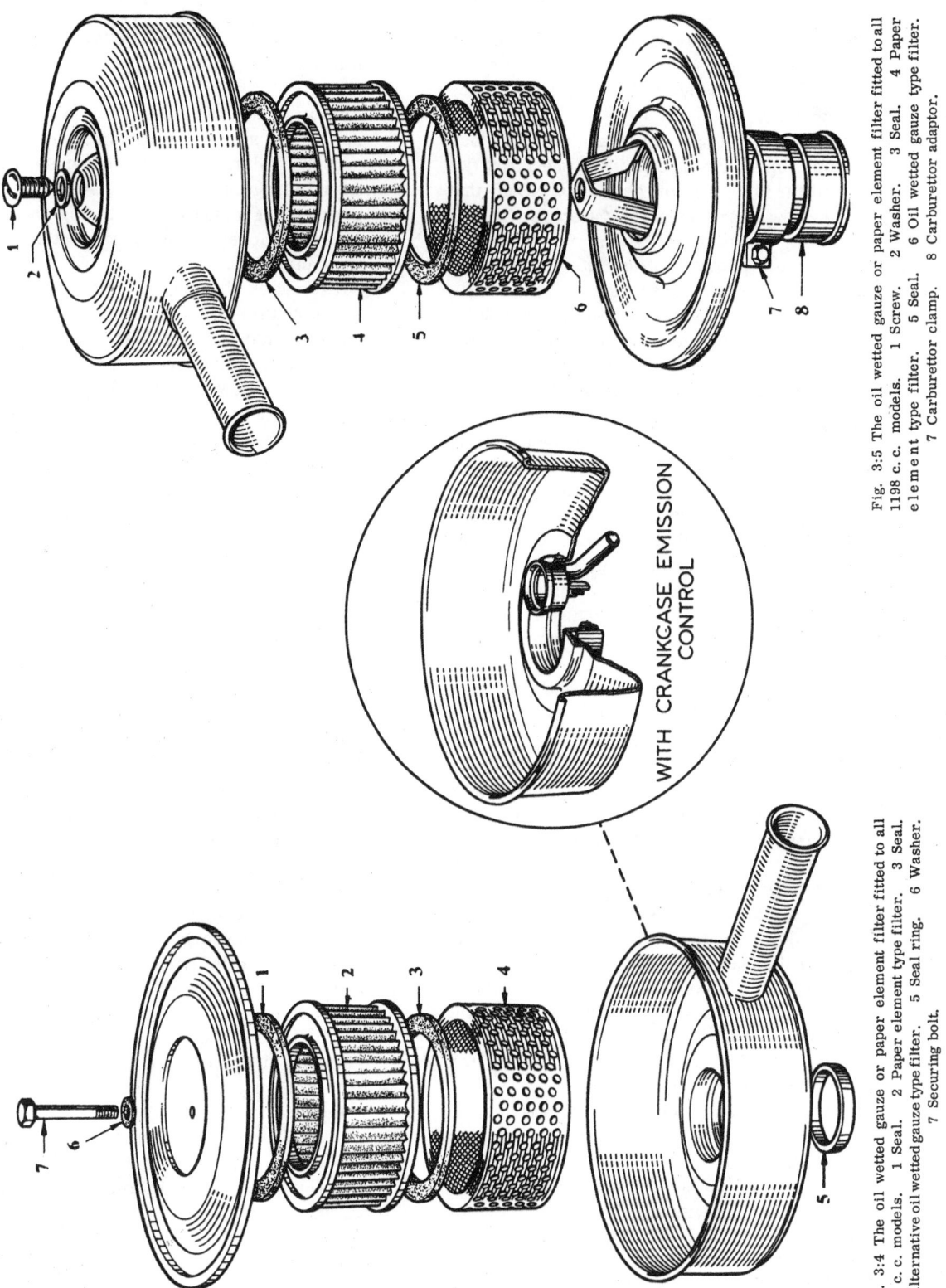

Fig. 3:5 The oil wetted gauze or paper element filter fitted to all 1198 c.c. models. 1 Screw. 2 Washer. 3 Seal. 4 Paper element type filter. 5 Seal. 6 Oil wetted gauze type filter. 7 Carburettor clamp. 8 Carburettor adaptor.

WITH CRANKCASE EMISSION CONTROL

Fig. 3:4 The oil wetted gauze or paper element filter fitted to all 997 c.c. models. 1 Seal. 2 Paper element type filter. 3 Seal. 4 Alternative oil wetted gauze type filter. 5 Seal ring. 6 Washer. 7 Securing bolt.

57

10. Unscrew the economiser and main jet air correction jets from the economiser body, lift off the body with the diffuser tube assembly.

11. Remove the starter jet, the main jet holder which includes the main jet, the idling jet and the idling air correction jet. NOTE that fibre washers must be fitted to all jets except the idling jet.

12. To remove the throttle plate and spindle, extract the two screws securing the plate in position and withdraw spindle and plate.

13. When refitting the throttle spindle ensure that, when the throttle is closed the mark (') stamped on the plate is towards the starting device and facing downwards.

14. Fit and tighten the two screws and lightly peen over the ends to lock them in position.

15. If the main jet has been removed, refit into its holder making certain that the fibre washer is in good order, otherwise there will be excessive fuel flow.

16. Check the washers on the economiser and starter jets before refitting. The idling jet has a taper on its seat and when refitting this do not overtighten.

17. If the discharge beak has been removed, refit by securing with the taper-ended screw.

18. Locate a new gasket on the economiser body and refit the body and diffuser tube assembly with one screw. Refit the economiser and main air correction jets.

19. Install the starter disc valve assembly in the taper cover, locate the ball and spring in the outer cover, set the disc valves with the slot in the inner valve vertical and install the operating lever.

20. Check this when the assembly is viewed from the front with the cable abutment bracket on the right, the locking ball hole on the lever is to the left. Fit and tighten the lever retaining nut.

21. Fit the starter device to the carburettor body and secure with the four screws, and then drop the float into its chamber with the cup washer upwards. Fit the float lever and hinge pin with the curve on the end of the lever towards the float.

22. Position a new gasket on top of the float chamber, fit the cover and secure with four screws and spring washers.

12. CARBURETTOR ADJUSTMENT

1. Once the carburettor is refitted to the intake manifold the engine is started up, all joints checked for possible fuel leakages, and the engine brought up to normal working temperature before adjustment is undertaken.

2. To obtain the exact setting for an individual engine the slow-running adjustment screw and the volume control screw should be adjusted together, and the most satisfactory results are obtained by tuning against a vacuum gauge which is connected to the inlet manifold.

3. First check that the air cleaner is clean because this affects the volume of air passing into the carburettor. Screw in the slow-running or throttle adjusting screw to allow the engine to idle a little faster than normal. Adjust the volume control screw to obtain the maximum reading on the gauge. Adjust the throttle control screw to bring the engine to a slower speed, adjusting the volume control until the maximum reading is obtained at the reasonable slow-running speed, the engine running evenly.

4. It is not advisable to have the engine running too slowly, otherwise this will place needless strains on the flexible rubber engine mountings.

13. SOLEX B 30 PSE CARBURETTOR - REMOVAL, DISMANTLING & REPLACEMENT

1. The carburettor fitted to later models is of the single venturi downdraught type incorporating an accelerator pump and economy device and a choke valve of the semi-automatic strangler type.

2. To remove the carburettor from the engine first remove the air cleaner, slacken back the clamp securing the cleaner hose to the carburettor top and lift off. Disconnect the fuel feed pipe union and the distributor vacuum pipe from the carburettor, and then disconnect the choke control cable at the operating cam, detaching the clip securing the outer cable in position. Remove the two nuts and spring washers which hold the flange to the manifold and lift off the carburettor.

3. To dismantle the carburettor first unscrew the five screws with spring washers securing the float chamber cover to the body, and lift away the body together with the gasket. Lift out the float arm and hinge pin and remove the float. Detach the split pin which retains the pushrod and spring, and then remove the four screws holding the accelerator pump in position, lifting away the pump body and operating arm

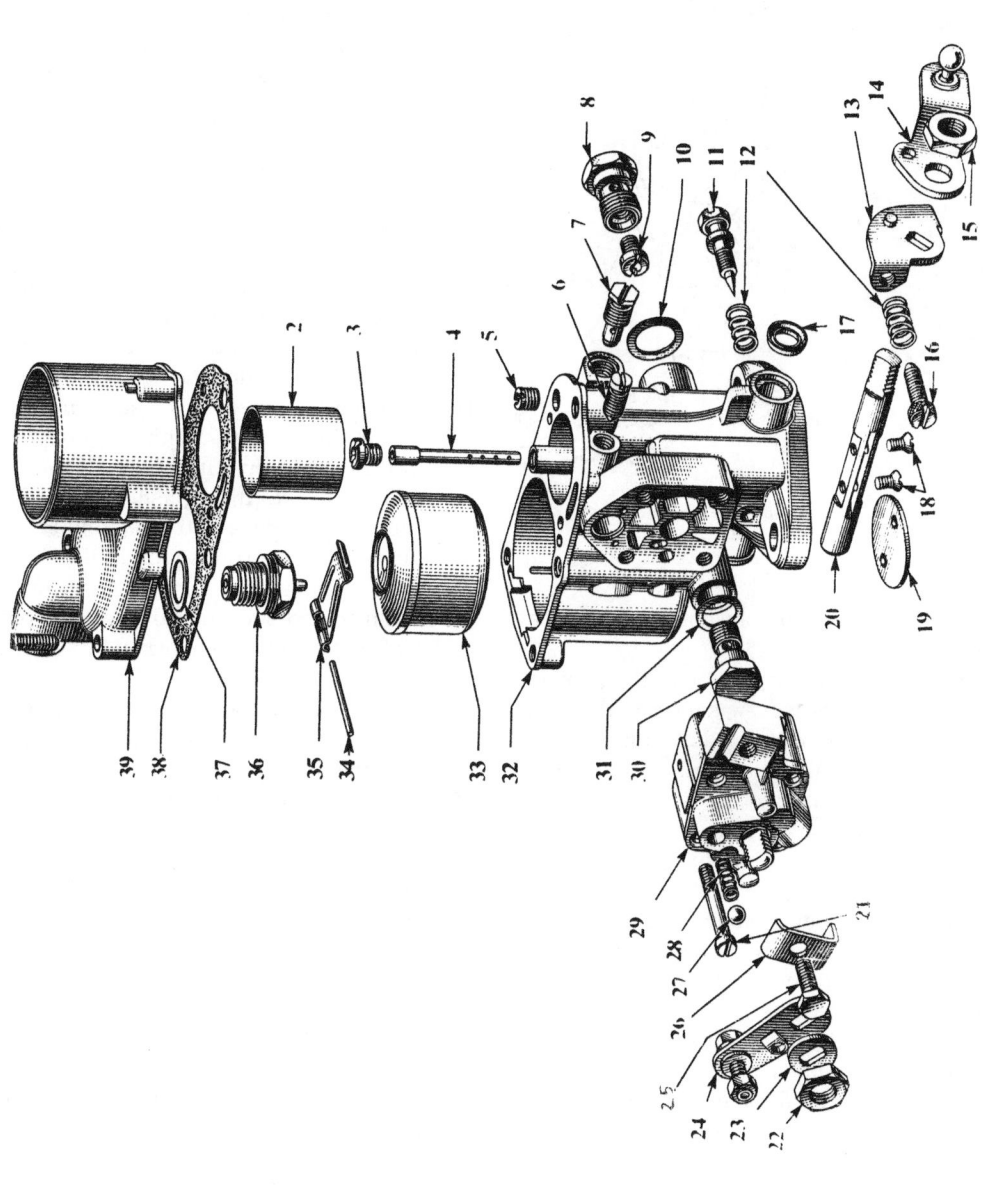

Fig. 3:6 THE SINGLE CHOKE CARBURETTOR FITTED TO THE ANGLIA VAN WITH LOW COMPRESSION.

1 Float chamber securing bolt.   2 Choke tube.   3 Main jet correction bleed.   4 Emulsion tube.   5 Auxiliary air jet bleed.   6 Choke tube fixing screw.   7 Auxiliary jet.   8 Main jet carrier bolt.   9 Main jet.   10 Washer.   11 Volume control screw.   12 Spring.   13 Throttle abutment plate.   14 Throttle lever.   15 Nut.
16 Idling adjustment screw.   17 Seal.   18 Screws.   19 Throttle disc.   20 Spindle.   21 Bolt.   22 Nut.   23 Washer.   24 Choke lever.   25 Bolt.   26 Clip.
27 Ball.   28 Spring.   29 Choke assembly.   30 Choke jet.   31 Washer.   32 Carburettor body.   33 Float.   34 Float lever pin.   35 Float lever.   36 Fuel
inlet valve.   37 Needle valve washer.   38 Gasket.   39 Float chamber cover.

59

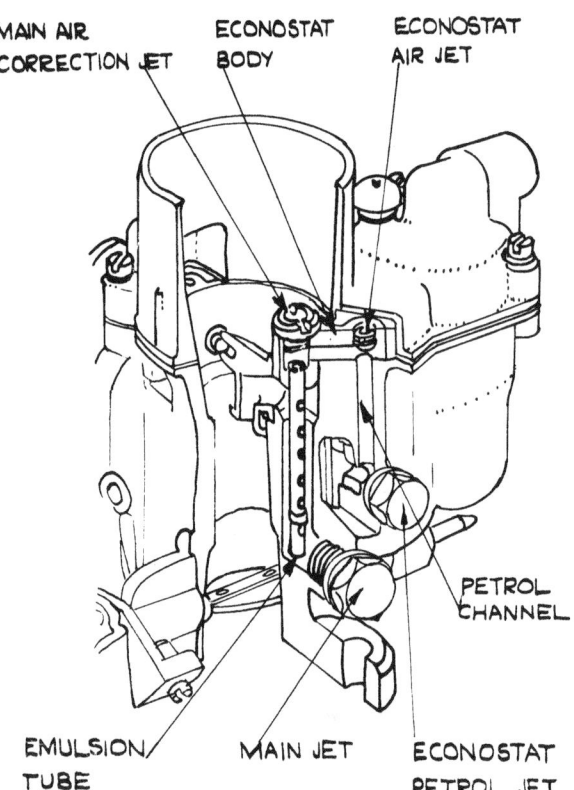

MAIN AIR CORRECTION JET   ECONOSTAT BODY   ECONOSTAT AIR JET

PETROL CHANNEL

EMULSION TUBE   MAIN JET   ECONOSTAT PETROL JET

Fig. 3:7 Section view of the carburettor — May, 1962 — showing the Econostat parts in relation to the main body.

together with the diaphragm and return spring.

4. Remove the spring clip securing the throttle link, unscrew the screw securing the link to the choke operating cam, and lift the link clear. Remove the bolt securing the operating cam and return spring and unscrew the cheese-headed screw holding the choke cable abutment bracket.

5. Unscrew the idling jet, high speed air correcting jet and emulsion tube assembly and lift off the accelerator pump discharge nozzle, then unscrew the anti-siphon valve and lift away the glass ball.

6. It is not normally necessary to remove the discharge beak but if this is removed then it will be essential to lock the taper end screw with lead shot when it is replaced. The shot should be inserted through the vertical drilling which will be located above the taper end screw.

7. Unscrew the bolt and flat washer which will give access to the main jet and allow this to be removed, and then to remove the throttle plate or spindle, extract the two screws which hold this plate in position and withdraw the spindle and plate.

8. First refit the throttle spindle into the carburettor body and then fit the throttle plate ensuring that the mark (') stamped on the plate is away from the accelerator pump and facing downwards when the throttle is closed. Fit and tighten the two securing screws and then lightly peen over the ends to prevent any possible loosening.

9. Replace the main jet and the blanking plug with its washer followed by the idling jet, main air correction jet and emulsion tube assembly and the accelerator pump discharge nozzle. Replace the glass ball and refit the anti-siphon valve, and then refit the choke cable abutment bracket, tightening the cheese-headed retaining screw finger-tight, while locating the choke operating cam and its retracting spring in position by using the hexagon headed bolt as a guide. Ensure that the inner end of the spring is located in the slot in the abutment bracket and that the outer end is against the 'V' in the operating cam. Both screws should then be tightened securely.

10. Replace the choke link, securing it to the choke-throttle link with a spring clip and to the choke operating cam with the adjustment bolt. Refit the pushrod to the spindle link, and secure with a spring clip. Replace the pushrod spring, attach the accelerator pump operating lever to the pushrod and secure with the split pin.

11. Install the return spring and diaphragm in the pump housing, refit the assembly to the carburettor body with the four retaining screws and then check the action of the return spring.

12. Drop the float into the float chamber with the cup washer to the top. Fit the float lever and hinge pin in position with the curve on the end of the lever towards the float.

13. Fit a new gasket on the top of the float chamber and offer to the cover while holding the choke plate in the fully open position. Secure firmly with the five screws and spring washers.

14. Once the carburettor is assembled it is fitted to the engine by first locating a new gasket on the manifold flange and then bolting down the carburettor flange, making quite certain that it is flat and level on the stud before tightening the nuts.

15. Connect up the distributor vacuum pipe to the rubber connection on the right-hand side, and refit the fuel pipe from the pump, Refit the throttle control rod to the upper end of the throttle lever connecting rod.

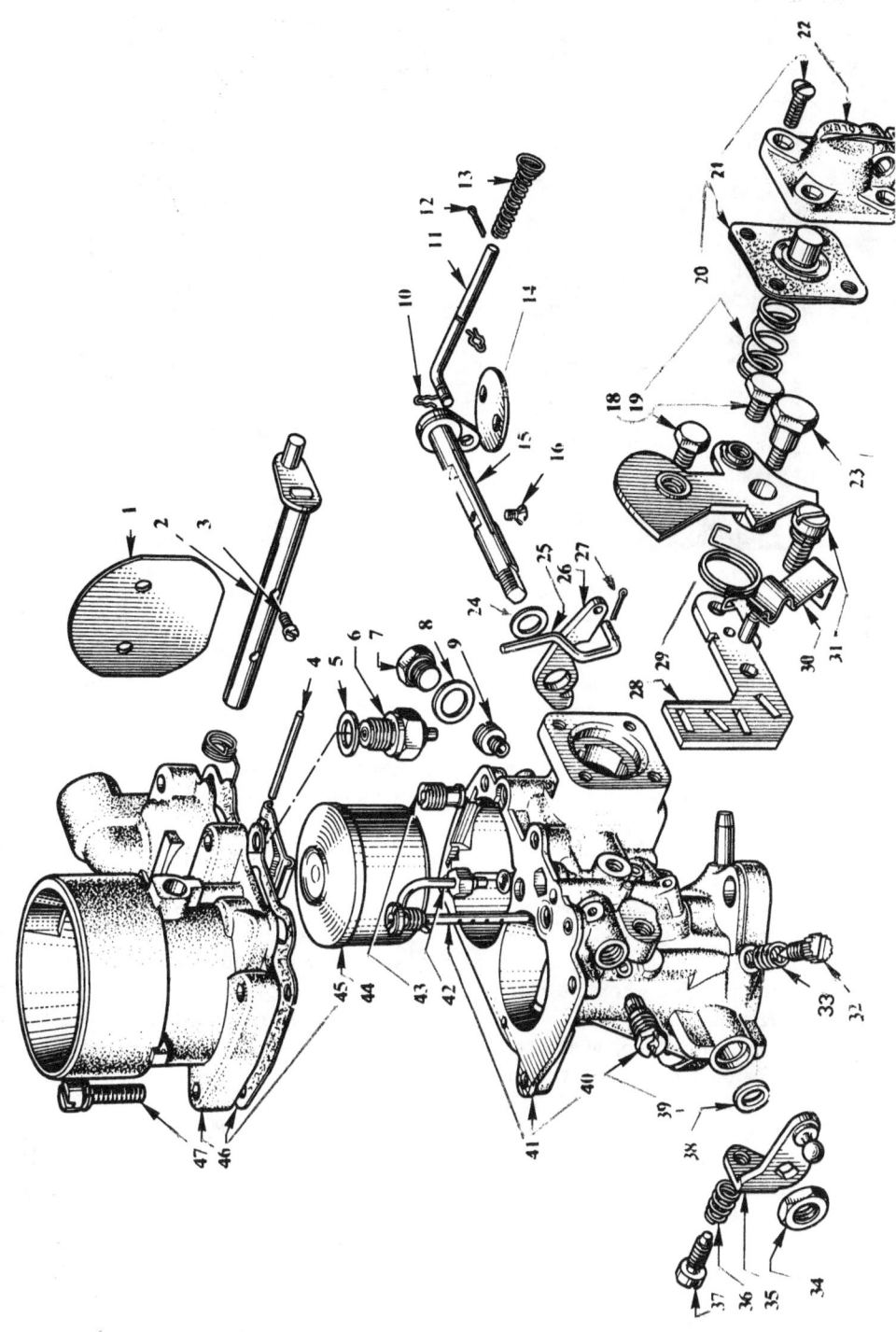

Fig. 3:8 THE CARBURETTOR FITTED TO THE SALOON AND ESTATE CAR AND VANS WITH HIGH COMPRESSION ENGINES.

1 Choke disc.   2 Choke spindle.   3 Grub screw.   4 Float chamber lever arm pin.   5 Washer.   6 Needle valve.   7 Bolt.   8 Washer.   9 Main jet.   10 Circlip.
11 Actuating arm.   12 Split pin.   13 Spring.   14 Throttle disc.   15 Throttle spindle.   16 Grub screw.   17 Carburettor choke lever assembly.   18 Bolts.
19 Spring.   20 Accelerator pump diaphragm.   21 Screw.   22 Accelerator pump cover.   23 Bolt.   24 Distance washer.   25 Fast idle rod.   26 Arm.   27 Split
pin.   28 Choke bracket.   29 Return spring.   30 Bracket.   31 Bolt.   32 Volume control screw.   33 Spring.   34 Nut.   35 Throttle control lever.   36 Spring.
37 Idling adjustment screw.   38 Washer.   39 Auxiliary jet.   40 Carburettor body.   41 Emulsion tube.   42 Accelerator pump jet.   43 Accelerator pump check
valve.   44 Float chamber.   45 Gasket.   46 Float chamber cover.   47 Bolt.

61

Fig. 3:9 The carburettor assembly in models from May, 1962 onwards.

Connect the choke control cable and tighten the clamp. Pass the cable inner wire through the choke operating cam trunnion and tighten the clamp screw. Check the operation of the choke to ensure that it opens and closes correctly and that there is a limited amount of slack in the cable when the control is pushed right home. Refit the air cleaner to the carburettor.

16. The choke control cable is adjusted at the operating cam to provide at least 1/8 in. free movement in the cable when the control is pushed right home.

17. The correct degree of throttle opening when the choke plate is closed for starting is obtained by placing a number 57 drill (1.1 mm.) between the edge of the throttle plate and the carburettor body at right angles to the throttle spindle.

18. Alternatively this setting can be obtained by screwing the throttle stop screw in three turns from the position which it abuts the throttle plate stop when the throttle is closed. It will be necessary to remove the throttle screw and remove the spring.

14. CARBURETTOR SLOW RUNNING ADJUSTMENT

1. To obtain the best slow-running adjustment the engine should be tuned against a vacuum gauge connected to the inlet manifold. To enable this to be accomplished a blanking plug will be found in the carburettor flange, and it is first necessary to remove this plug and fit in a screwed adaptor.

2. To this is connected a plastic tube which in turn is connected to the rear of a vacuum gauge.

3. Before commencing any adjustments make sure that the air cleaner is clean and not blocked, since this will affect the amount of air in the fuel mixture.

4. It is important to appreciate that the correct use of a vacuum gauge allows for checking the condition of the engine, the correct timing of the ignition and the general running characteristics as well as the correct tuning of the carburettor, and these points are dealt with in the Section dealing with tuning the engine for satisfactory running.

5. No adjustments to the carburettor should be attempted until the engine has been run to bring it up to working temperature.

6. To obtain correct mixture, screw in the throttle stop until a reasonable idling speed is attained, and then turn the volume control screw either one way or the other until the maximum vacuum reading, usually between 19° and 22° is attained, and the needle remains steady. Ease back the throttle screw and continue adjustment of the volume control screw, watching the vacuum gauge needle at each adjustment until the maximum reading is obtained with the engine at a reasonable slow-running speed.

7. To attain the most satisfactory result it may be necessary to adjust the ignition setting described later.

8. If a satisfactory reading cannot be obtained the reasons are set out in the section dealing with the engine fault diagnosis.

15. ACCELERATOR PUMP ADJUSTMENT — SOLEX B 30 PSE UNIT

1. For normal operating conditions set the accelerator pump so that the pushrod passes through the outer elongated hole in the operating lever and the split pin through the outer hole in the pushrod.

2. For cold climatic conditions the setting requires that the pushrod passes through the inner elongated hole in the operating lever and the split pin through the inner hole in the pushrod.

16. FUEL SYSTEM - FAULT FINDING

There are three main types of fault the fuel system is prone to, and they may be summarised as follows:

a) Lack of fuel at engine
b) Weak mixture
c) Rich mixture.

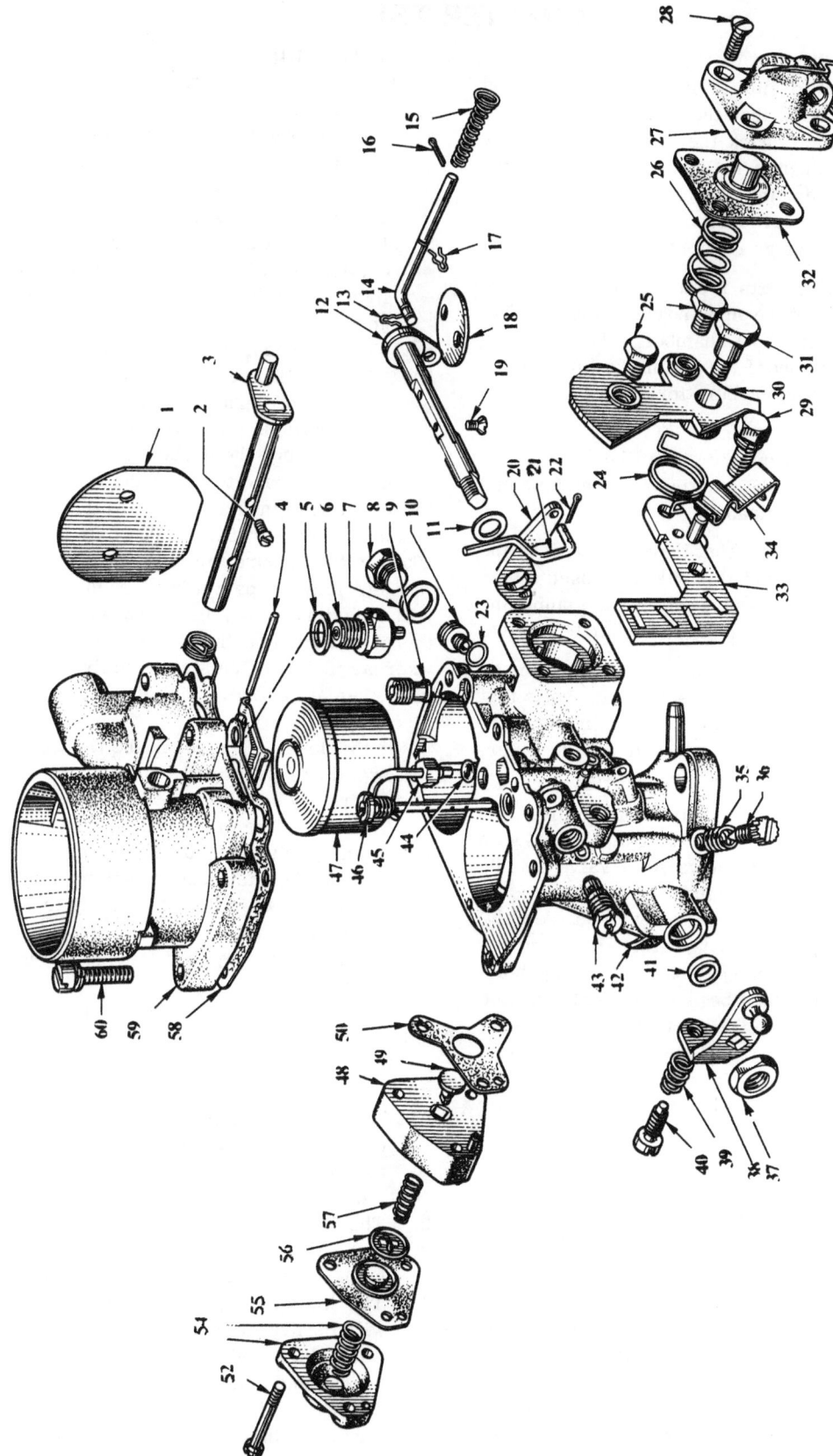

Fig. 3:10 THE CARBURETTOR FITTED TO 1198 c. c. ENGINES — EXPLODED VIEW.

1 Choke disc. 2 Grub screw. 3 Choke spindle. 4 Float chamber lever arm pin. 5 Washer. 6 Needle valve. 7 Washer. 8 Bolt. 9 Accelerator pump check valve. 10 Main jet. 11 Washer. 12 Throttle spindle. 13 Circlip. 14 Actuating arm. 15 Spring. 16 Split pin. 17 Circlip. 18 Throttle disc. 19 Grub screw. 20 Arm. 21 Fast idle rod. 22 Split pin. 23 Washer. 24 Spring. 25 Bolts. 26 Spring. 27 Accelerator pump cover. 28 Screw. 29 Bolt. 30 Carburettor choke lever assembly. 31 Bolt. 32 Accelerator pump diaphragm. 33 Choke bracket. 34 Bracket. 35 Spring. 36 Volume control screw. 37 Nut. 38 Throttle control lever. 39 Spring. 40 Idling adjustment screw. 41 Washer. 42 Carburettor body. 43 Auxiliary jet. 44 Seal. 45 Accelerator pump jet. 46 Emulsion tube. 47 Float chamber. 48 Economiser body. 49 Economiser valve. 50 Gasket. 51 Economiser jet. 52 Bolt. 53 Cover. 54 Diaphragm spring. 55 Economiser diaphragm. 56 Washer. 57 Spring. 58 Gasket. 59 Float chamber cover assembly. 60 Bolt.

17. LACK OF FUEL AT ENGINE

If it is not possible to start the engine, first positively check that there is fuel in the fuel tank, and then check the ignition system as detailed in Chapter 4. If the fault is not in the ignition system then disconnect the fuel inlet pipe from the carburettor and turn the engine over by the starter relay switch.

If petrol squirts from the end of the inlet pipe, reconnect the pipe and check that the fuel is getting to the float chamber. This is done by unscrewing one of the jets on the float chamber portion of the carburettor, when fuel should run out.

If fuel runs out then it is likely that there is a blockage in the starting jet, which should be removed and cleaned.

No fuel indicates that there is no fuel in the float chamber, and this will be caused either by a blockage in the pipe between the pump and float chamber or a sticking float chamber valve.

If it is decided that it is the float chamber valve that is sticking, remove the bolts that secure the float chamber cover in position, remove the fuel inlet pipe, and lift the cover, complete with valve and floats, away.

Remove the valve spindle and valve and thoroughly wash them in petrol. Petrol gum may be present on the valve or valve spindle and this is usually the cause of a sticking valve. Replace the valve in the needle valve assembly, ensure that it is moving freely, and then re-assemble the float chamber. It is important that the same washer be placed under the needle valve assembly as this determines the height of the floats and therefore the level of petrol in the chamber.

Reconnect the fuel pipe and refit the air cleaner.

If no petrol squirts from the end of the pipe leading to the carburettor then disconnect the pipe leading to the inlet side of the fuel pump. If fuel runs out of the pipe then there is a fault in the fuel pump, and the pump should be checked as has already been detailed.

No fuel flowing from the tank when it is known that there is fuel in the tank indicates a blocked pipe line. The line to the tank should be blown out. It is unlikely that the fuel tank vent would become blocked, but this could be a reason for the reluctance of the fuel to flow. To test for this, blow into the tank down the fill orifice. There should be no build up of pressure in the fuel tank, as the excess pressure should be carried away down the vent pipe.

18. WEAK MIXTURE

If the fuel/air mixture is weak there are six main clues to this condition:
1. The engine will be difficult to start and will need much use of the choke, stalling easily if the choke is pushed in.
2. The engine will overheat easily.
3. If the sparking plugs are examined (as detailed in Chapter 4), they will have a light grey/white deposit on the insulator nose.
4. The fuel consumption may be light.
5. There will be a noticeable lack of power.
6. During acceleration and on the overrun there will be a certain amount of spitting back through the carburettor.

As the carburettor is of the fixed jet type, these faults are invariably due to circumstances outside the carburettor. The only usual fault likely in the carburettor is that one or more of the jets may be partially blocked. If the car will not start easily but runs well at speed, then it is likely that the starting jet is blocked, whereas if the engine starts easily but will not rev. then it is likely that the main jets are blocked.

If the level of petrol in the float chamber is low this is usually due to a sticking valve or incorrectly set floats.

Air leaks either in the fuel lines, or in the induction system should also be checked for. Also check the distributor vacuum pipe connection as a leak in this is directly felt in the inlet manifold.

The fuel pump may be at fault as has already been detailed.

19. RICH MIXTURE

If the fuel/air mixture is rich there are also six main clues to this condition:
1. If the sparking plugs are examined (as detailed in Chapter 4), they will be found to have a black sooty deposit on the insulator nose.
2. The fuel consumption will be heavy.
3. The exhaust will give off a heavy black smoke, especially when accelerating.
4. The interior deposits on the exhaust pipe will be dry, black and sooty (if they are wet, black and sooty this indicates worn bores, and much oil being burnt).
5. There will be a noticeable lack of power.
6. There will be a certain amount of backfiring through the exhaust system.

The faults in this case are usually in the carburettor and the most usual is that the level of petrol in the float chamber is too high. This is due either to dirt behind the needle valve, or

FUEL SYSTEM AND CARBURATION

a leaking float which will not close the valve properly, or a sticking needle.

With a very high mileage (or because someone has tried to clean the jets out with wire), it may be that the jets have become enlarged.

If the air correction jets are restricted in any way the mixture will become very rich.

Occasionally it is found that the choke control is sticking or has been mal-adjusted.

Again, occasionally the fuel pump pressure may be excessive so forcing the needle valve open slightly until a higher level of petrol is reached in the float chamber.

FAULT FINDING CHART

Cause	Trouble	Remedy
SYMPTOM:	FUEL CONSUMPTION EXCESSIVE	
Carburation and ignition faults	Air cleaner choked and dirty giving rich mixture	Remove, clean and replace air cleaner.
	Fuel leaking from carburettor(s), fuel pumps, or fuel lines	Check for and eliminate all fuel leaks. Tighten fuel line union nuts.
	Float chamber flooding	Check and adjust float level.
	Generally worn carburettor(s)	Remove, overhaul and replace.
	Distributor condenser faulty	Remove, and fit new unit.
	Balance weights or vacuum advance mechanism in distributor faulty	Remove, and overhaul distributor.
Incorrect adjustment	Carburettor(s) incorrectly adjusted mixture too rich	Tune and adjust carburettor(s).
	Idling speed too high	Adjust idling speed.
	Contact breaker gap incorrect	Check and reset gap.
	Valve clearances incorrect	Check rocker arm to valve stem clearances and adjust as necessary.
	Incorrectly set sparking plugs	Remove, clean, and regap.
	Tyres under-inflated	Check tyre pressures and inflate if necessary.
	Wrong sparking plugs fitted	Remove and replace with correct units.
	Brakes dragging	Check and adjust brakes.
SYMPTOM:	INSUFFICIENT FUEL DELIVERY OR WEAK MIXTURE DUE TO AIR LEAKS	
Dirt in system	Petrol tank air vent restricted	Remove petrol cap and clean out air vent.
	Partially clogged filters in pump and carburettor(s)	Remove and clean filters.
	Dirt lodged in float chamber needle housing	Remove and clean out float chamber and needle valve assembly.
	Incorrectly seating valves in fuel pump	Remove, dismantle, and clean out fuel pump.

CHAPTER FOUR

IGNITION SYSTEM

CONTENTS

SPECIFICATIONS

At the time of writing no information was available concerning overhaul of the Ford Motorcraft distributor fitted to 1966 on models.

Spark plugs
    Type ... ... Champion N5 or Autolite AG.32
    Gap:
        Champion N5 ... ... 0.028 to 0.033 in (0.71 mm to 0.84 mm)
        Autolite AG.32 ... ... 0.023 in (0.59 mm)
    Firing order 1, 2, 4, 3

Distributor
    Type ... ... Lucas or Ford
    Identification:
        Lucas:
            High compression engine ... ... Red or yellow washer on LT terminal
            Low compression engine ... ... Green or brown washer on LT terminal
        Ford:
            High compression engine... ... ... Red paint spot on vacuum diaphragm plug
            Low compression engine... ... ... Green paint spot on vacuum diaphragm plug

Contact breaker points gap
    Lucas ... ... 0.014 to 0.016 in (0.35 to 0.40 mm)
    Ford ... ... 0.025 in (0.64 mm)

Static ignition timing
    997 cc engine:
        High and low compression before Sept 1963 ... 10° BTDC
        Low compression after Sept 1963 ... ... 8° BTDC
    1198 cc engine:
        High and low compression before Feb 1965 ... 6° BTDC
        Low compression after Feb 1965 ... ... 10° BTDC

1. GENERAL DESCRIPTION

In order that the engine can run correctly it is necessary for an electrical spark to ignite the fuel/air mixture in the combustion chamber at exactly the right moment in relation to engine speed and load. The ignition system is based on feeding low tension voltage from the battery to the coil where it is converted to high tension voltage. The high tension voltage is powerful enough to jump the sparking plug gap in the cylinders many times a second under high compression pressures, providing that the system is in good condition and that all adjustments are correct.

The ignition system is divided into two circuits. The low tension circuit and the high tension circuit.

The low tension (sometimes known as the primary) circuit consists of the battery, lead to the control box, lead to the ignition switch, lead from the ignition switch to the low tension or primary coil windings (terminal SW), and the lead from the low tension coil windings (coil terminal CB) to the contact breaker points and condenser in the distributor.

The high tension circuit consists of the high tension or secondary coil windings, the heavy ignition lead from the centre of the coil to the centre of the distributor cap, the rotor arm, and the sparking plug leads and sparking plugs.

The system functions in the following manner. Low tension voltage is changed in the coil into high tension voltage by the opening and closing of the contact breaker points in the low tension circuit. High tension voltage is then fed via the carbon brush in the centre of the distributor cap to the rotor arm of the distributor. The rotor arm revolves inside the dis-

Fig. 4:1 Position of some of the ignition and electrical equipment in the engine compartment which is not directly attached to the engine. 1 Ignition coil. 2 High tension lead. 3 Low tension lead. 4 lamp lead connector. 5 Battery. 6 Heavy duty cable to starter switch. 7 Starter switch.

tributor cap and, each time it comes in line with one of the four metal segments in the cap, which are connected to the sparking plug leads, the opening and closing of the contact breaker points causes the high tension voltage to build up, jump the gap from the rotor arm to the appropriate metal segment. The voltage then passes via the sparking plug lead to the sparking plug, where it finally jumps the spark plug gap before going to earth.

The ignition is advanced and retarded automatically, to ensure the spark occurs at just the right instant for the particular load at the prevailing engine speed.

The ignition advance is controlled both mechanically and by a vacuum operated system. The mechanical governor mechanism comprises two lead weights, which move out from the distributor shaft, due to centrifugal force, as the engine speed rises. As they move outwards they rotate the cam relative to the distributor shaft, and so advance the spark. The weights are held in position by two light springs and it is the tension of the springs which is largely responsible for correct spark advancement.

The vacuum control consists of a diaphragm, one side of which is connected via a small bore tube to the carburettor, and the other side to the contact breaker plate. Depression in the inlet manifold and carburettor, which varies with engine speed and throttle opening, causes the diaphragm to move, so moving the contact breaker plate, and advancing or retarding the spark. A fine degree of control is achieved by a spring in the vacuum assembly.

2. DISTRIBUTOR DIFFERENCES

The distributor fitted to low compression engines is externally identical to that fitted to high compression engines. Internally the only difference lies in the advance weight springs and the vacuum advance assembly. Although these differences are small it is essential that only the correct type of distributor is used in each application. The advance curves of the two units are different and if incorrectly fitted will result in poor running and loss of power.

The distributor for the low compression engine can be recognised by a green or brown washer on the low tension terminal and by the numbers 5 13 10 on the vacuum unit. The high compression distributor has a red or yellow washer on the low tension terminal and the numbers 5 12 6 on the vacuum unit.

3. CONTACT BREAKER ADJUSTMENT

1. To adjust the contact breaker points to the correct gap, first pull off the two clips

securing the distributor cap to the distributor body, and lift away the cap. Clean the cap inside and out with a dry cloth. It is unlikely that the four segments will be badly burned or scored, but if they are the cap will have to be renewed.

2. Push in the carbon brush located in the top of the cap once or twice to make sure that it moves freely.

3. Gently prise the contact breaker points open to examine the condition of their faces. If they are rough, pitted, or dirty, it will be necessary to remove them for resurfacing, or for replacement points to be fitted.

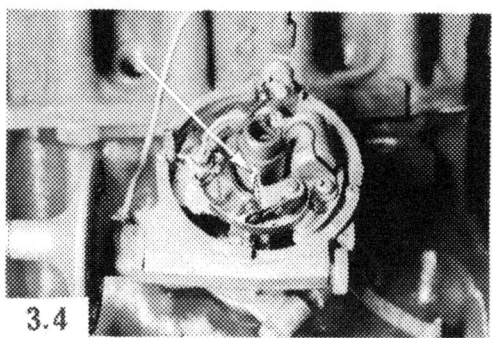

3.4

4. Presuming the points are satisfactory, or that they have been cleaned and replaced, measure the gap between the points by turning the engine over until the contact breaker arm is on the peak of one of the four cam lobes (arrowed).

5. A 0.015 in. feeler gauge should now just fit between the points.

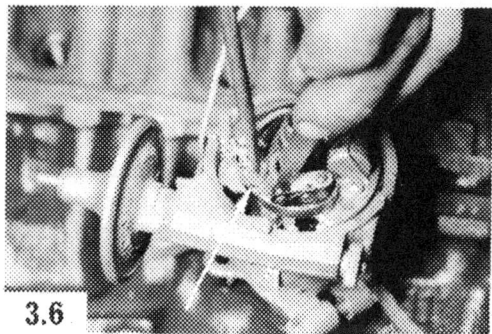

3.6

6. If the gap varies from this amount, slacken the contact plate securing screw (arrowed).

7. Adjust the contact gap by inserting a screwdriver in the notched hole (arrowed) at the end of the plate. Turning clockwise to decrease and anti-clockwise to increase the gap. Tighten the securing screw and check the gap again (small arrow).

8. Replace the rotor arm and distributor cap and clip the spring blade retainers into position.

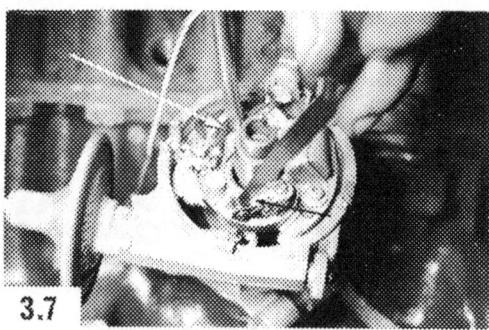

3.7

4 REMOVING & REPLACING CONTACT BREAKER POINTS.

1. If the contact breaker points are burned, pitted or badly worn, they must be removed and either replaced, or their faces must be filed smooth.

2. To remove the points unscrew the terminal nut and remove it together with the steel washer under its head. Remove the flanged nylon bush and then the condenser lead and the low tension lead from the terminal pin. Lift off the contact breaker arm and then remove the large fibre washer from the terminal pin.

3. The adjustable contact breaker plate is removed by unscrewing the one holding down screw and removing it, complete with spring and flat washer.

4. To reface the points, rub their faces on a fine carborundum stone, or on fine emery paper. It is important that the faces are rubbed flat and parallel to each other so that there will be complete face to face contact when the points are closed. One of the points will be pitted and the other will have deposits on it.

5. It is necessary to completely remove the built-up deposits, but not necessary to rub the pitted point right down to the stage where all the pitting has disappeared, though obviously if this is done it will prolong the time before the operation of refacing the points has to be repeated.

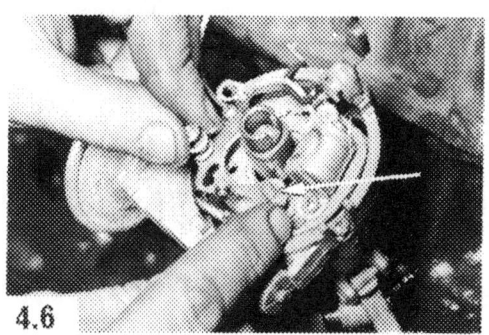

4.6

6. To replace the points first position the adjustable contact breaker plate over the terminal pin (arrowed, see photo).

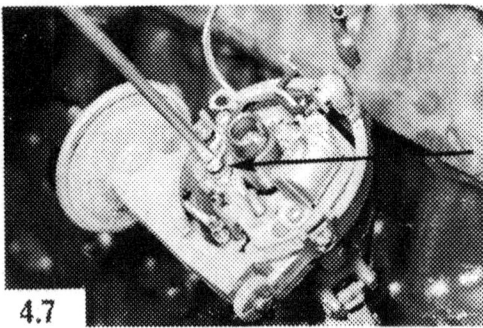

4.7

7. Secure the contact plate by screwing in the screw (arrowed) which should have a spring and a flat washer under its head.

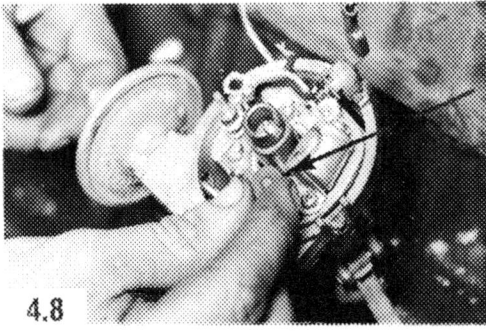

4.8

8. Then fit the fibre washer (arrowed) over the terminal pin.
9. Next fit the contact breaker arm complete with spring over the terminal pin.
10. Drop the fibre washer over the terminal bolt (arrowed).
11. Then bend back the spring of the contact breaker arm and fit it over the terminal bolt (arrowed).
12. Place the terminals of the low tension lead and the condenser over the terminal bolt.
13. Then fit the flanged nylon bush over the terminal bolt with the two leads immediately under its flange.
14. Next fit a steel washer and then a 'star' washer over the nylon bush.
15. Then fit the nut over the terminal bolt and tighten it down.
16. The points are now reassembled and the gap should be set as described in the previous section.
17. Finally replace the rotor arm (arrowed) and then the distributor cap.

5. CONDENSER REMOVAL, TESTING & REPLACEMENT
   1. The purpose of the condenser, (sometimes known as a capacitor) is to ensure that when the contact breaker points open there is no sparking across them which would waste voltage and cause wear.
   2. The condenser is fitted in parallel with the contact breaker points. If it develops a short circuit, it will cause ignition failure as the points will be prevented from interrupting the low tension circuit.
   3. If the engine becomes very difficult to start or begins to miss after several miles running and the breaker points show signs of excessive burning, then the condition of the condenser must be suspect. A further test can be made by separating the points by hand with the ignition switched on. If this is accompanied by a flash it is indicative that the condenser has failed.
   4. Without special test equipment the only sure way to diagnose condenser trouble is to replace a suspected unit with a new one and note if there is any improvement.
   5. To remove the condenser from the distributor, remove the distributor cap and the rotor arm. Unscrew the contact breaker arm terminal nut, and remove the nut, washer, and flanged nylon bush and release the condenser lead from the bush. Unscrew the condenser retaining screw from the breaker plate and remove the condenser. Replacement of the condenser is simply a reversal of the removal process. Take particular care that the condenser lead does not short circuit against any portion of the breaker plate.

6. DISTRIBUTOR LUBRICATION
   1. It is important that the distributor cam is lubricated with petroleum jelly at the specified mileages, and that the breaker arm, governor weights, and cam spindle, are lubricated with engine oil once every 1,000 miles. In practice it will be found that lubrication every 2,000 miles is adequate, although this is not recommended by the factory.
   2. Great care should be taken not to use too much lubricant, as any excess that might find its way onto the contact breaker points could cause burning and misfiring.
   3. To gain access to the cam spindle, lift away the rotor arm. Drop no more than two drops of engine oil onto the screw head. This will run down the spindle when the engine is hot and lubricate the bearings.

No more than ONE drop of oil should be applied to the pivot post.

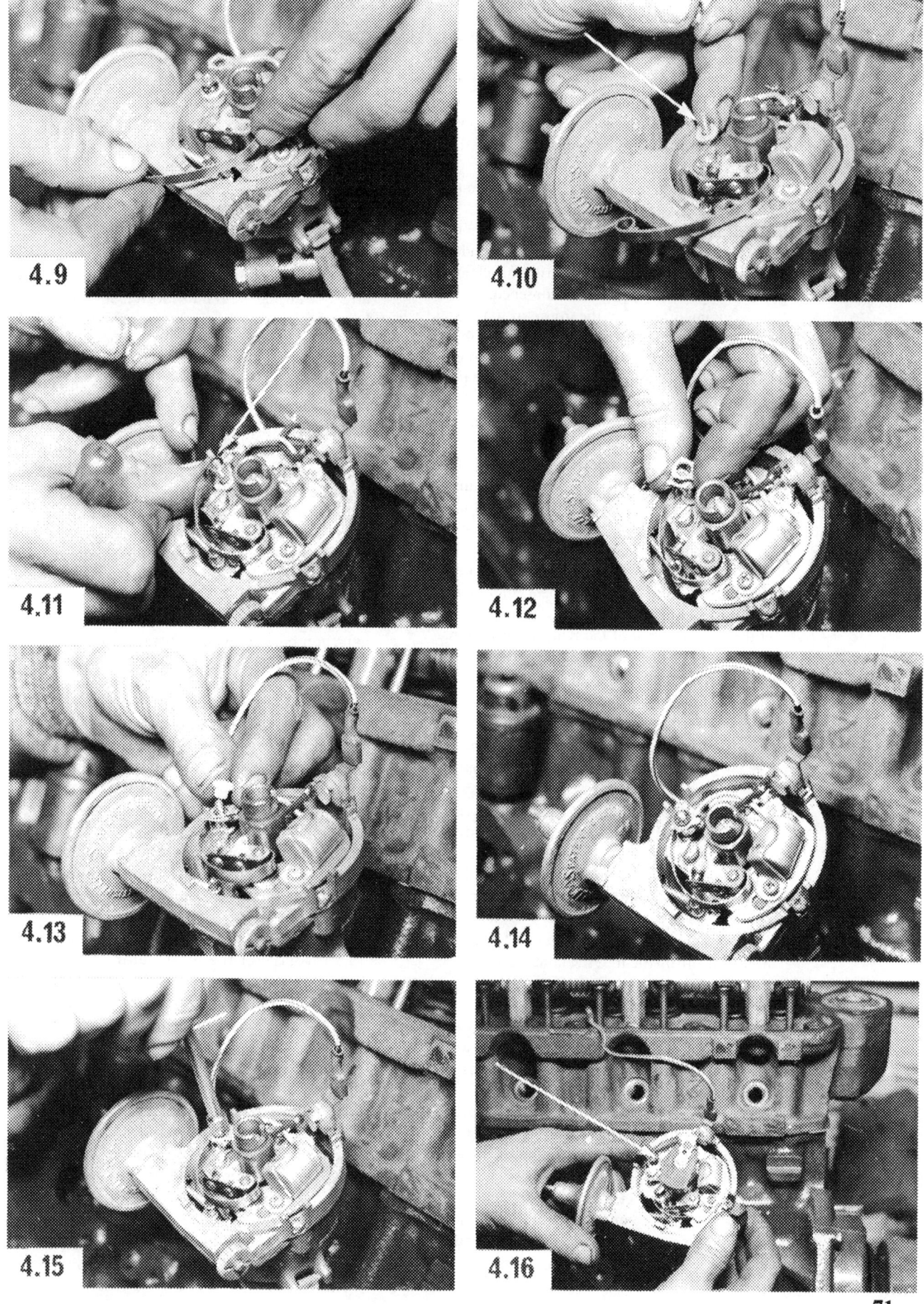

4.9

4.10

4.11

4.12

4.13

4.14

4.15

4.16

CHAPTER FOUR

7. DISTRIBUTOR REMOVAL & REPLACEMENT

1. Release the two spring clips securing the distributor cap, lift off the cap and position away from the distributor.

2. Undo and remove the nut securing the low tension lead to the terminal on the side of the distributor and remove the lead.

3. Unscrew the union securing the vacuum pipe to the distributor vacuum body.

4. If the distributor is being removed but it is not wished to disturb the ignition timing, then under no circumstances must the distributor clamp pinch bolt (item 12, Fig. 4.2) be loosened.

5. It is also important for the rotor arm to be positioned correctly when refitting the distributor. Turn the engine over until the timing notch on the crankshaft pulley is aligned with the correct timing mark on the timing case with No 1 piston on its firing stroke. Using white paint, alignment marks should be made to indicate the fitted position of the rotor arm relative to the distributor body, and the location of the clamp bolt within the elongated slot of the clamp itself.

6. Undo and remove the distributor clamp-to-engine securing bolt and withdraw the distributor. Note that the distributor drive is by skew gear and the rotor arm movement should be noted for refitting purposes.

7. Refitting is a reversal of the removal procedure providing the engine has not been rotated in the meantime and the paint marks align when the distributor is correctly positioned.

8. DISTRIBUTOR DISMANTLING (See Fig. 4:1)

1. With the distributor removed from the car and on the bench, remove the distributor cap 1 and lift off the rotor arm 41. If very tight, lever it off gently with a screwdriver.

2. Remove the points 37,38 from the distributor as detailed in Chapter 4/4.

3. Remove the condenser 43 from the contact breaker plate 36 by releasing its securing screw 42.

4. Unhook the vacuum unit spring from its mounting pin on the moving contact breaker plate.

5. Unscrew the two screws and lockwashers which hold the contact breaker base plate 32 in position and remove the earth lead from the relevant screw. Remember to replace this lead on reassembly.

6. Slide the low tension terminal complete with nylon block and wire 33 up out of its slot in the edge of distributor body 16 and side of the base plate 32.

7. Lift out the contact breaker base plate 32 together with the securing contact breaker plate 36. To separate the two plates turn the top plate 36 until the peg under it sits

in the hole 'A' at the end of the slot in the base plate 32. Free the small spring clip under the base plate 32 at the same time separating both plates.

8. This exposes the weights and springs of the centrifugal governor. Unhook the two springs 21 and 29 then undo the screw 31 which holds the cam 30 to the distributor shaft 27. Lift off the cam 30 and then the weights 29.

9. To remove the vacuum unit 19, spring off the small circlip 'B' which secures the advance adjustment nut 3 which should then be unscrewed. With the micrometer adjusting nut removed, release the spring 4 and the micrometer adjusting nut lock spring clip 5. This is the clip that is responsible for the 'clicks' when the micrometer adjuster is turned, and it is small and easily lost as is the circlip, so put them in a safe place. Do not forget to replace the lock spring clip on reassembly.

10. It is only necessary to remove the distributor drive shaft 27 or spindle if it is thought to be excessively worn. With a thin punch drive out the retaining pin 25 from the driving tongue collar on the bottom end of the distributor drive shaft. The shaft can then be removed. The distributor is now completely dismantled.

9. DISTRIBUTOR INSPECTION & REPAIR

1. Check the points as has already been described in Chapter 4/4. Check the distributor cap for signs of tracking, indicated by a thin black line between the segments. Replace the cap if any signs of tracking are found.

2. If the metal portion of the rotor arm is badly burned or loose, renew the arm. If slightly burnt clean the arm with a fine file.

3. Check that the carbon brush moves freely in the centre of the distributor cover.

4. Examine the fit of the breaker plate on the bearing plate and also check the breaker arm pivot for looseness or wear and renew as necessary.

5. Examine the balance weights and pivot pins for wear, and renew the weights or cam assembly if a degree of wear is found.

6. Examine the shaft and the fit of the cam assembly on the shaft. If the clearance is excessive compare the items with new units, and renew either, or both, if they show excessive wear.

7. If the shaft is a loose fit in the distributor bushes and can be seen to be worn, it will

72

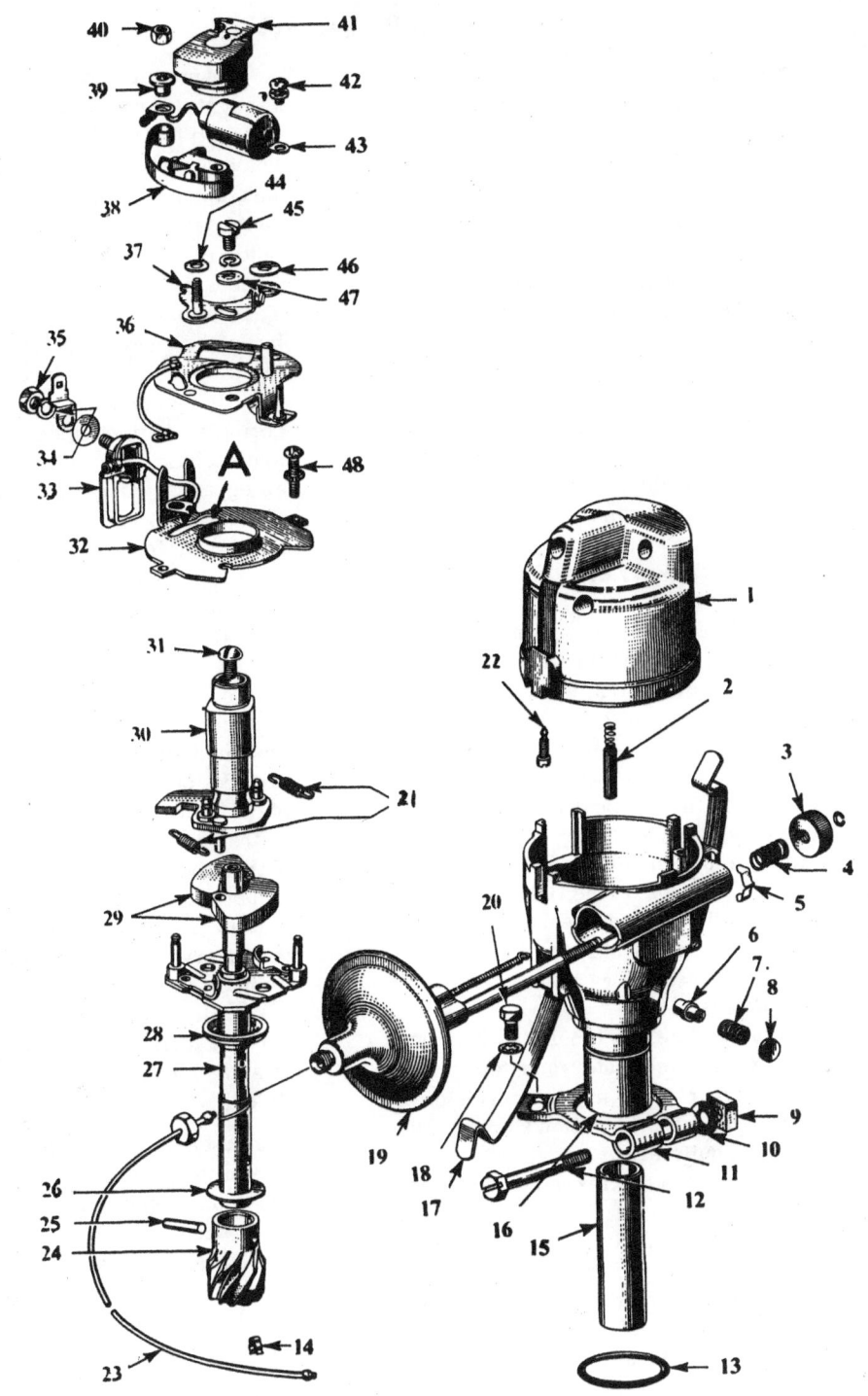

Fig. 4:2 EXPLODED VIEW OF THE DISTRIBUTOR.

1 Distributor cap.　2 Brush and spring.　3 Knurled adjusting nut.　4 Spring.　5 Ratchet spring.　6 Distributor shaft pressure pad.　7 Spring.　8 Disc.　9 Nut.　10 Washer.　11 Distributor timing clamp.　12 Clamp securing bolt.　13 Seal.　14 Clip. 15 Bush.　16 Distributor body.　17 Distributor clips.　18 Washer.　19 Vacuum advance & retard.　20 Fixing bolt.　21 Weight springs.　22 H.T. wires to distributor cap screw.　23 Vacuum pipe.　24 Distributor drive gear.　25 Drive gear securing pin. 26 Thrust washer.　27 Distributor shaft & weight plate.　28 Spacing washer.　29 Balance weights.　30 Distributor cam.　31 Securing screw.　32 Contact breaker base plate.　33 Low tension terminal.　34 Spring washer.　35 Nut.　36 Contact breaker plate. 37 Fixed point.　38 Spring point.　39 Insulating bush.　40 Nut.　41 Rotor arm.　42 Screw.　43 Condenser.　44 Washer. 45 Screw.　46 Washer.　47 Washer.　48 Screw.

be necessary to fit a new shaft and bushes. The old bushes in the early distributor, or the single bush in the later ones, are simply pressed out.   NOTE that before inserting new bushes they should be stood in engine oil for 24 hours.

8. Examine the length of the balance weight springs and compare them with new springs. If they have stretched they must be renewed.

10. DISTRIBUTOR REASSEMBLY

1. Reassembly is a straight reversal of the dismantling process, but there are several points which should be noted in addition to those already given in the section on dismantling.

2. Lubricate with S. A. E. 20 engine oil the balance weights and other parts of the mechanical advance mechanism, the distributor shaft, and the portion of the shaft on which the cam bears, during assembly. Do not oil excessively but ensure these parts are adequately lubricated.

3. Check the action of the weights in the fully advanced and fully retarded positions and ensure they are not binding.

4. Tighten the micrometer adjusting nut to the middle position on the timing scale.

5. Finally, set the contact breaker gap to the correct clearance of . 016 in.

11. IGNITION TIMING

1. If the clamp plate pinch bolt has been loosened on the distributor and the static timing lost, or if for any other reason it is wished to set the ignition timing, this can be done quite easily.

2. The static advance is checked at the exact moment of opening of the points relative to the position of the timing marks and to the position of the rotor arm relative to the metal segments in the distributor cap.

3. The static advance of 10 degrees before top dead centre is a feature of these engines and when Number 1 cylinder is on compression stroke and the notch on the crankshaft pulley aligns with the upper timing mark of the timing cover as shown in Fig. 1:8 the crankshaft is at the correct position for the distributor timing to be set.

4. Make certain the distributor is at its central point of adjustment to allow the ignition to be advanced or retarded by the micro adjuster.   The central position is when the fourth line on the ignition timing scale is in line with the edge of the distributor body connecting from the vacuum diaphragm.

5. At this position the initial timing setting of the ignition can be made by slackening off the distributor body clamp and rotating the body clockwise until the breaker points are just opening when the rotor is adjacent to Number 1 plug lead contact in the distributor cap. Tighten the clamp bolt.

6. To ensure No. 1 piston is coming up to T. D. C. on the compression stroke check by removing No. 1 sparking plug and feeling the pressure being developed in the cylinder, or by removing the rocker cover and noting when the valves in No. 4 cylinder are rocking, i. e. , the inlet valve just opening and exhaust valve just closing. If this check is not made it is all too easy to set the timing 180° out, as both No. 1 and 4 cylinders come up to T.D.C. at the same time but only one is on the firing stroke.

7. With the notch in the pulley wheel adjacent to the mark on the timing case and the rotor arm opposite the correct segment for No. 1 cylinder, turn the advance/retard knob on the distributor until the contact points are just beginning to open. Eleven clicks of the knurled micrometer adjuster nut represent 1° of timing movement.

8. If the range of adjustment provided by this adjuster is not sufficient, then, if the clamp bolt is not already slackened, it will be necessary to slacken it and turn the distributor body slightly.   Sufficient adjustment will normally be found available using the distributor micrometer adjuster. When this has been done the engine is statically timed.

9. Difficulty is sometimes experienced in determining exactly when the contact breaker points open.   This can be ascertained most accurately by connecting a 12-volt bulb in parallel with the contact breaker points (one lead to earth and the other from the distributor low tension terminal). Switch on the ignition, and turn the advance and retard adjuster until the bulb lights up indicating that the points have just opened.

10. A better result can sometimes be obtained by making slight readjustments under running conditions.

11. First start the engine and allow to warm up to normal temperature, and then accelerate in top gear from 30 to 50 m. p. h. , listening for heavy pinking of the engine. If this occurs, the ignition needs to be retarded slightly until just the faintest trace of pinking can be heard under these operating conditions.

12. Since the ignition advance adjustment enables the firing point to be related correctly in relation to the grade of fuel used, the fullest advantage of any change of fuel will only be attained by re-adjustment of the ignition settings.

13. This is done by varying the setting of the index scale on the vacuum advance mechanism one or two divisions, checking to make sure that the best all-round result is attained.

12. SPARKING PLUGS & LEADS

1. The correct functioning of the sparking plugs are vital for the correct running and efficiency of the engine.

2. At intervals of 5,000 miles the plugs should be removed, examined, cleaned, and if worn excessively, replaced. The condition of the sparking plug will also tell much about the overall condition of the engine.

3. If the insulator nose of the sparking plug is clean and white, with no deposits, this is indicative of a weak mixture, or too hot a plug (A hot plug transfers heat away from the electrodes slowly - a cold plug transfers it away quickly).

4. The plugs fitted as standard are the Champion N5 or Autolite AG32 14 mm. type. If the tip and insulator nose is covered with hard black-looking deposits, then this is indicative that the mixture is too rich. Should the plug be black and oily, then it is likely that the engine is fairly worn, as well as the mixture being too rich.

5. If the insulator nose is covered with light tan to greyish brown deposits, then the mixture is correct and it is likely that the engine is in good condition.

6. If there are any traces of long brown tapering stains on the outside of the white portion of the plug, then the plug will have to be renewed, as this shows that there is a faulty joint between the plug body and the insulator, and compression is being allowed to leak away.

7. Plugs should be cleaned by a sand blasting machine, which will free them from carbon more thoroughly than cleaning by hand. The machine will also test the condition of the plugs under compression. Any plug that fails to spark regularly at the recommended pressure should be renewed.

8. The sparking plug gap is of considerable importance, as, if it is too large or too small, the size of the spark and its efficiency will be seriously impaired. The sparking plug gap should be set to 0.025

in. for the best results.

9. To set it, measure the gap with a feeler gauge, and then bend open, or close, the outer plug electrode until the correct gap is achieved. The centre electrode should never be bent as this may crack the insulation and cause plug failure if nothing worse.

10. When replacing the plugs, remember to use new plug washers, and replace the leads from the distributor in the correct firing order, which is 1, 2, 4, 3, No. 1 cylinder being the one nearest the radiator.

11. The plug leads require no routine attention other than being kept clean and wiped over regularly. At intervals of 5,000 miles, however, pull each lead off the plug in turn and remove them from the distributor by unscrewing the knurled moulded terminal knobs. Water can seep down into these joints giving rise to a white corrosive deposit which must be carefully removed from the brass washer at the end of each cable, through which the ignition wires pass.

13. IGNITION SYSTEM FAULT-FINDING

By far the majority of breakdown and running troubles are caused by faults in the ignition system either in the low tension or high tension circuits.

14. IGNITION SYSTEM FAULT SYMPTOMS

1. There are two main symptoms indicating ignition faults. Either the engine will not start or fire, or the engine is difficult to start and misfires. If it is a regular misfire, i.e., the engine is only running on two or three cylinders, the fault is almost sure to be in the secondary, or high tension, circuit. If the misfiring is intermittent, the fault could be in either the high or low tension circuits. If the car stops suddenly, or will not start at all, it is likely that the fault is in the low tension circuit. Loss of power and overheating, apart from faulty carburation settings, are normally due to faults in the distributor or incorrect ignition timing.

15. FAULT DIAGNOSIS - Engine fails to start

1. If the engine fails to start it is likely that the fault is in the low tension circuit. The way the starter motor spins over will indicate whether there is a good charge in the battery. If the battery is evidently in good condition, then check the distributor.

2. Remove the distributor cap and rotor arm, and check that the contact points are not burnt, pitted or dirty. If the points are

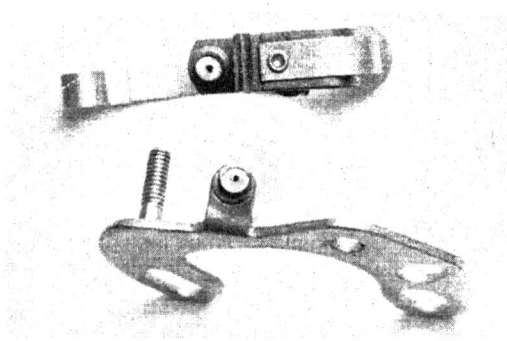

badly pitted, or burnt or dirty, clean and reset them as described in Chapter 4/4. Shown are two badly pitted points.

3. If the engine still refuses to fire check the low tension circuit further. Check the condition of the condenser as described in Chapter 4/5.

4. Switch on the ignition and turn the crankshaft until the contact breaker points have fully opened. With either a voltmeter or bulb, and length of wire, connect the contact breaker plate terminal to earth on the engine. If the bulb lights, the low tension circuit is in order, and the fault is in the points. If the points have been cleaned and reset, and the bulb still lights, then the fault is in the high tension circuit.

5. If the bulb fails to light, connect it to the ignition coil terminal CB and earth. If it lights, it points to a damaged wire or loose connection in the cable from the CB terminal on the contact breaker plate.

6. If the bulb fails to light, connect it between the ignition coil terminal SW and earth. If the bulb lights it indicates a fault in the primary winding of the coil, and it will be necessary to fit a replacement unit.

7. Should the bulb not light at this stage, then check the cable to SW for faults or a loose connection. Connect the bulb from the negative terminal of the battery to the SW terminal of the coil. If the bulb lights, then the fault is somewhere in the switch, or wiring and control box.

8. If the fault is not in the low tension circuit check the high tension circuit. Disconnect each plug lead in turn at the sparking plug end, and hold the end of the cable about 3/16 in. away from the cylinder block. Spin the engine on the starter motor by pressing the rubber button on the starter motor solenoid switch (under the bonnet). Sparking between the end of the cable and the block should be fairly strong with a regular blue spark. (Hold the lead with rubber to avoid electric shocks.).

9. Should there be no spark at the end of the plug leads, disconnect the lead at the distributor cap, and hold the end of the lead about 1/4 in. from the block. Spin the engine as before, when a rapid succession of blue sparks between the end of the lead and the block, indicate that the coil is in order, and that either the distributor cap is cracked, or the carbon brush is stuck or worn, or the rotor arm is faulty.

10. Check the cap for cracks and tracking, and the rotor arm for cracks or looseness of the metal portion and renew as necessary.

11. If there are no sparks from the end of the lead from the coil, then check the connections of the lead to the coil and distributor head, and if they are in order, and the low tension side is without fault, then it will be necessary to fit a replacement coil.

16. FAULT DIAGNOSIS - Engine misfires

1. If the engine misfires regularly, run it at a fast idling speed, and short out each of the plugs in turn by placing a short screwdriver across from the plug terminal to the cylinder. Ensure that the screwdriver has a WOODEN or PLASTIC INSULATED HANDLE.

2. No difference in engine running will be noticed when the plug in the defective cylinder is short circuited. Short circuiting the working plugs will accentuate the misfire.

3. Remove the plug lead from the end of the defective plug and hold it about 3/16 in. away from the block. Restart the engine. If the sparking is fairly strong and regular the fault must lie in the sparking plug.

4. The plug may be loose, the insulation may be cracked, or the points may have burnt away giving too wide a gap for the spark to jump. Worse still, one of the points may have broken off. Either renew the plug, or clean it, reset the gap, and then test it.

5. If there is no spark at the end of the plug lead, or if it is weak and intermittent, check the ignition lead from the distributor to the plug. If the insulation is cracked or perished, renew the lead. Check the connections at the distributor cap.

6. If there is still no spark, examine the distributor cap carefully for tracking. This can be recognised by a very thin black line running between two or more electrodes, or between an electrode and some other part of the distributor. These lines are paths which now conduct electricity across

the cap thus letting it run to earth. The only answer is a new distributor cap.

Apart from the ignition timing being incorrect, other causes of misfiring have already been dealt with under the section dealing with the failure of the engine to start. To recap - these are that:

a) The coil may be faulty giving an intermittent misfire.

b) There may be a damaged wire or loose connection in the low tension circuit.

c) The condenser may be short circuiting.

d) There may be a mechanical fault in the distributor (Broken driving spindle or contact breaker spring).

8. If the ignition timing is too far retarded, it should be noted that the engine will tend to overheat, and there will be a quite noticeable drop in power. If the engine is overheating and the power is down, and the ignition timing is correct, then the carburettor should be checked, as it is likely that this is where the fault lies.

Plug too hot - white deposits

A chipped electrode

Typical damage caused by pre-ignition

Plug too cold - dry black fuel deposits

Badly burnt electrodes

A normal plug with light tan deposits

CHAPTER FIVE

CLUTCH AND ACTUATING MECHANISM

CONTENTS

SPECIFICATION

Type ... ... Single dry plate.
Diameter ... ... 7.25 in. (18.42 cm.).
Total frictional area... ... ... 43.28 sq. in. (279 sq. cm.).
Thickness of linings ... ... 0.125 in. (3.18 mm.).
No. of pressure springs ... ... Six.
Clutch release arm free travel ... ... $1/16$ in. (1.5 mm.).
Flywheel bolts tightening torque ... ... 12 to 15 lb/ft. (1.658 to 2.073 kg.m.).
Method of actuation ... ... Hydraulic.

1. GENERAL DESCRIPTION

The clutch assembly comprises a steel cover which is bolted and doweled to the rear face of the flywheel and contains the pressure plate, pressure plate springs, release levers, and clutch disc or driven plate.

The pressure plate, pressure springs, and release levers are all attached to the clutch assembly cover. The clutch disc is free to slide along the splined first motion shaft and is held in position between the flywheel and the pressure plate by the pressure of the pressure plate springs.

Friction lining material is riveted to the clutch disc and it has a spring cushioned hub to absorb transmission shocks and to help ensure a smooth take-off.

The clutch is actuated hydraulically. The pendant clutch pedal is connected to the clutch master cylinder and hydraulic fluid reservoir by a short pushrod. The master cylinder and hydraulic reservoir are mounted on the engine side of the bulkhead in front of the driver.

Depressing the clutch pedal moves the piston in the master cylinder forwards, so forcing hydraulic fluid through the clutch hydraulic pipe to the slave cylinder.

The piston in the slave cylinder moves forward on the entry of the fluid and actuates the clutch release arm by means of a short pushrod. The opposite end of the release arm is forked and is located behind the release bearing.

As this pivoted clutch release arm moves backwards it bears against the release bearing pushing it forwards to bear against the release bearing thrust plate and three clutch release levers. These levers are also pivoted so as to move the pressure plate backwards against the pressure of the pressure plate springs, in this way disengaging the pressure plate from the clutch disc.

When the clutch pedal is released, the pressure plate springs force the pressure plate into contact with the high friction linings on the clutch disc, at the same time forcing the clutch disc against the flywheel and so taking the drive up.

The clutch pedal is of the suspended type and is mounted together with the brake and accelerator pedals on a bracket, which is held to the front bulkhead by four bolts. On the engine side of the bulkhead the clutch and brake master cylinders are held in place on these same four bolts by nuts and washers which also serve to hold the bracket against the bulkhead.

Two further bolts hold the top of the bracket to the upper portion of the front bulkhead.

2. MAINTENANCE

1. Routine maintenance consists of checking the level of the hydraulic fluid in the master cylinder every 1,000 miles and topping up with the correct fluid if the level falls; and checking that there is the necessary free movement between the clutch release arm and the pushrod in the slave cylinder.
2. If it is noted that the level of the liquid has fallen then an immediate check should be made to determine the source of the leak.
3. Before checking the level of the fluid in the master cylinder reservoir, carefully clean the cap and body of the reservoir unit with clean rag so as to ensure that no dirt enters the system when the cap is removed. On no account should paraffin or any other cleaning solvent be used in case the hydraulic fluid becomes contaminated.
4. Check that the level of the hydraulic fluid is up to within $1/2$ in. of the filler neck and that the vent hole in the gap is clear. Do not overfill.
5. When the clutch mechanism is correctly adjusted the pedal will return to its stop at once, and there will be a $1/16$ in. clearance between the clutch release arm and the domed nut on the operating cylinder pushrod.
6. After a new clutch disc has been fitted this clearance should be increased to $1/10$ in. since if the clearance is reduced the clutch release bearing will be in permanent contact with the clutch fingers, causing exces-

sive wear and resulting in clutch slip.
7. The adjustment is effected by first disconnecting the retracting spring, slacken the locknut and turn the domed nut on the pushrod until the correct clearance is obtained between the end of the release arm and the nut. Tighten the locknut, recheck the adjustment and reconnect the spring.

3. CLUTCH SYSTEM - BLEEDING
1. Gather together a clean jam jar, a 9 in. length of rubber tubing which fits tightly over the bleed nipple in the slave cylinder, a tin of hydraulic brake fluid, and a friend to help.
2. Check that the master cylinder is full and if not, fill it, and cover the bottom inch of the jar with hydraulic fluid.
3. Remove the rubber dust cap from the bleed nipple on the slave cylinder and, with a suitable spanner, open the bleed nipple one turn.
4. Place one end of the tube securely over the nipple and insert the other end in the jam jar so that the tube orifice is below the level of the fluid.
5. The assistant should now pump the clutch pedal up and down slowly until air bubbles cease to emerge from the end of the tubing. He should also check the reservoir frequently, to ensure that the hydraulic fluid does not disappear, so letting air into the system.
6. When no more air bubbles appear, tighten the bleed nipple on the downstroke.
7. Replace the rubber dust cap over the bleed nipple. Allow the hydraulic fluid in the jar to stand for at least 24 hours before using it, in order that all the minute air bubbles may escape.

4. CLUTCH SLAVE CYLINDER - REMOVAL, DISMANTLING, EXAMINATION & REASSEMBLY
The clutch slave cylinder is located in a hole drilled in an extension on the lower left-hand side of the bellhousing. The cylinder is retained in place by a circlip.
1. To remove the slave cylinder, completely disconnect the hydraulic pipe at the cylinder, remove the retaining circlip and pull the cylinder out of its hole on the side of the bellhousing. If it is wished to remove the cylinder because the gearbox is being removed, there is no need to disconnect the hydraulic pipe; the slave cylinder being tied back out of the way. Always blank off the open end of the hydraulic pipe.

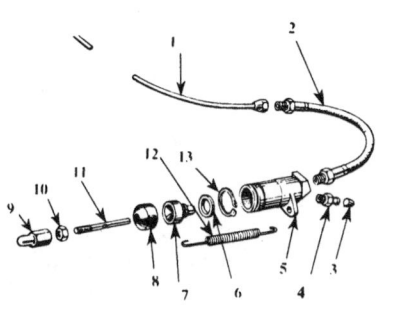

Fig. 5:1 EXPLODED VIEW OF THE CLUTCH SLAVE CYLINDER
1 Hydraulic steel pipe. 2 Flexible pipe. 3 Cap. 4 Bleed screw.
5 Slave cylinder. 6 Seal. 7 Piston. 8 Dust cover. 9 Adjusting
screw. 10 Locknut. 11 Pushrod. 12 Return spring. 13 Retaining
circlip.

2. Clean the outside of the cylinder before dismantling. Remove the pushrod and rubber dust cap and shake the piston and seal out of the cylinder. Clean all the components thoroughly with hydraulic fluid or alcohol and then dry them off.

3. Carefully examine the rubber components for signs of swelling, distortion, splitting or other wear, and check the piston and cylinder wall for wear and score marks. Replace any parts that are found faulty.

4. Reassembly is a straight reversal of the dismantling procedure, but NOTE the following points:
   a) As the component parts are refitted to the slave cylinder barrel, smear them with hydraulic fluid.
   b) When reassembling the operating cylinder, locate the piston seal on the spigot at the front end of the piston so that the sealing lip is away from the body of the piston.
   c) On completion of reassembly, top up the reservoir tank with the correct grade of hydraulic fluid and bleed the system.

5. CLUTCH MASTER CYLINDER - REMOVAL, DISMANTLING, EXAMINATION & REASSEMBLY
   1. Free the master cylinder pushrod from the clutch pedal after undoing and removing the nut and bolt which hold them together. The numbers in the text refer to Fig. 5:2.
   2. Place a rag under the master cylinder to catch any hydraulic fluid which may be spilt. Unscrew the union nut from the end of the hydraulic pipe where it enters the clutch master cylinder and gently pull the pipe clear.

3. Unscrew the two bolts and spring washers holding the clutch cylinder mounting flange to the mounting bracket.

4. Remove the master cylinder and reservoir, unscrew the filler cap 1, and drain the hydraulic fluid into a clean container.

5. Pull off the rubber boot 12, which exposes the circlip 13 which must be removed so the pushrod complete with metal retaining washer 14 can be pulled out of the master cylinder.

6. Pull the piston 15 and valve assembly 6 as one unit from the master cylinder.

7. The next step is to separate the piston and valve assemblies. With the aid of a small screwdriver prise up the inner leg of the piston return spring retainer 10 which engages under a shoulder in the front of the piston and holds the retainer 10 in place.

8. The retainer 10, spring 9, and valve assembly 5-8, can then be separated from the piston.

9. To dismantle the valve assembly compress the spring 9, and move the retainer 10 (which has an offset hole) to one side in order to release the valve stem 6 from the retainer 10.

10. With the seat spacer 8 and valve seal washer 7 removed, the rubber seals can be taken off and inspected.

11. Clean and carefully examine all the parts, especially the piston cup and rubber washers, for signs of distortion, swelling, splitting, or other wear and check the piston and cylinder for wear and scoring. Replace any parts that are faulty.

   During the inspection of the piston seal it has been found advisable to maintain the shape of this seal as regular as possible and for this reason do not turn it inside out as slight distortion may be caused.

12. Rebuild the piston and valve assembly in the following sequence.
    a) Fit the piston seal 16 to the piston 15 so the larger circumference of the rubber lip will enter the cylinder bore first. The seal sits in the groove 'B'.
    b) Then fit the valve seal 5 to the valve 6 in the same way.
    c) Place the valve spring seal washer 7 so its convex face abuts the valve stem flange 6 and then fit the seat spacer 8 and spring 9.

d) Fit the spring retainer 10 to the spring 9 which must then be compressed so the valve stem 6 can be reinserted in the retainer 10.

e) Replace the front of the piston 15 in the retainer 10, and then press down the retaining leg so it locates under the shoulder 'A' at the front of the piston 15.

f) Generously lubricate the assembly with hydraulic fluid and carefully replace it in the master cylinder taking great care not to damage the rubber seals as they are inserted into the cylinder bore.

g) Fit the pushrod 11 and washer 14 in place and secure with the circlip 13. Replace the rubber boot 12.

13. Replacement of the unit in the car is a straightforward reversal of the removal sequence. Finally, bleed the system as described earlier in section 3.

6. CLUTCH PEDAL - ADJUSTMENT, REMOVAL & REPLACEMENT

On early cars it was possible to alter the height of the clutch pedal by as much as 1 in. by means of an eccentric bolt which was used instead of an ordinary bolt to connect the clutch pedal lever to the master cylinder pushrod. If the bolt is rotated through 180° the pedal will go from the 'high' to 'low' positions and vice versa. Later models make use of a normal bolt so no adjustment is available. To remove the clutch pedal proceed as follows:

1. From inside the car undo and remove the nut and bolt which holds the pushrod arm to the clutch pedal lever.

2. Free the pedal return spring from the clutch pedal lever by judicious levering with a screwdriver.

3. Take off the circlip from the end of the pedal shaft and then push the shaft out of the mounting bracket. NOTE the sintered bronze washers between the clutch and brake pedal bosses. The pedal can now be removed.

4. Clean and oil the pedal bearing bush prior to replacement, which is a reversal of the removal sequence.

7. CLUTCH REMOVAL

The clutch can be removed after dropping the gearbox as described in Chapter 6/3. This is the easiest method. Other ways to remove the clutch are to first remove the engine as described in Chapter 1/4. or to remove the engine and gearbox together and then split to give access to the clutch.

1. Remove the clutch assembly by unscrewing the six bolts holding the cover to the rear face of the flywheel. Unscrew the bolts diagonally half a turn at a time to prevent distortion to the cover flange.

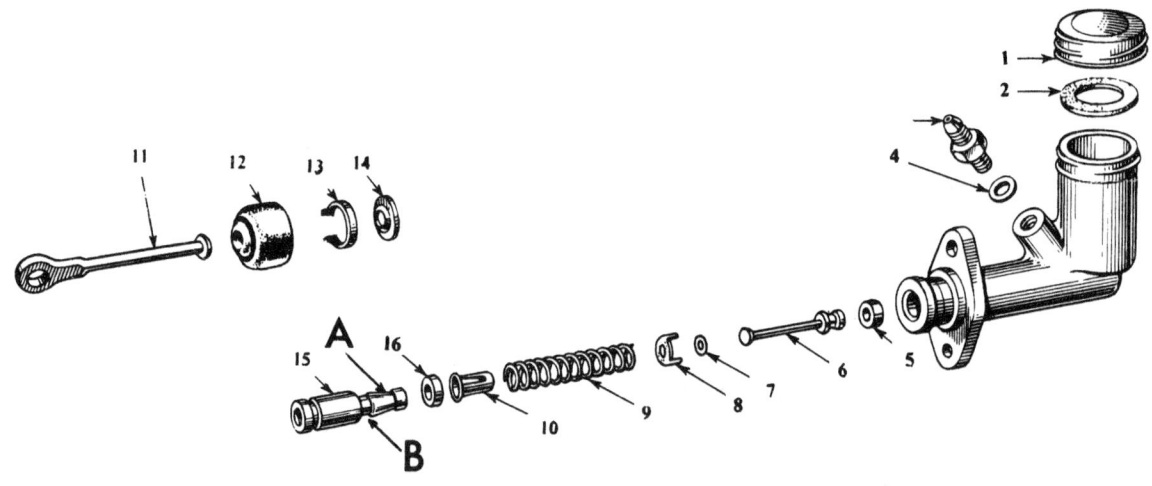

Fig. 5:2 EXPLODED VIEW OF THE CLUTCH MASTER CYLINDER.

1 Master cylinder cap.	5 Valve seal.	9 Piston return spring.	13 Circlip.
2 Sealing ring.	6 Valve stem.	10 Piston return spring retainer.	14 Washer.
3 Adaptor for hydraulic pipe.	7 Valve seal spring washer.	11 Pushrod.	15 Piston.
4 Sealing washer.	8 Seat spacer.	12 Rubber boot.	16 Inner seal.

CLUTCH AND ACTUATING MECHANISM

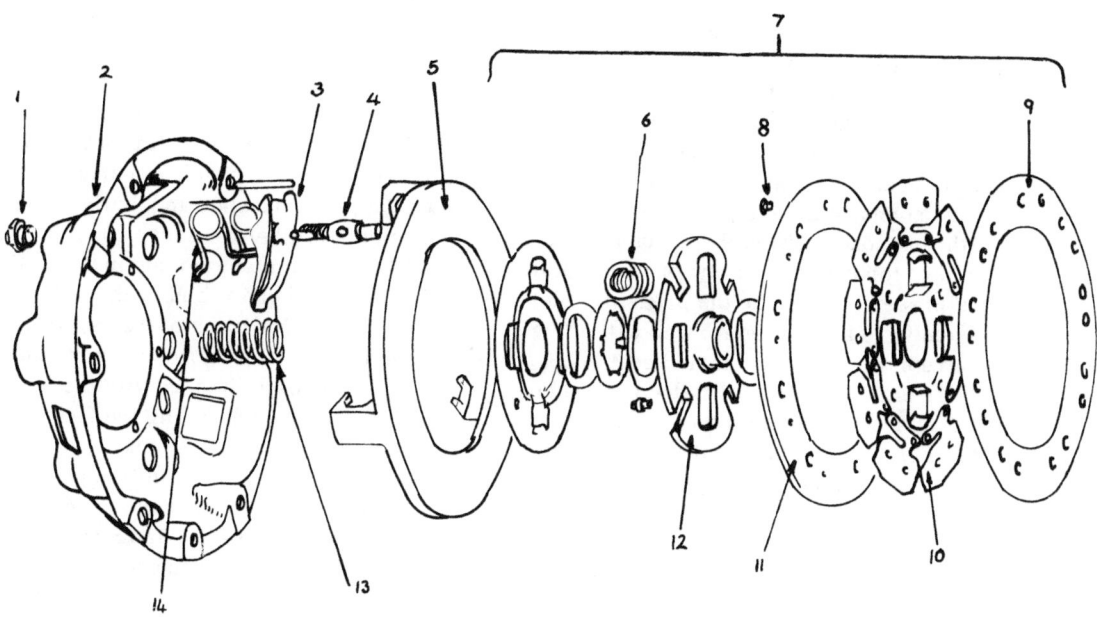

Fig. 5:3 EXPLODED DRAWING OF THE CLUTCH DISC AND PRESSURE PLATE PARTS IN THEIR RELATIVE POSITIONS. Clutch pressure plate assembly parts on the left, disc assembly parts on the right. 1 Eyebolt nut.   2 Clutch cover.   3 Release lever. 4 Eyebolt.   5 Pressure plate.   6 Driven plate spring.   7 Driven plate assembly.   8 Rivet.   9 Clutch lining.   10 Driven plate outer.   11 Clutch lining.   12 Driven plate inner.   13 Thrust spring.   14 Anti-rattle spring.

2. With all the bolts and spring washers removed, lift the clutch assembly off the three locating dowels.   The driven plate or clutch disc will fall out at this stage as it is not attached to either the clutch cover assembly or the flywheel.

8. CLUTCH INSPECTION
   1. Examine the clutch disc friction linings for wear and loose rivets and the disc for rim distortion, cracks, broken hub springs, and worn splines. If the linings are worn down or close to the rivets the driven plate should be renewed. At the same time examine the colour of the linings. If they have a shiny glazed surface but the colour and grain of the material are clearly visible all is well.   If the surface has darkened but the grain is still clearly visible then small amounts of oil have been deposited. If the surface is very dark and the grain largely lost, then this glazed surface will shortly result in clutch slip and difficulty in engaging gear from rest.   The linings should certainly be renewed if in this latter state, and a fresh oil seal fitted to the gearbox at the same time.

2. It is always best to renew the clutch driven plate as an assembly to preclude further trouble, but, if it is wished to merely renew the linings, the rivets should be drilled out and not knocked out with a punch. The manufacturers do not advise that only the linings are renewed and personal experience dictates that it is far more satisfactory to renew the driven plate complete than to try and economise by only fitting new friction linings.

3. Check the machined faces of the flywheel and the pressure plate. If either are badly grooved, they should be machined until smooth.   If the pressure plate is cracked or split it must be renewed, also if the portion on the other side of the plate in contact with the release lever tips are grooved.

4. The clutch cover and pressure plate assembly should not be dismantled. In the normal course of events clutch replacement is the term used for simply fitting a new clutch disc.

5. If a new clutch disc is being fitted it is a false economy not to renew the release bearing at the same time. This will preclude having to replace it at a later date

when wear on the clutch linings is still very small.

6. Examine the clutch cover and pressure plate assembly and check the release bearing thrust plate for cracks. Examine the tips of the release levers and note if more than a small flat has been worn on their ends. The best way to estimate wear is to compare the old pressure plate unit with a new one. Check the clutch pressure springs for breaks. If any of these faults are present, then take the pressure plate assembly to a Ford Agent, who will advise if a replacement unit should be fitted.

7. The reason why no attempt should be made to dismantle and rebuild the pressure plate assembly is that to perform adequately a rebuilt unit must be accurately balanced and there is no way round using special tools.

8. Examine the clutch release bearing in the gearbox bellhousing and if it is worn, loose, cracked or pitted, it must be removed and replaced.

9. CLUTCH RELEASE BEARING - REMOVAL & REPLACEMENT

1. To remove the clutch release bearing, disconnect the retracting spring, remove the spring clip securing the gaiter and detach the gaiter. Pull the forked end of the release arm from the spring clips of the release bearing hub and disengage the arm from the fulcrum pin. Pull the hub off the main drive gear bearing retainer and withdraw the release arm.

2. The clutch release bearing assembly is a light press fit on the hub; and to dismantle, hold the bearing downwards and tap the shoulder of the hub sharply on the bench. Check that the release arm fork spring clips on the rear face of the hub are sound and assemble the new bearing on the hub with the thrust face away from the hub. Press the hub into position, ensuring that it enters squarely into the bearing bore.

3. Pass the clutch release arm through the opening in the side of the clutch housing with the fulcrum pin spring clip facing to the rear and engine the clip around the pin head. Check carefully that the machined sleeve of the gearbox main shaft bearing is free from burrs and dirt, then lightly smear the sleeve with high melting point grease and replace the release bearing assembly, engaging the fork in the end of the release arm with the spring clips on the hub. Check the movement on the outer end of the release arm to ensure that it is freely transmitted to the bearing.

10. CLUTCH REPLACEMENT

It is important that no oil or grease gets on the clutch disc friction linings, or the pressure plate and flywheel faces. It is advisable to replace the clutch with clean hands and to wipe down the pressure plate and flywheel faces with a clean dry rag before assembly begins.

1. Place the clutch disc against the flywheel with the shorter end of the hub, which is the end with the chamfered splines, facing the flywheel. On no account should the clutch disc be replaced with the longer end of the centre hub facing the flywheel as on reassembly it will be found quite impossible to operate the clutch in this position.

2. Replace the clutch cover assembly loosely on the three dowels. Replace the six bolts and spring washers and tighten them finger tight so that the clutch disc is gripped but can still be moved.

3. The clutch disc must now be centralised so that when the engine and gearbox are mated the gearbox input shaft splines will pass through the splines in the centre of the driven plate hub.

4. Centralisation can be carried out quite easily by inserting a round bar or long screwdriver through the hole in the centre of the clutch, so that the end of the bar rests in the small hole in the end of the crankshaft containing the input shaft bearing bush.

5. Using the input shaft bearing bush as a fulcrum, moving the bar sideways or up and down will move the clutch disc in whichever direction is necessary to achieve centralisation.

6. Centralisation is easily judged by removing the bar and viewing the driven plate hub in relation to the hole in the release bearing. When the hub appears exactly in the centre of the release bearing hole all is correct.

7. Tighten the clutch bolts in a diagonal sequence to ensure that the cover plate is pulled down evenly and without distortion of the flange.

8. Mate the engine and gearbox, and check that the clutch is operating properly.

11. CLUTCH FAULTS

There are four main faults which the clutch and release mechanism are prone to. They may occur by themselves or in conjunction with any of the other faults. They are clutch squeal, slip, spin, and judder.

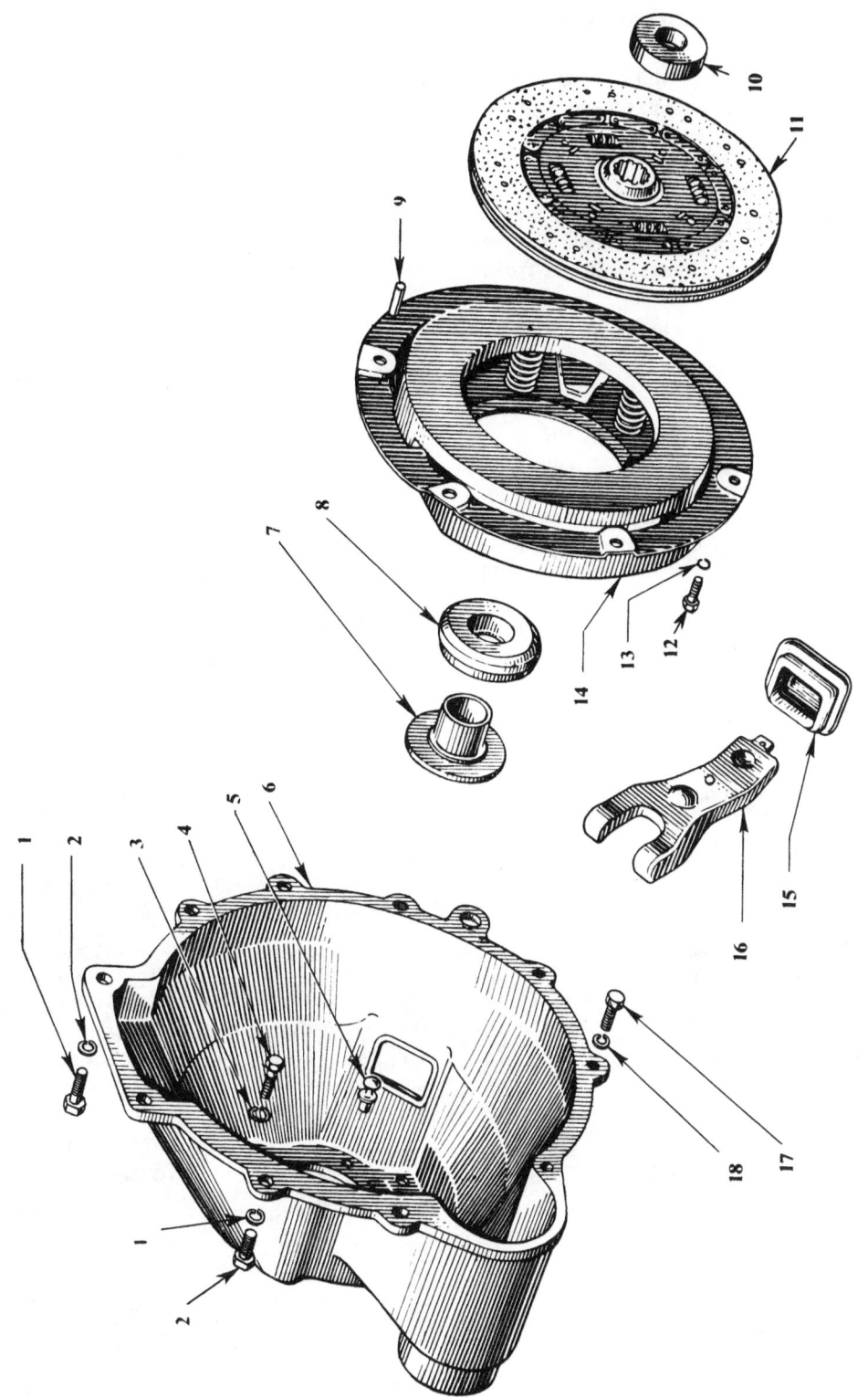

Fig 5·4 EXPLODED VIEW OF THE CLUTCH AND RELEASE BEARING COMPONENTS.

1 Bellhousing bolt.   2 Spring washer.   3 Washer.   4 Bolt.   5 Clutch release fork fulcrum pin.   6 Bellhousing.   7 Clutch release hub.   8 Clutch release bearing.   9 Dowel.   10 Clutch pilot bearing.   11 Clutch driven disc.   12 Bolt.   13 Spring washer.   14 Pressure plate assembly.   15 Rubber cover.   16 Clutch release arm.   17 Bolt.   18 Spring washer.

12. CLUTCH SQUEAL - DIAGNOSIS & CURE

If, on taking up the drive or when changing gear, the clutch squeals, this is a sure indication of a badly worn clutch release bearing. As well as regular wear due to normal use, wear of the clutch release bearing is much accentuated if the clutch is ridden, or held down for long periods in gear, with the engine running. To minimise wear of this component, the car should always be taken out of gear at traffic lights and for similar hold-ups.

The clutch release bearing is not an expensive item.

13. CLUTCH SLIP - DIAGNOSIS & CURE

Clutch slip is a self-evident condition which occurs when the clutch friction plate is badly worn, the release arm free travel is insufficient, oil or grease have got onto the flywheel or pressure plate faces, or the pressure plate itself is faulty.

The reason for clutch slip is that, due to one of the faults listed above, there is either insufficient pressure from the pressure plate, or insufficient friction from the friction plate to ensure solid drive.

If small amounts of oil get onto the clutch, they will be burnt off under the heat of clutch engagement, in the process gradually darkening the linings. Excessive oil on the clutch will burn off, leaving a carbon deposit which can cause quite bad slip, or fierceness, spin and judder.

If clutch slip is suspected, and confirmation of this condition is required, there are several tests which can be made.

1. With the engine in second or third gear and pulling lightly up a moderate incline, sudden depression of the accelerator pedal may cause the engine to increase its speed without any increase in road speed. Easing off on the accelerator will then give a definite drop in engine speed without the car slowing.

2. Drive the car at a steady speed in top gear and braking with the left leg, try and maintain the same speed by pressing down on the accelerator. Providing the same speed is maintained a change in the speed of the engine confirms that slip is taking place.

3. In extreme cases of clutch slip the engine will race under normal acceleration conditions.

Fig. 5:5 EXTERNAL VIEW OF THE CLUTCH SLAVE CYLINDER. 1 Bleed nipple. 2 Slave cylinder. 3 Dust cover. 4 Pushrod. 5 Adjusting nut. 6 Return spring. 7 Bellhousing.

CLUTCH AND ACTUATING MECHANISM

If slip is due to oil or grease on the linings a temporary cure can sometimes be effected by squirting carbon tetrochloride into the clutch, The permanent cure, of course, is to renew the clutch driven plate and trace and rectify the oil leak.

14. CLUTCH SPIN - DIAGNOSIS & CURE

Clutch spin is a condition which occurs when there is either a leak in the clutch hydraulic actuating mechanism where this system of actuation is used; the release arm free travel is excessive; there is an obstruction in the clutch either on the primary gear splines, or in the operating lever itself; or the oil may have partially burnt off the clutch linings and have left a resinous deposit which is causing the clutch disc to stick to the pressure plate or flywheel.

The reason for clutch spin is that due to any, or a combination of, the faults just listed, the clutch pressure plate is not completely freeing from the centre plate even with the clutch pedal fully depressed.

If clutch spin is suspected, the condition can be confirmed by extreme difficulty in engaging first gear from rest, difficulty in changing gear, and very sudden take-up of the clutch drive at the fully depressed end of the clutch pedal travel as the clutch is released.

Check the operating lever free travel. If this is correct examine the clutch master and slave cylinders and the connecting hydraulic pipe for leaks. Fluid in one of the rubber boots fitted over the end of either the master or slave cylinders, where fitted, is a sure sign of a leaking piston seal.

If these points are checked and found to be in order then the fault lies internally in the clutch, and it will be necessary to remove the clutch for examination.

15. CLUTCH JUDDER - DIAGNOSIS & CURE

Clutch judder is a self-evident condition which occurs when the gearbox or engine mountings are loose or too flexible, when there is oil on the faces of the clutch friction plate, or when the clutch pressure plate has been incorrectly adjusted.

The reason for clutch judder is that due to one of the faults just listed, the clutch pressure plate is not freeing smoothly from the friction disc, and is snatching.

Clutch judder normally occurs when the clutch pedal is released in first or reverse gears, and the whole car shudders as it moves backwards or forwards.

CHAPTER SIX

GEARBOX

CONTENTS

SPECIFICATIONS

Type	Four-speed constant mesh with helical cut gears. Synchromesh on top three gears of 997 cc and on all gears of 1200 cc models

Gear Ratios:	997 cc	1200 cc
1st	4.118:1	3.543:1
2nd	2.396:1	2.396:1
3rd	1.412:1	1.412:1
4th	1.000:1	1.000:1
Reverse	5.404:1	3.963:1

Layshaft Gear end float	0.008 in. to 0.020 in. (0.203 to 0.508 mm.)
Mainshaft Bearing end float	0.001 in. to 0.008 in. (0.025 to 0.203 mm.)
Third Gear end float	0.005 in. to 0.015 in. (0.127 to 0.381 mm.)
Second Gear end float	0.005 in. to 0.0187 in. (0.127 to 0.475 mm.)
Oil Capacity	1¾ pints
Grade of Lubricant	S.A.E. 80 E.P. Gear oil

Gear Identification - Early Cars

Main drive constant mesh laygear ...	⅝ in. tooth length Pt. No. 105E-7113-C
Primary Gear	¾ in. tooth length Pt. No. 105E-7017-B
Third Gear	11⁄16 in. tooth length Pt. No. 105E-7101-D
Second Gear	11⁄16 in. tooth length Pt. No. 105E-7102-C

Gear Identification - Later Cars

Main drive constant mesh laygear ...	11⁄16 in. tooth length Pt. No. 105E-7113-D
Main drive gear	13⁄16 in. tooth length Pt. No. 105E-7017-C
Third Gear	¾ in. tooth length Pt. No. 105E-7101-E
Second Gear	¾ in. tooth length Pt. No. 105E-7102-D

1. GENERAL DESCRIPTION

The gearbox is of the constant mesh type having four forward speeds and one reverse, with synchromesh engagement on second, third and top gears. Improvements have been incorporated since the introduction of this gearbox including increased helix angle on all helical gears.

The specification table given at the beginning of this chapter gives the numbers of the former and current gears.

Since the current and former gears are very similar in appearance, care must be taken to ensure that they are not intermixed in service.

Another change effective from about engine number 105E 34518, affects the mainshaft assembly which incorporates a nut and spacer to replace three circlips, two of which retain the speedometer gear and one locating the rear gearbox bearing.

2. GEARBOX MAINTENANCE

1. Once every 1,000 miles check the level of oil in the gearbox. To do this remove the filler plug on the side of the box and ensure the oil is up to the bottom of the plug orifice.

2. Top up with S.A.E. 80 E.P. gear oil using a syringe or oil gun.

3. Every 5,000 miles the oil must be changed. This is best done after a run when the lubricant is hot and will drain more quickly than when cold. Undo the square headed drain plug on the bottom of the gearbox and catch the oil in a container with a minimum capacity of 2 pints. Replace the drain plug, remove the filler plug and pour in $1\frac{3}{4}$ pints of the recommended lubricant. Replace the filler plug.

3. GEARBOX REMOVAL FROM THE CAR

1. To remove the gearbox from the car, first disconnect the battery leads, drain the oil from the gearbox and disconnect the battery lead from the starter motor. Unscrew the two bolts securing the starter motor and lift this away allowing it to lie on the engine shield. Unscrew and remove the bolts securing the clutch housing to the cylinder block and then remove the splash shield from the lower half of the flywheel housing.

2. Disconnect the clutch release arm retracting spring, remove the circlip from the cylinder body and push the cylinder out of its location.

3. Unscrew the bolt securing the speedometer drive cable retainer to the extension housing and withdraw the cable.

4. Disconnect the earthing strap from the bracket.

5. Unscrew the four self-locking nuts and remove the four bolts from the drive shaft coupling flange.

6. Unscrew the four self-locking nuts and take away the four bolts holding the drive shaft coupling after marking the two flanges in order to ensure correct re-assembly. Tap the coupling free, lower the rear end of the shaft and slide it back so that the front end will clear the gearbox main shaft.

7. Disconnect the exhaust pipe from the engine, and then make sure that the gear lever is in the neutral position, remove the gaiter, unscrew the gear lever cap and lift out the lever.

8. Support the rear end of the engine, remove the four bolts with their locking washers from the engine rear support member to the floor pan and then remove the gearbox complete with the rear support.

9. Release the locking tabs on the two bolts which secure the gearbox mounting to the extension housing, unscrew the bolts and remove the mounting and cross member.

4. GEARBOX DISMANTLING

1. Undo the four bolts and spring washers holding the gearlever cover in place and lift the cover off. (See Photograph).

4.1

4.2

2. Undo the four bolts and spring washers holding the gearbox cover in place and lift the cover away (see Photograph), so exposing the gearchange selector rods and the three springs for the locking balls.

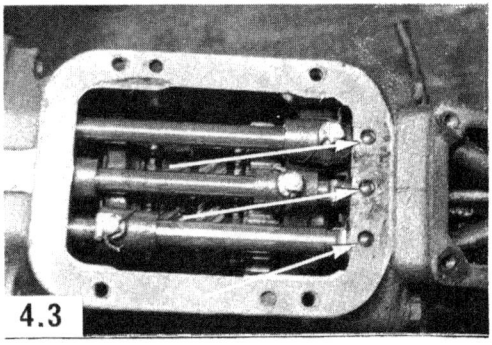

4.3

3. Seen here are the three gearchange selector rods and the locking balls (arrowed).

4. Remove the locking balls with the aid of a magnet. Alternatively turn the gearbox over so the balls fall out.

5. From inside the bellhousing free the springs retaining the release bearing to the release arm, and pull off the spring holding the release arm to its pivot post. (See Photograph). Remove the release arm and bearing.

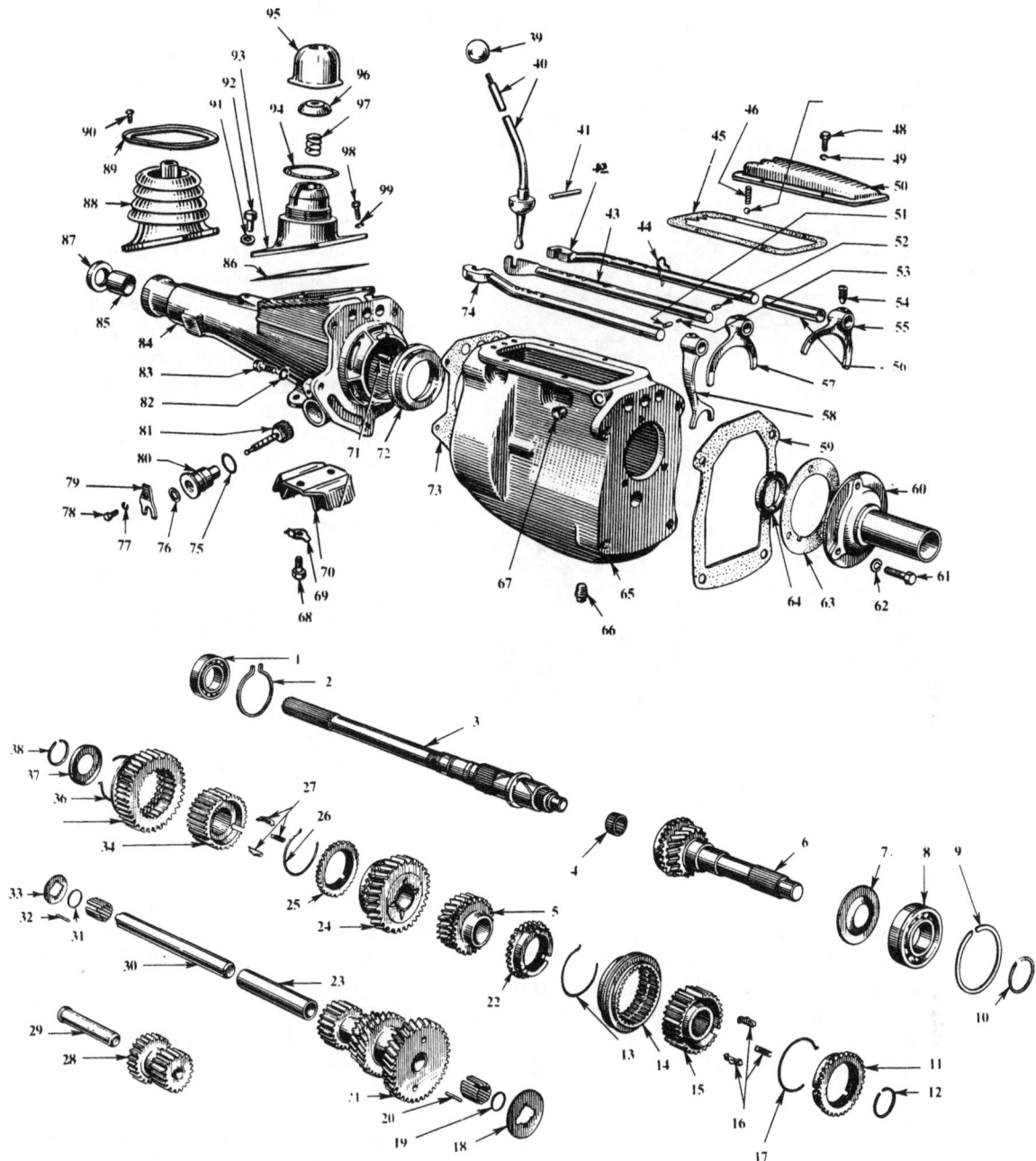

Fig. 6:1 EXPLODED VIEW OF THE 997 c.c. GEARBOX.

1 Mainshaft bearing. 2 Retaining circlip. 3 Mainshaft. 4 Mainshaft roller bearing. 5 Third gear. 6 Primary gear and input shaft. 7 Baffle. 8 Primary gear bearing. 9 Circlip. 10 Inner circlip. 11 First and second gear synchroniser ring. 12 Circlip for first gear. 13 Third and fourth gear synchroniser spring. 14 Third and fourth gear synchroniser hub. 15 Synchroniser hub. 16 Synchroniser hub inserts. 17 Synchroniser spring. 18 Layshaft front thrust washer. 19 Layshaft washer. 20 Roller bearing. 21 Laygear. 22 Ring. 23 Laygear bearing spacer tube. 24 Second gear. 25 Synchro ring. 26 Circlip. 27 Synchroniser hub inserts. 28 Reverse gear. 29 Reverse gear shaft. 30 Layshaft. 31 Layshaft washer. 32 Roller bearing. 33 Layshaft rear thrust washer. 34 First and second gear synchroniser hub. 35 First gear. 36 Circlip. 37 First and second gear hub insert retainer. 38 Circlip. 39 Gearlever Knob. 40 Gearlever. 41 Gearlever trunnion. 42 Third and fourth gear selector rod. 43 First and second gear selector rod. 44 Spring. 45 Gasket. 46 Selector spring. 47 Selector ball. 48 Bolt. 49 Spring washer. 50 Gearbox cover plate. 51 Selector rod interlock plunger. 52 Selector rod interlock plunger. 53 Interlock pin. 54 Selector for securing screw. 55 Third and fourth gear selector fork. 56 Tube. 57 First and second gear selector fork. 58 Reverse gear selector fork. 59 Gasket. 60 Primary shaft bearing retainer. 61 Bolt. 62 Spring washer. 63 Gasket. 64 Oilseal. 65 Gearbox casing. 66 Drain plug. 67 Plug. 68 Bolt. 69 Tab washer. 70 Gearbox mounting bracket. 71 Dowel. 72 Mainshaft bearing housing. 73 Gasket. 74 Reverse gear selector rod. 75 Sealing ring. 76 Washer. 77 Spring washer. 78 Bolt. 79 Securing clip. 80 Speedometer terminal. 81 Speedometer drive gear. 82 Spring washer. 83 Bolt. 84 Gearbox extension casing. 85 Extension bearing. 86 Gasket. 87 Oilseal. 88 Rubber bellows. 89 Securing plate. 90 Screw. 91 Spring washer. 92 Bolt. 93 Gearlever cover. 94 Gasket. 95 Gearlever cap. 96 Gearlever retaining seat. 97 Spring. 98 Bolt. 99 Spring washer.

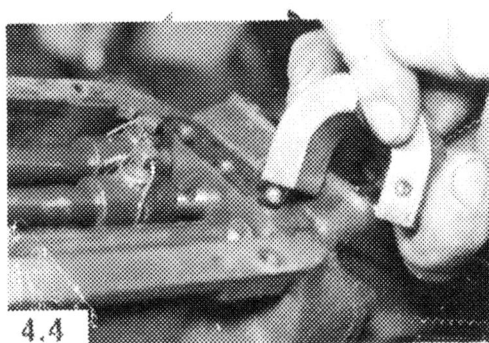

4.4

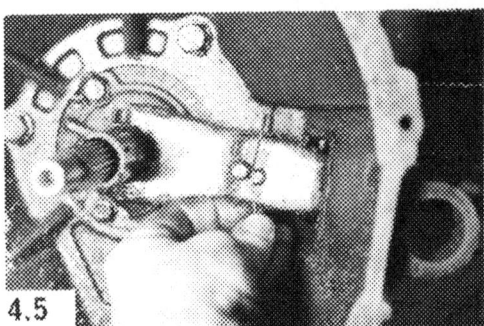

4.5

forward end of the shaft. Before the rod can be removed it must be turned through 90° as shown.

15. The first and second gear selector fork can then be lifted out of the gearbox. (See Photograph).

16. Moving to the front of the gearbox remove the third and fourth gear selector fork. (See Photograph).

17. Undo and remove the three bolts and spring washers (see Photograph) holding the primary shaft bearing retainer in place and pull the bearing retainer off the nose of the primary shaft.

18. Undo and remove the five bolts and spring washers holding the gearbox extension to the gearbox casing.

19. Pull the gearbox extension back about ¼ in. and then turn the extension anti-clockwise about 90° until the semi-circular cut-out (arrowed) in the extension flange lines up with the hole in the gearbox for the layshaft. (NOTE. In the photograph the layshaft has already been removed for clarity).

20. Then from the other end of the gearbox tap out the layshaft with a long rod and remove the shaft as shown. (The 40 layshaft needle roller bearings will now be free and care must be taken to ensure none are lost.) A 5/16 in. U.N.F. bolt must then be screwed into the threaded hole (arrowed) in the centre of the reverse gear shaft.

21. Turn the extension casing further anti-clockwise until the semi-circular cut-out lines up with the reverse shaft hole. With a screwdriver or cold chisel under the head of the bolt, tap the shaft out of the gearbox as shown.

6. Then undo and remove the four bolts and washers holding the bellhousing to the gearbox. (See Photograph).

7. Pull the gearbox away from the bellhousing as shown. It is now helpful to place the gearbox in a large vice.

8. A forked securing clip holds the speedometer drive in place. Undo the single bolt and spring washer holding the clip in position and then lift out the drive gear. (See Photograph).

9. Make sure the gearbox is in neutral by lining up the cut outs for the gearlever in the ends of the selector rods. Cut through the locking wire on the three securing bolts. (See Photograph).

10. Undo and remove the three securing bolts from the three selector forks. The bolts have a tapered end and serve to hold the forks securely to the rods. (See Photograph).

11. Pull out the reverse gear selector rod as shown.

12. Then lift out the reverse gear selector fork. (See Photograph).

13. Pull out the third and top gear selector rod through the gearlever cover hole as shown and lift out the sleeve (arrowed) which will slide off the rod as it is withdrawn.

14. Partially remove the first and second gear selector rod (the one in the middle), and take out the floating pin from its hole in the

4.21

22. Pull the extension housing complete with the mainshaft and gears from the gearbox housing. (See Photograph).

23. With a pair of circlip pliers release the circlip which is fitted in a groove round the primary shaft ball bearing.

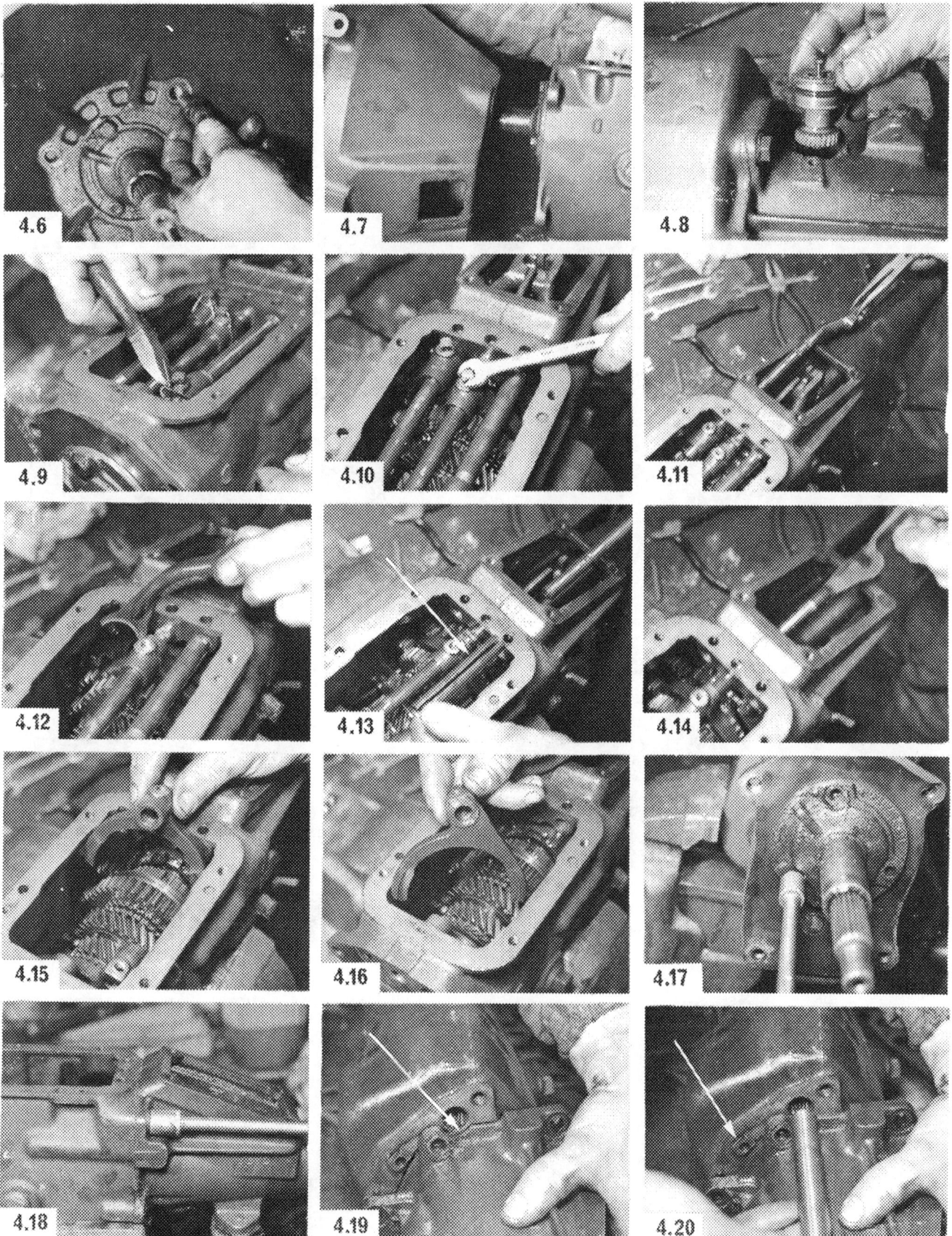

4.6

4.7

4.8

4.9

4.10

4.11

4.12

4.13

4.14

4.15

4.16

4.17

4.18

4.19

4.20

93

4.22

4.23

4.24

24. Push the primary gear assembly into the gearbox casing and remove the assembly through the hole in the top of the box. (See Photograph).

4.25

25. Lift out the reverse idler gear from the gearbox. (See Photograph).

4.26

26. Then pull out the laygear. (See Photograph).

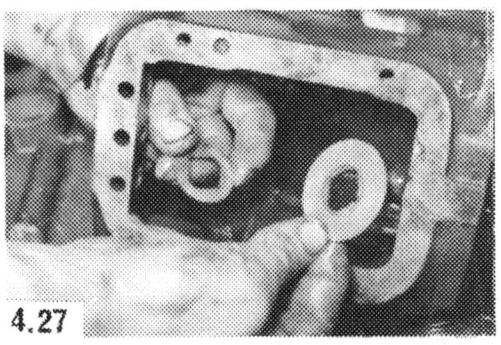

4.27

27. Remove the two laygear thrust washers. Note that the larger washer fits on the bell-housing end of the gearbox while the smaller washer fits on the gearbox extension end.

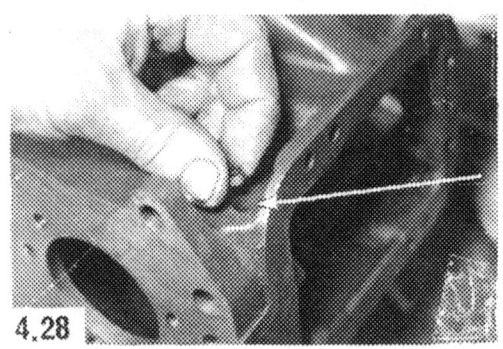

4.28

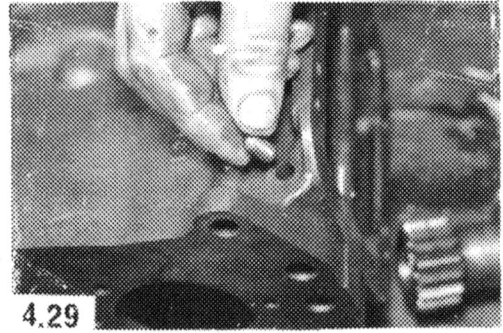

4.29

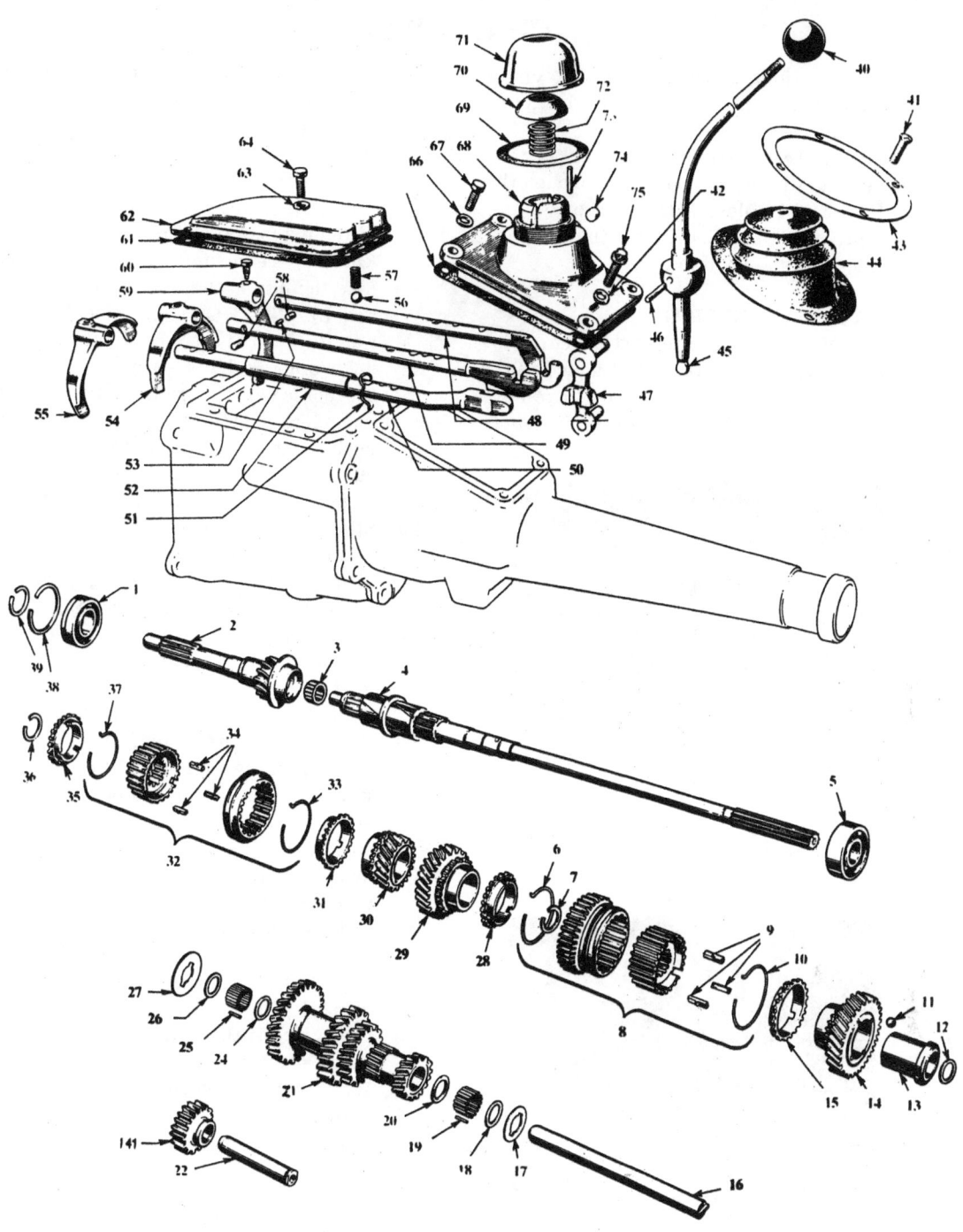

Fig. 6:2 EXPLODED VIEW OF THE 1198 c.c. GEARBOX.

1 Primary gear bearing. 2 Primary gear and shaft. 3 Roller bearing. 4 Mainshaft. 5 Mainshaft roller bearing. 6 Circlip.
7 Small circlip. 8 First and second gear synchroniser unit. 9 Synchroniser hub inserts. 10 Circlip. 11 Ball bearing. 12 First
gear thrust washer. 13 Bush. 14 First gear. 15 First and second gear synchroniser ring. 16 Layshaft. 17 Rear thrust washer.
18 Laygear washer. 19 Roller bearing. 20 Laygear washer. 21 Laygear. 22 Reverse gear shaft. 23 Reverse gear. 24 Laygear washer. 25 Roller bearing. 26 Laygear washer. 27 Front thrust washer. 28 First and second gear synchroniser ring.
29 Second gear. 30 Third gear. 31 Third and fourth gear synchroniser ring. 32 Third and fourth gear synchroniser unit.
33 Circlip. 34 Synchroniser hub inserts. 35 Third and fourth gear synchroniser ring. 36 Locating circlip. 37 Circlip.
38 Primary gear retaining circlip. 39 Inner circlip. 40 Gearlever knob. 41 Screw. 42 Spring washer. 43 Sealing ring.
44 Rubber boot. 45 Gearlever. 46 Pin. 47 Selector gate. 48 Reverse gear selector. 49 First and second gear selector.
50 Third and fourth gear selector. 51 Retaining spring. 52 Sleeve. 53 Interlock pin. 54 Third and fourth gear selector fork.
55 First and second gear selector fork. 56 Ball. 57 Spring. 58 Interlock plungers. 59 Reverse gear selector fork. 60 Selector
fork locking screw. 61 Gasket. 62 Metal cover. 63 Spring washer. 64 Bolt. 65 Gasket. 66 Spring washer. 67 Bolt.
68 Gearlever cover. 69 Gasket. 70 Gearlever retaining seat. 71 Gearlever cap. 72 Spring. 73 Pin. 74 Bar. 75 Bolt.

28. Remove the plug (arrowed) from the cross drilling in the bellhousing end of the gearbox casing.

29. Shake out the two interlock plungers if they have not already dropped out through the selector rod holes. The gearbox is now completely dismantled. One of the plungers is shown in the photograph.

MAINSHAFT DISMANTLING

It is easier to dismantle part of the mainshaft assembly while it is still attached to the gearbox extension. If it is wished to remove the mainshaft in one piece, follow the instructions in 6/5. 6 and 7.

5.1

1. Slide off the outside synchronising ring. (See Photograph).

5.2

2. With a pair of circlip pliers remove the circlips which hold the third and top gear synchroniser in position. (See Photograph).

3. With the aid of a tyre lever carefully prise off the third and top gear synchroniser; the synchro ring; and third gear; as shown. Take great care not to damage the teeth of second gear against which the lever pivots. If available use a proper puller.

4. Shown in the photograph are the synchroniser hub, synchro ring, and third gear in the order in which they are removed.

5. It is not possible to dismantle the mainshaft further until it is removed from the extension casing because of the flange (arrowed) which separates third and second gears.

6. With a pair of pliers compress the legs of the circlip (arrowed) which holds the mainshaft bearing in the extension housing.

7. Then pull the mainshaft from out of the front of the extension casing. (See Photograph).

8. Knock up the locking tab on the washer behind the nut on the mainshaft. (See Photograph). NOTE On early models a circlip was used instead of a nut to retain the speedometer drive gear.

9. The nut is very large and difficulty may be experienced in finding a spanner large enough to fit it. If this is the case start the nut with the aid of a cold chisel against one of the edges as shown in the photograph.

10. Slide the speedometer drive gear off the mainshaft. NOTE the locating ball in the shaft and the corresponding groove in the drive gear. (See Photograph).

11. Tap out the locating ball or remove it with the aid of a magnet as shown in the photograph.

12. Slide the spacer off the mainshaft as shown.

13. With a soft metal drift carefully tap the bearing off the mainshaft. (See Photograph). If available a puller can be located behind second gear and second gear: first gear; the first and second gear synchroniser; the synchro ring; and the bearing all pulled off together after the circlip has been removed.

14. Release the circlip from the first and second gear synchroniser. (See Photograph).

15. Then with the aid of a pair of tyre levers carefully lever the synchroniser hub and first gear off the splines on the mainshaft (See Photograph).

16. Withdraw the synchroniser hub together with first gear as shown in the photograph.

17. With the aid of a soft drift carefully tap off second gear and remove it together with the synchroniser ring. (See Photograph).

6. GEARBOX INSPECTION & OVERHAUL

1. The first gear and second gear synchroniser and hub assembly must be serviced as a unit, and therefore the synchro bar retaining plate must not be dismantled from the hub, nor must the sleeves and hubs be interchanged between assemblies. All the circlips on the mainshaft assembly are the same size.

2. To remove the third and top gear synchroniser from the hub extract the blocker bars and front spring, and then remove the circlip from the synchroniser to the mainshaft.

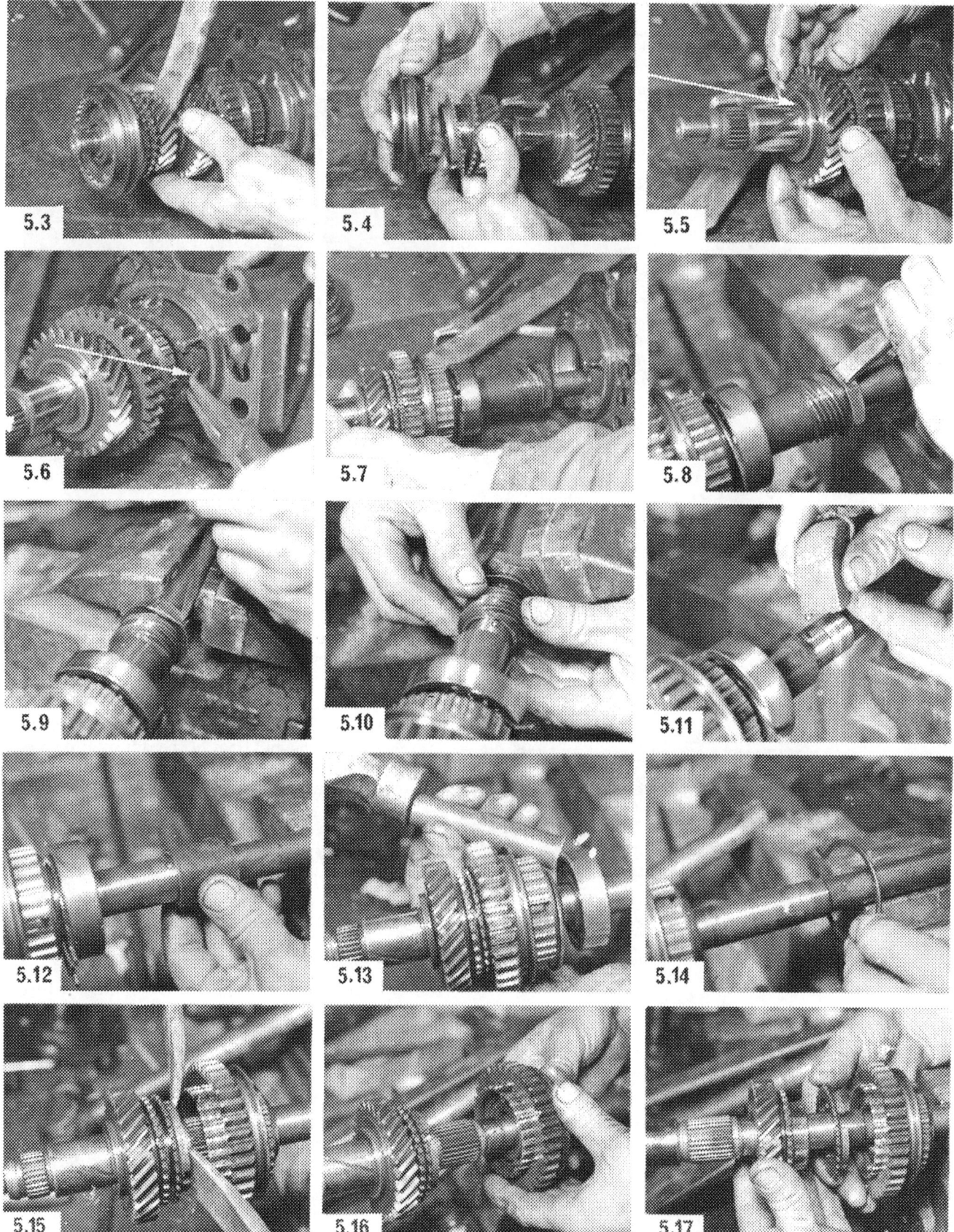

3. Locate a spit adaptor tool behind the third gear, support the assembly in the support ring and base plate and press off the third and top gear synchroniser hub, blocking plate and third gear.

4. The synchroniser hub and sleeve are mated together and lines are etched on each part to enable them to be assembled in correct position.

6.5

5. To dismantle the primary gear assembly remove the circlip which secures the main drive gear bearing to the gear, (see Photograph), support the bearing and press the main drive gear from the bearing. Note that an oil slinger is fitted between the gear and the bearing.

6.6

6. To overhaul the extension housing extract the oil seal as shown in the photograph from the rear of the housing, and then examine the rear bearing and if necessary drive this into the housing.

7. When fitting in a new bearing enter it into the housing with the split in the bush towards the top. Drive the bearing into position until the rear end is flush with the recess of the extension housing.

8. Locate the new oil seal so that the lip of the seal faces into the housing. This seal may be fitted after the housing has been refitted to the gearbox.

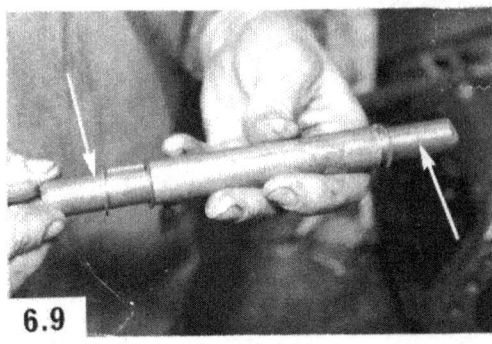

6.9

9. Examine the layshaft for wear or scuffing and replace it if wear is evident. Renew the needle roller bearings if these are worn. The arrows in the photograph show the areas to check. Shown fitted is the tubular spacer, one needle roller, and the retaining washers.

10. Examine the condition of the main ball bearings, one on the first motion shaft and the other on the mainshaft. If there is looseness between the inner and outer races the bearing must be renewed.

7. GEARBOX REASSEMBLY

In general rebuilding the gearbox is a straightforward reversal of the dismantling sequence. The following notes will ensure that the gearbox is assembled correctly in the minimum of time. Throughout the assembly process check that the end float of the different components corresponds with that given in the specification. Where the end float is incorrect your local Ford agent will be able to supply over or undersize thrust washers and circlips.

1. Starting with the mainshaft, when a new unit is fitted, slide the synchroniser sleeve from the hub, locate the blocker bars in the hub so that the flat extensions are within the retaining plate and the tag on the end of the spring is inside the bar. Leave the other end of the spring free. Next determine which blocker bar the spring tag is located in and also the direction of rotation of the spring, and slide the second gear sleeve with the selector fork to the rear, onto the hub, making sure that the mating marks on the hub and sleeve are in line. Fit in the front blocker bar spring with the tag located in the same bar as the rear spring with the springs running in opposite directions.

2. To reassemble the mainshaft, slide the second gear on to the shaft with the teeth toward the thrust collar. Position the synchro ring on the tapered face of the second

gear and then locate the first gear and second gear synchroniser on the shaft, making certain that the mating splines on the hub and shaft correspond. (See Fig. 6.3)

3. The hub needs to be pressed on the shaft until the rear face is level with the bearing shoulder.

4. Fit the large circlip over the mainshaft and locate the bearing to ensure that the radius on the outside diameter of the bearing faces the extension housing.

5. Support the shaft in a vice and press home the bearing with the aid of an 18 in. piece of tube whose diameter should not exceed that of the inner race.

6. Slide the third gear onto the shaft with the teeth toward the thrust collar and then locate the synchro ring on the taper face of the gear.

7. Fit one of the blocker bar springs in the rear of the third and top gear synchroniser hub and locate the hub on the shaft with the long boss toward the front of the shaft.

8. Support the assembly of the third and top gear synchroniser, and locate the shaft so that the mating marks on the hub and shaft are in line and then press the hub right home.

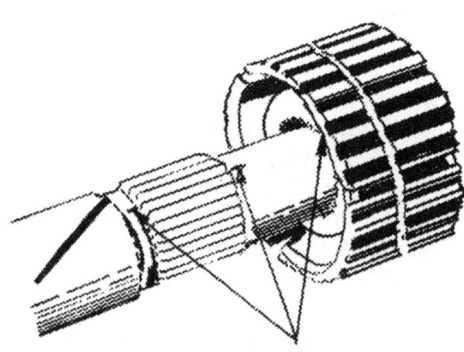

Fig. 6:3 Method of mating up the second gear synchroniser hub, with the mating marks which must be in line (arrowed.)

9. Fit the circlip in the groove. Install the blocker bars and front spring as previously, refit the sleeve to the hub and then slide the spacer onto the mainshaft and install the locating ball for the speedometer drive gear in its seating followed by the gear, which should have the shoulder to the rear.

10. Fit on the tab washer, screw on the nut and tighten this to a torque value of between 20 and 25 lb. ft.

11. Turning next to the installation of the main shaft assembly in the extension housing, take care not to damage the oil seal as the splines pass through. Make sure that the mainshaft bearing is located in the extension housing before fitting the circlip in such a manner that the two legs are located in the portion of the extension housing which is cut away to receive them.

12. Refit the speedometer driven gear, and then reassemble the layshaft by locating the tubular washer spacer in the laygear and fit to a dummy layshaft. Grease the needle rollers and locate twenty around this dummy shaft at each end of the gear.

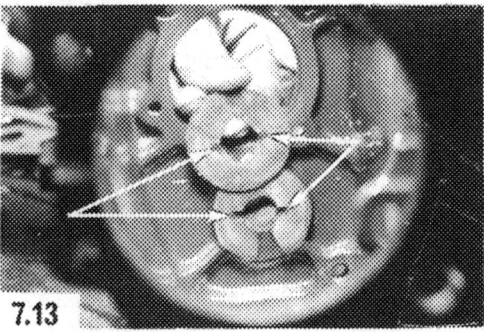

7.13

13. Fit the retaining washers over each end of the shaft, locate the two thrust washers with the large diameter washer to the front in position in the gearbox, and ensure that the tongue of each washer is located within the recess. The arrows in the photograph show the tongues and recesses on the larger of the two thrust washers.

14. Now place the laygear in the bottom of the box making sure that the thrust washers are not displaced. Install the reverse idler gear with the larger gear towards the rear and allow it to rest in the box.

15. Next assemble the primary gear, and then install the thirteen needle rollers in the bore of the primary gear and fit the gear to the front face of the gearbox casing. When fitting these rollers, use grease to retain twelve in position and then slide the last one longitudinally into the remaining space. This will lock them in position.

16. Fit the large diameter circlip in its location on the bearing.

17. Place a new gasket on the gearbox front face making sure that the oil groove is in line with the oil passage in the gearbox casing as the retainer is placed over the shaft. Bolt up the retainer with three bolts and lockwashers.

18. To fit the main shaft and extension housing, fit a new gasket to the rear face of the gearbox and pass the main shaft assembly through the rear of the box, locating the

main shaft spigot in the bore of the main drive gear. Next install the reverse idler shaft in the gear so that the flats will line up with the recess in the extension housing.

19. To complete the layshaft gear assembly, rotate the extension h o u s i n g 90 degrees anti-clockwise from its normal position, lift the gear into mesh with the main shaft and primary gear, making sure that the thrust washers are not moved, and carefully, fit in the l a y s h a f t from the rear, keeping it in contact with the dummy shaft.

20. Ensure that the locking face of the layshaft and the reverse idler shaft will engage with the recess cast in the extension housing, rotate the housing and push the assembly home.

21. Secure the housing with the five bolts and lockwashers, and note that an e a r t h i n g strap should be fitted to the lower right-hand bolt.

22. Next refit the bellhousing with the four bolts and lockwashers and then a s s e m b l e the clutch release mechanism.

23. To reassemble the selector mechanism, first make sure that the two interlocking plungers are located in the front face of the box, and then position the selector forks on the gears, making sure that the gearbox is in neutral before fitting in the second gear selector shaft.

24. Before this s h a f t is pushed home check that the floating pin is located in the shaft, set the shaft in the neutral position, aligning the hole in the shaft with the bolt hole in the selector fork and fit the square taper bolt, tighten bolts and lock up, securing with a length of wire.

25. Next install the reverse selector shaft and then the third and top gear selector shaft, fitting the securing bolts and locking these with a length of wire.

26. Fit a new gasket on the top face of the gearbox and fit the selector shaft locking balls and their springs into the three holes in the end of the gearbox flange, and then place the cover in position with the three springs in their drillings. Bolt down the cover with the four bolts and lockwashers.

27. Fit a new gasket to the gear lever housing and secure this to the extension housing with four bolts and lockwashers.

8. GEARBOX REPLACEMENT IN THE CAR

1. When offering up the gearbox to the engine, ensure that the clutch housing is aligned with the tubular dowels. Fit and tighten the clutch housing bolts, and then secure the support member to the floor pan with two bolts and lockwashers on each side.

2. Fit a paper gasket between the speedometer drive cable and the bearing and refit the drive cable which is secured in place with a horseshoe retainer, one bolt and a lockwasher. Reconnect the earth strap to the bracket on the floor pan.

3. Replace the drive shaft, slide the front universal joint sleeve on to the splines of the mainshaft, and align the mating marks on the rear flange and pinion drive flange. Fit the retaining bolts and tighten up the self-locking nuts.

4. Connect up the exhaust pipe to the manifold, refit the clutch operating cylinder, assemble the splash shield to the lower half of the clutch housing, refit the starter motor and connect the cable, insert the gear lever and refit the ball joint securely together with the rubber gaiter.

5. Fill the gearbox to the correct level with the correct lubricant, and then check the hydraulic operating gear of the clutch, filling with brake fluid and bleeding to release the air as required.

FAULT FINDING CHART

Cause	Trouble	Remedy
SYMPTOM:	WEAK OR INEFFECTIVE SYNCHROMESH	
General wear	Synchronising cones worn, split or damaged.	Dismantle and overhaul gearbox. Fit new gear wheels and synchronising cones.
	Baulk ring synchromesh dogs worn, or damaged	Dismantle and overhaul gearbox. Fit new baulk ring synchromesh.
SYMPTOM:	JUMPS OUT OF GEAR	
General wear or damage	Broken gearchange fork rod spring	Dismantle and replace spring.
	Gearbox coupling dogs badly worn	Dismantle gearbox. Fit new coupling dogs.
	Selector fork rod groove badly worn	Fit new selector fork rod.
	Selector fork rod securing screw and locknut loose	Remove side cover, tighten securing screw and locknut.
SYMPTOM:	EXCESSIVE NOISE	
Lack of maintenance. General wear	Incorrect grade of oil in gearbox or oil level too low	Drain, refill, or top up gearbox with correct grade of oil.
	Bush or needle roller bearings worn or damaged	Dismantle and overhaul gearbox. Renew bearings.
	Gearteeth excessively worn or damaged	Dismantle, overhaul gearbox. Renew gearwheels.
	Laygear thrust washers worn allowing excessive end play	Dismantle and overhaul gearbox. Renew thrust washers.
SYMPTOM:	EXCESSIVE DIFFICULTY IN ENGAGING GEAR	
Clutch not fully disengaging	Clutch pedal adjustment incorrect	Adjust clutch pedal correctly.

CHAPTER SEVEN

PROPELLER SHAFT AND UNIVERSAL JOINTS

CONTENTS

1. GENERAL DESCRIPTION

Drive is transmitted from the gearbox to the rear axle by means of a finely balanced tubular propeller shaft. Fitted at each end of the shaft is a universal joint which allows for vertical movement of the rear axle. Each universal joint comprises a four legged centre spider, four needle roller bearings and two yokes.

Fore and aft movement of the rear axle is absorbed by a sliding spline in the front of the propeller shaft which slides over a mating spline on the rear of the gearbox mainshaft. A supply of oil through very small oil holes from the gearbox lubricates the splines, and a grease nipple is fitted to each universal joint so that the needle roller bearings can be lubricated. The propeller shaft is a relatively simple component, and to overhaul and repair it is fairly easy.

2. PROPELLER SHAFT - REMOVAL & REPLACEMENT

1. Jack up the rear of the car, or position the rear of the car over a pit or on a ramp.
2. If the rear of the car is jacked up supplement the jack with support blocks so that danger is minimised should the jack collapse.
3. If the rear wheels are off the ground place the car in gear or put the handbrake on to ensure that the propeller shaft does not turn when an attempt is made to loosen the four nuts securing the propeller shaft to the rear axle.
4. Unscrew and remove the four self-locking nuts, bolts, and securing washers which hold the flange on the propeller shaft to the flange on the rear axle.

5. The propeller shaft is carefully balanced to fine limits and it is important that it is replaced in exactly the same position it was in prior to its removal. Scratch a mark on the propeller shaft and rear axle flanges to ensure accurate mating when the time comes for reassembly.
6. Slightly push the shaft forward to separate the two flanges, and then lower the end of the shaft and pull it rearwards to disengage the gearbox mainshaft splines.
7. Place a large can or a tray under the rear of the gearbox extension to catch any oil which is likely to leak through the spline lubricating holes, when the propeller shaft is removed.
8. Replacement of the propeller shaft is a reversal of the above procedure. Ensure that the mating marks scratched on the propeller shaft and rear axle flanges line up.

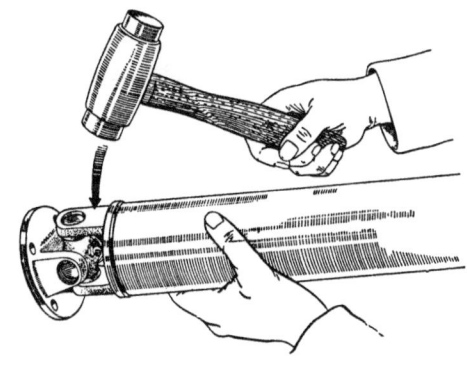

Fig. 7:1 Tap the universal joint with a hammer to free the bearing.

3. UNIVERSAL JOINTS - INSPECTION & REPAIR

1. Wear in the needle roller bearings is characterised by vibration in the transmission, 'clonks' on taking up the drive, and in extreme cases of lack of lubrication, metallic squeaking, and ultimately grating and shrieking sounds as the bearings break up.

2. It is easy to check if the needle roller bearings are worn with the propeller shaft in position, by trying to turn the shaft with one

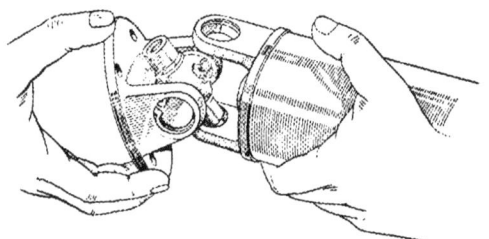

Fig. 7:2 Separate the universal joint as shown above.

Fig. 7:2

hand, the other hand holding the rear axle flange when the rear universal is being checked, and the front half coupling when the front universal is being checked. Any movement between the propeller shaft and the front and the rear half couplings is indicative of considerable wear. If worn, the old bearings and spiders will have to be discarded and a repair kit, comprising new universal joint spiders, bearings, oil seals, and retainers purchased. Check also by trying to lift the shaft and noticing any movement in the joints.

3. Examine the propeller shaft splines for wear. If worn it will be necessary to purchase a new front half coupling, or if the yokes are badly worn, an exchange propeller shaft. It is not possible to fit oversize bearings and journals to the trunnion bearing holes.

4. UNIVERSAL JOINTS - DISMANTLING
(See Fig. 7:3).

1. Clean away all traces of dirt and grease from circlips (8) located on the ends of the spiders (4), and remove the circlips by pressing their open ends together with a pair of pliers and lever them out with a screwdriver. NOTE If they are difficult to remove tap the bearing face resting on top of the spider with a mallet which will ease the pressure on the circlip.

2. Hold the propeller shaft in one hand and remove the bearing cups (7) and needle rollers by tapping the yoke at each bearing with a copper or hide faced hammer. As soon as the bearings start to emerge they can be drawn out with your fingers. If the bearing cup refuses to move then place a thin bar against the inside of the bearing and tap it gently until the cup starts to emerge.

3. With the bearings removed it is relatively easy to extract the spiders (4) from their yokes. If the bearings and spider journals are thought to be badly worn this can easily be ascertained visually with the universal joints dismantled.

5. UNIVERSAL JOINTS - REASSEMBLY

1. Thoroughly clean out the yokes and journals.

2. Fit new oil seals (6) and retainers (5) on the spider journals, place the spider on the propeller shaft yoke, and assemble the needle rollers in the bearing races with the assistance of some thin grease.

3. Refit the bearing cups on the spider and tap the bearings home so that they lie squarely in position.

4. Replace the circlips (8) and lubricate the bearings well with a lithium based grease.

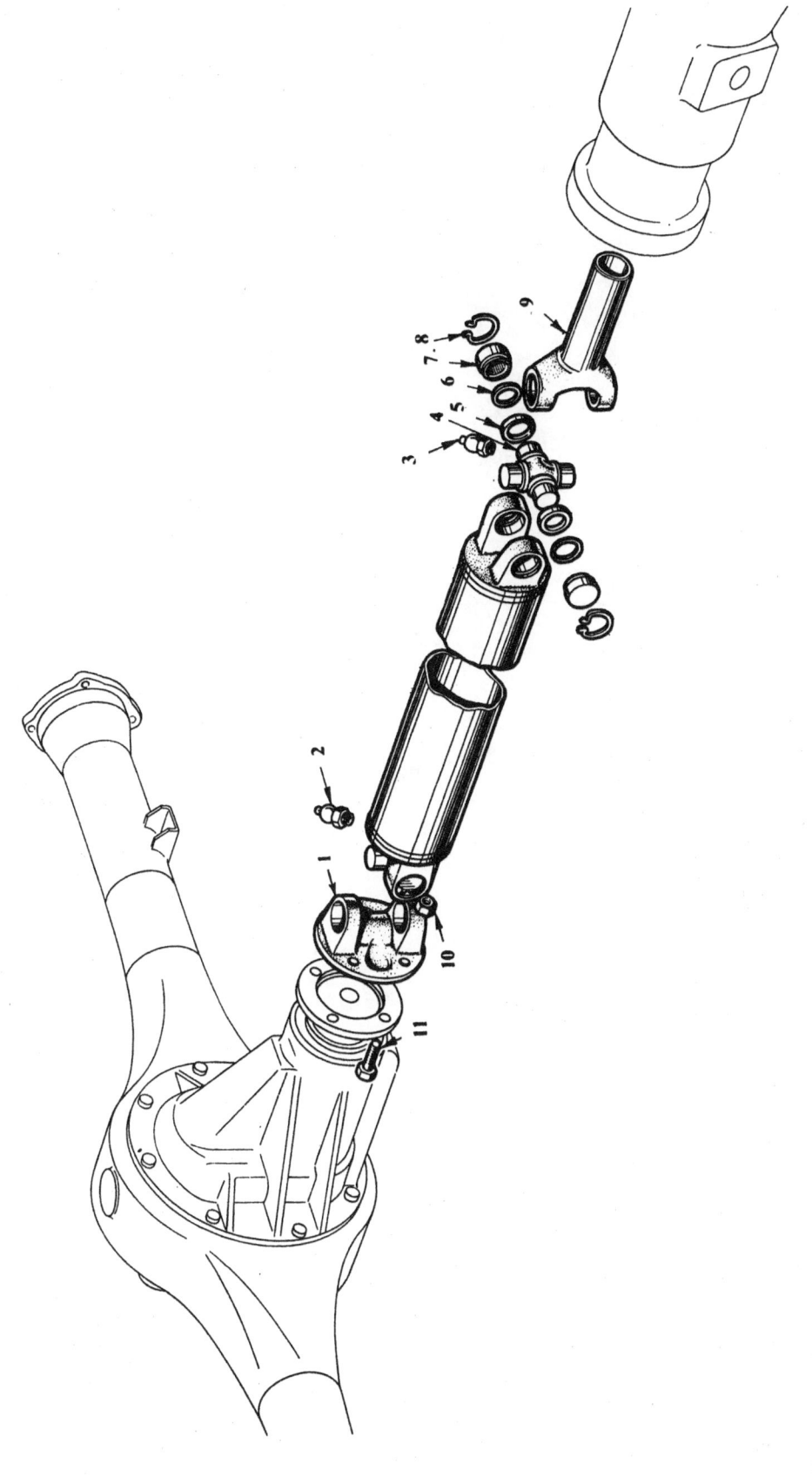

Fig. 7:3 EXPLODED VIEW OF THE PROPELLER SHAFT AND UNIVERSAL JOINTS.

1 Drive shaft flange yoke.   2 Grease nipple.   3 Grease nipple.   4 Spider.   5 Oil seal retainer.   6 Oil seal.   7 Needle roller bearings and cap.   8 Retaining circlip.   9 Universal joint knuckle.   10 Nut.   11 Bolt.

CHAPTER EIGHT

REAR AXLE

CONTENTS

SPECIFICATIONS

Type	Semi-floating
Axle Ratio	4.125:1 or 4.44 to 1
Crown Wheel - Number of Teeth	33 or 31
Pinion - Number of Teeth	8 or 7
Pinion Bearing Preload	9 to 11 lb. in. without oil seal
Recommended Lubricant	Hypoid oil S.A.E. 90
Rear Axle Capacity	2 pints (1.13 litres)

TORQUE WRENCH SETTINGS

Crown wheel to differential case bolts	30 to 35 lbs. ft.
Differential carrier to axle housing	15 to 18 lbs. ft.
Differential bearing locking plate bolts	12 to 15 lbs. ft.
Bearing cap bolts	45 to 50 lbs. ft.
Axle shaft bearing retainer nuts	15 to 18 lbs. ft.
Drive flange nuts	15 to 18 lbs. ft.

1.

GENERAL DESCRIPTION

The rear axle is of the semi-floating type and is held in place by two semi-elliptic springs. These provide the necessary lateral and longitudinal support for the axle.

The banjo type casing carries the differential assembly which consists of a hypoid crown wheel and pinion and the two star pinion differential bolted in a carrier to the casing nose piece.

All repairs can be carried out to the component parts of the rear axle without removing the axle casing from the car. It will be found simpler in practice to fit a guaranteed second hand axle from a car breakers yard rather than dismantle the differential unit which calls for special tools which very few garages will have.

As an alternative a replacement differential carrier assembly can be fitted which means that the axle can be left in position and dismantling is reduced to a minimum.

2. REAR AXLE - REMOVAL & REPLACEMENT

1. Remove the rear wheel hub caps and loosen the wheel nuts.

2. Raise and support the rear of the body and the differential casing with chocks or jacks so that the rear wheels are clear of the ground. This is most easily done by placing a jack under the centre of the differential, jacking up the axle and then fitting chocks under the mountings points at the front of the rear springs to support the body.

3. Remove both rear wheels and place the wheel nuts in the hub caps for safe keeping.

4. Free the check strap from its attachment to the rear axle.

5. Mark the propeller shaft and differential drive flanges to ensure replacement in the same relative positions. Undo and remove the nuts and bolts holding the two flanges together.

6. Release the handbrake and disconnect the cable at the clevis joint on the left hand brake plate. Free the transverse brake rod by removing the split pin and pulling out the clevis pin on the other backplate.

7. Undo the nuts and bolts holding the shock absorbers attachments to the spring seats.

8. Unscrew the union on the flexible brake pipe where it enters the bracket on the axle casing and have handy either a jar to catch the hydraulic fluid or a plug to block the end of the pipe.

9. Check that the jack is under the differential casing and taking the weight of the rear axle and then unscrew the nuts from under the spring retaining plates. These nuts screw onto the ends of inverted 'U' bolts which retain the axle to the spring.

10. The axle will now be resting on the jack and can be lowered and removed from under the car. Replacement is a r e v e r s a l of the above process. Note that the two inverted 'U' bolts on each side of the car are not identical. The inner bolts have an offset cut on the i n s i d e of the curved portion. (See Fig 8.1). On reassembly the inner 'U' bolts should be replaced so the offset cut is towards the front of the car and contains the front edge of the bump stop mounting plate.

11. After the axle has been replaced adjust the hand brake and bleed the brakes as described in Chapter 9/5 and 6

3. HALF SHAFTS AND OIL SEALS - REMOVAL & REPLACEMENT

1. When it is necessary to replace half shafts or damaged oil seals the shaft may be withdrawn without disturbing the differential assembly.

2. If an oil seal provided at the outer ends of the shafts is to be replaced, then the remover tool number P 3072 - 3 is required.

3. After jacking up the vehicle and removing the road wheel unscrew the cheese head screw retaining the brake drum.

4. Remove the four self-locking nuts retaining the half shaft bearing housing to the axle. These nuts can be reached through the large hole in the axle shaft flange. Withdraw the shaft. Secure the base drawer tool to the flange by means of the wheel nuts, and by operating the slide hammer mounted on the

tool shaft, withdraw the shaft complete with the flange. Remove the half shaft bearing if required with the tool adaptors, and then support the assembly in the base plate on the bed of a hydraulic press. The ram adaptor is fitted to the press ram, and then the splined end of the axle shaft can be pushed out of the bearing and its retainer.

5. To renew the axle shaft oil seal, screw the oil seal remover tool, number P 3072 - 3 onto the centre bolt and slide hammer assembly, and pass the o i l s e a l remover through the seal so that the wings locate behind the metal casing. Hold the centre bolt and apply the hammer in order to extract the oil seal.

6. Locate the new seal on the adaptor tool number 4078, so that its sealing edge is towards the centre of the car. Fit the adaptor handle in place and drive the oil seal into

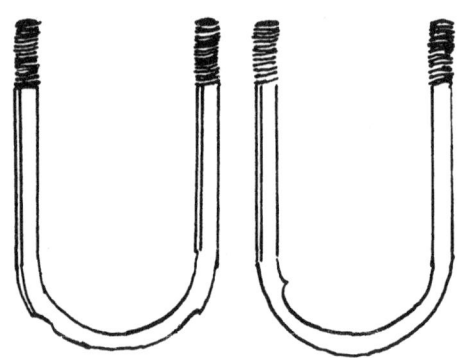

Fig. 8:1 The difference in the inner and outer rear spring U-bolts are shown here. The inner clip — left — has an offset cut-out, while the outer clip is plain on the curved inner face.

its position in the axle casing.

7. When refitting the axle shaft, take care in passing it through the seal not to damage the edges with the splines.

8. Note that when pressing on the bearing to the axle shaft a m i n i m u m pressure of 1200 lb. should be needed. If considerably less than this is required this indicates an incorrect fit between the shaft and bearing. Similarly, when fitting the bearing retaining ring the minimum pressure should be 800 lb.

9. Replacing the axle shaft is otherwise the reverse to that of dismantling.

4. DIFFERENTIAL CARRIER - REMOVAL & REPLACEMENT

1. To remove the differential carrier assembly, jack up the rear of the vehicle, and remove both rear road wheels, and brake

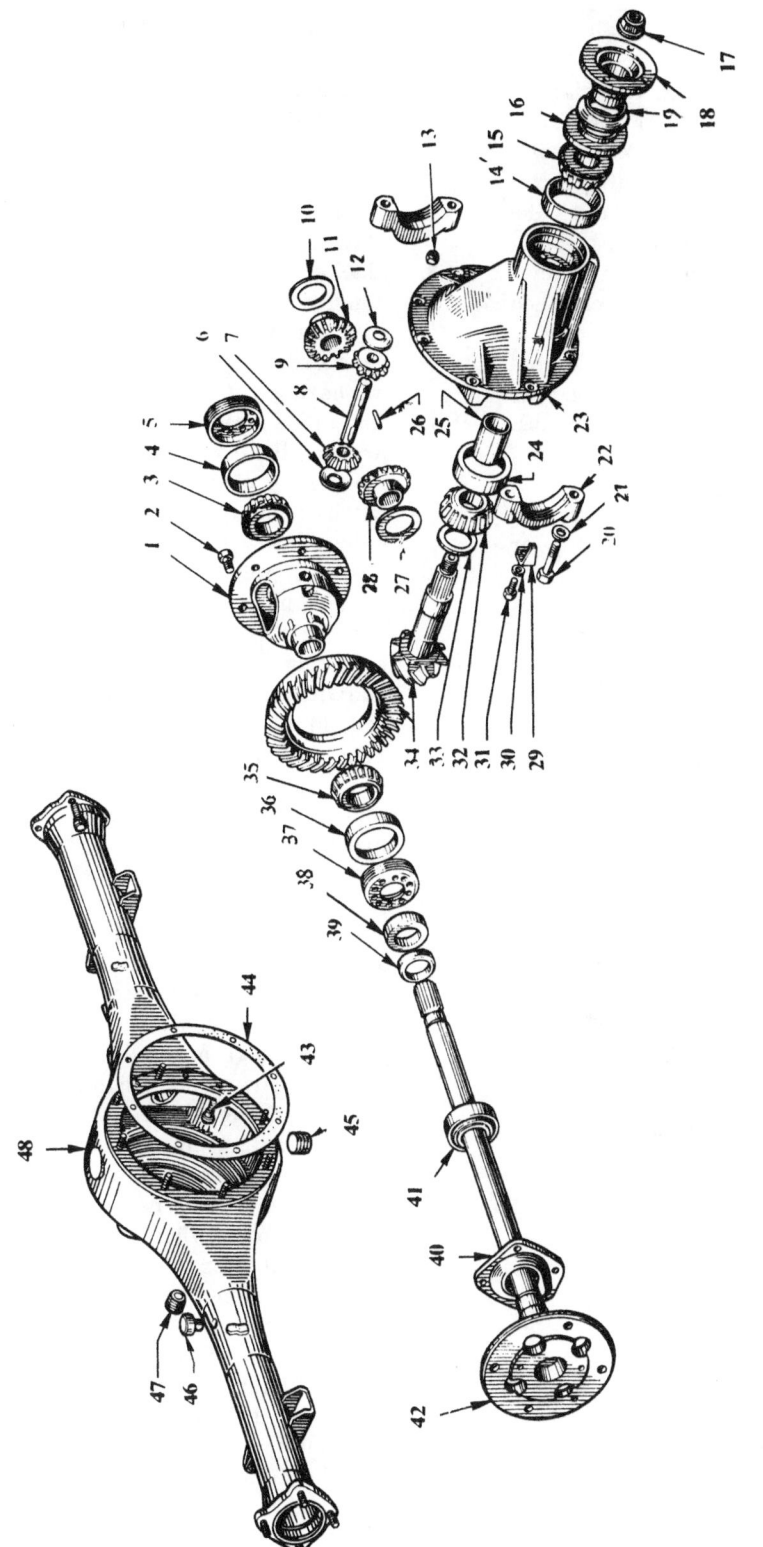

Fig. 8:2 EXPLODED VIEW OF THE REAR AXLE.

1 Differential cage. 2 Cage to crown wheel bolt. 3 Differential roller bearing. 4 Differential bearing cup. 5 Bearing adjusting nut. 6 Pinion thrust washer.
7 Differential pinion. 8 Pinion shaft. 9 Differential pinion. 10 Differential gear thrust washer. 11 Differential gear. 12 Pinion thrust washer. 13 Nut.
14 Driving pinion bearing cup. 15 Driving pinion roller bearing. 16 Oil seal. 17 Flange nut. 18 Drive shaft flange. 19 Oil seal dust deflector. 20 Bearing
cap bolt. 21 Washer. 22 Bearing cap carrier. 23 Differential carrier. 24 Driving pinion bearing cup. 25 Driving pinion bearing spacer. 26 Pinion shaft
lock pin. 27 Differential gear thrust washer. 28 Differential gear. 29 Locknut. 30 Washer. 31 Bolt. 32 Driving pinion cone roller bearing. 33 Bearing
adjusting shim. 34 Driving pinion. 35 Differential roller bearing. 36 Cup. 37 Bearing adjusting cup. 38 Oil seal. 39 Seal. 40 Flange. 41 Bearing.
42 Half shaft. 43 Bolt. 44 Gasket. 45 Drain plug. 46 Vent. 47 Filler plug. 48 Rear axle housing.

drums and then withdraw both half shafts as described in Chapter 7/3.

2. Drain the oil from the casing, and disconnect the drive shaft at the rear end as detailed in 7/2.5. Unscrew the eight self-locking nuts w h i c h hold the differential carrier to the axle casing and withdraw the hydraulic pipe connector from its locating stud. The carrier, complete with crown wheel and differential assembly can then be lifted away.

3. Replacement is a straightforward reversal of the removal instructions. Refill the rear axle with two pints of Hypoid S.A.E. 90 oil.

5. DIFFERENTIAL - DISMANTLING

1. Under normal circumstances it is wisest to take the unit to a Ford main dealer for

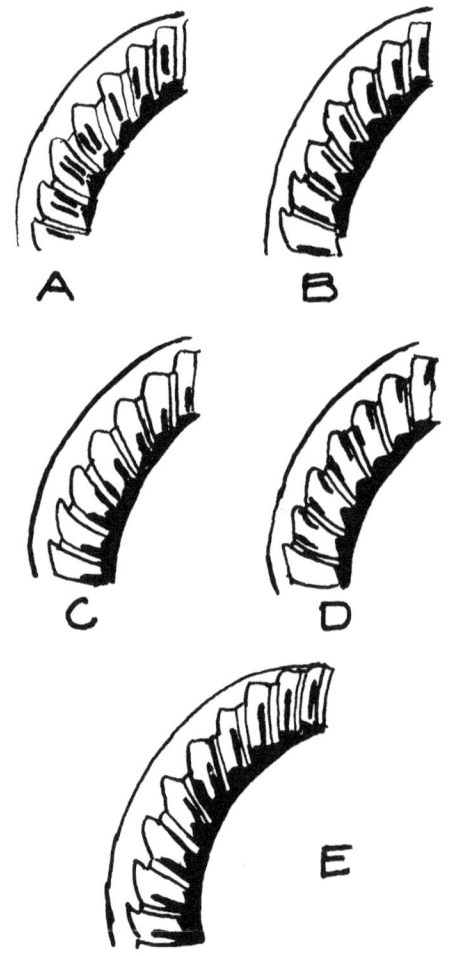

Fig. 8:3 S k e t c h of c r o w n wheel tooth marks when checked with mating pinion wheel. A Heavy flank contact. B Heavy face contact. C Contact on toe. D Contact on heel. E Correct tooth mating.

dismantling. Special tools must be used and these are listed as required.

2. It is advisable to mount the unit in a vice before starting to dismantle. First check that mating marks are clearly defined on the bearing caps and then unscrew the locking plate bolts and r e m o v e the locking plates.

3. Slacken the differential cap bolts and then, using spanner No. P 4079, back off the adjusting nuts, and then remove the bearing caps after withdrawing the bolts and lockwashers.

4. The drive pinion is secured by a nut which presses the c o u p l i n g flange against the inner face of the front pinion bearing. It will be found that a tubular spacer is provided between the pinion bearings - and the length of this spacer controls the pinion bearing preload. Once the crown wheel is lifted out, together with the bearings and adjusting nuts, the staking can be relieved and with the aid of spanner number P 4028 to hold the pinion flange, the drive flange retaining nut is unscrewed. With the drive flange pulled from the pinion splines the pinion and its tubular spacer can be withdrawn from the carrier.

5. Next remove the pinion b e a r i n g s caps, front bearing and oil seal. Using driver tool P 4015, drive out the front bearing and oil seal, and then drive out the rear pinion bearing cap from the front.

6. If it is only necessary to renew the drive pinion oil seal this is done at this stage.

7. With the drive pinion assembly withdrawn, and the existing oil seal levered out with the correct tool, a new seal is fitted with the sealing edge facing into the carrier. Oil the seal lightly, fit a new collapsible spacer to the pinion and adjust the bearing pre-load as detailed later. The assembly can then be re-assembled to the c a r r i e r and the crown wheel and pinion backlash set, together w i t h the differential pre-load as detailed later.

8. However, if it is necessary to continue to dismantle the pinion assembly, first detach the collapsible spacer from the pinion shaft and locate the pinion assembly in the adaptor segments of tool P 4000 - 28 behind the bearing cone.

9. Mount the assembly on a base plate in the bed of a press and press out the pinion. The spacer can then be removed from the pinion shaft.

10. To dismantle the crown wheel and differential assembly first remove the six bolts

holding the crown wheel to the case, and then press the case through the crown wheel. The differential spider locking shaft can then be driven out, and it should be noted that this is tapered at one end, so that it should be removed from the crown wheel side of the case.

11. The pinion shaft is pushed out of the case and by revolving the pinions around the axle shaft they are extracted through the openings in the case, together with the spherical thrust washers.

12. Lift out the axle shaft gears and flat thrust washers which will be found located between the gears and the case, and then remove the bearing cones using tool number P 4000 - 27.

13. With all the parts stripped down, clean them thoroughly, examine for damage and wear and renew as required.

6. DIFFERENTIAL REASSEMBLY

1. To obtain smooth quiet running of the differential it is important to reassemble in the correct order, using the correct tools and making quite sure that all parts are thoroughly clean.

2. First lubricate the flat thrust washers and position them on the backs of the axle shaft gears, and then off the gears into the differential case. Then lubricate the spherical thrust washers and locate these on the back of the pinions and position these opposite each other in the openings in the case, rotating them so that they can line up with the holes for the spider shaft. Take care that the thrust washers have not been displaced before inserting the spider shaft, and note this needs to be inserted so that the locking pin hole lines up with the hole in the case. With the shaft pushed home, insert the pin, taper end first, and drive home, lightly peening over the end to prevent the pin from working out.

3. Refit the crown wheel by locating on the case with the bolt holes in alignment, and press home with the correct tool number 4080. Fit new self-locking bolts and tighten to a torque of 30 to 35 lb. ft. Fit in the bearing cones, and press these on to the case using tool number P 4080.

4. Place the rear bearing cup on the body of tool number P 4013 - 3 and pass this through the carrier throat from the rear, and then assemble the front bearing cup loose adaptor and wing nut and press the bearing cups home, and then remove the tool.

5. The axle is now ready for adjustment, and for this the correct equipment is absolutely essential to obtain satisfactory results.

6. Select the pinion bearing shim to control depth of mesh, and slide the rear bearing cone onto its location on a dummy pinion tool number P 4075 - 4 with the large diameter of the bearing facing the pinion flange. Fit this assembly to the throat of the carrier, and then slide the front bearing cone with its smaller diameter inwards, onto the dummy pinion, fit the drive shaft flange to the splines and screw the pre-load adaptor nut onto the threaded end of the pinion.

7. Next pre-load the pinion bearings by holding the drive flange with the special spanner and gradually tighten the flange retaining nut while rocking the pinion back and forth in order to ensure that the bearing rollers are seating. Continue this rocking movement until the bearing drag can be felt to remain constant, indicating that the bearings are seating correctly.

8. Fit the pre-load gauge number P 4030 to set the pinion bearing pre-load to a running torque of between 9 and 11 lbs. in.

9. It may be necessary to slacken back the drive flange retaining nut and remove all pre-load and then gradually retighten in order to obtain the correct pre-loading.

10. Next check the pinion depth of mesh in the crown wheel teeth. To obtain this the pinion is moved in or out in relation to the centre line of the crown wheel by fitting a shim between the bearing cone and the forward face of the pinion. The thickness of this shim is obtained by employing a depth gauge tool number P 4075 together with adaptors.

11. The dial of the gauge must be set to zero, and then by sliding the setting button across the machined face of the gauge adjust the dial as required to give the zero reading.

12. Position the gauge so that the dial plunger rests on the top face of the dummy pinion, and rock the gauge very slightly to ensure that a minimum reading is obtained. Add 0.10 in. to the gauge reading to obtain the exact thickness of shim to be introduced. Shims of several thicknesses are available, identified by the part number suffix marked on one face.

13. Having established the correct depth, remove the dummy pinion from the carrier, unscrew the pre-load gauge adaptor nut, pull off the drive flange and front bearing cone and extract the dummy pinion and rear bearing cone from the housing.

14. Fit the selected shim to the drive pinion, fit the rear bearing cone to the pinion shaft, and s u p p o r t the bearing in the adaptors while pressing the bearing right home on the pinion. Fit the front pinion bearing cone to its cup, locate the oil seal in the axle throat with the lip toward the bearing and with the c o r r e c t tool press the oil seal right home.

15. Oil the seal and then assemble the pinion to the differential carrier. Using a new collapsible spacer on the pinion shaft fit the pinion into the front bearing, and then fit the flange drive retaining nut and gradually tighten until only a very slight endfloat can be felt on the pinion shaft.

16. Using the pre-load gauge adaptor and pre-load gauge, check the running torque required to rotate the assembly, allowing the pre-load gauge to drop through the horizontal position. This torque is the resistance offered by the oil seal, and when the final setting of the pinion bearing pre-load is determined this figure must be added to the 9 to 11 lbs. for the pinion bearings alone.

17. Gradually tighten the drive flange nut, rotating the pinion throughout in order to ensure that the rollers are seating, until the established pinion b e a r i n g pre-load is obtained.

18. Note particularly that frequent checks on the pre-load must be made while this nut is being tightened, as if overtightening takes place, the whole assembly must be dismantled and the collapsible s p a c e r removed and replaced, and the process started again.

19. Once the c o r r e c t pre-load has been attained, stake the drive flange nut securely to the pinion with a centre punch.

20. Turn next to the adjustment of the crown wheel and pinion backlash and differential bearing pre-load adjustment. These are of extreme importance for correct tooth contact, and first locate the differential bearing caps in the cones and position the assembly in the carrier. Refit the bearing caps making sure that the mating marks mentioned earlier correspond, and replace the bearing cap bolts so that they just hold the caps in position but are not tight.

21. Fit the bearing adjusting nuts, and then install the bearing cap spread gauge number P 4009 by bolting to the differential cap.

22. Set up the plunger of the cap spread gauge so that it locates on the vertical face of the locking plate. Set the dial face to zero and screw in the bearing adjusting nuts without spreading the caps so that only a very slight b a c k l a s h can be felt between the crown wheel and pinion.

23. Next mount the b a c k l a s h gauge number P 4008 - 1 on one of the holes in the differential carrier flange and fit the plunger of the gauge so that it is resting on the heel of a wheel tooth at right angles to it. Zero the gauge, and then by means of the bearing adjusting nuts, adjust the backlash until a reading of between 0. 001 and 0. 002 backlash is obtained. The adjusting nut on the crown wheel side must be tightened last.

24. Now s w i n g the b a c k l a s h gauge out of position, and by rotating the crown wheel, screw in the bearing adjusting nut on the differential side with the spanner until a constant cap spread r e a d i n g of between 0. 005 and 0. 007 in. is obtained.

25. Now swing the backlash gauge back into position and zero. Hold the pinion and rock the crown wheel back and forth noting the maximum and minimum readings. The correct backlash between the crown wheel and pinion should be 0. 005 to 0. 007 in.

26. If the readings are outside these limits, adjustment is obtained by slackening the adjusting nut on one side and tightening the nut on the other side by a corresponding a m o u n t so that the cap s p r e a d is not affected. It is e s s e n t i a l that the final tightening is made on the crown wheel side. Check and recheck until the correct reading is obtained, and when this is correct, refit the adjusting nut locking plate.

27. Tighten the locking plate retaining bolts to a torque of 12 lbs. ft. ; and the differential bearing cap retaining bolts to a torque of 45 to 50 lbs. ft.

28. Finally check the tooth contact area at the crown wheel and pinion by applying a thin coating of red lead or engineer's blue to the crown wheel teeth.

29. Fit the shafts to the differential gears, hold the shafts to apply the load and rotate the pinion in both directions. This will mark up the mating teeth, and if the pre-load and backlash have been set correctly, the contact area should show up clearly and evenly on each tooth. Check the patterns on both sides of the gear teeth and compare with the incorrect patterns shown in the drawings. If the pattern is incorrect, the method of operation is given under each drawing.

30. Once correct mating has been attained, the differential c a r r i e r is assembled to the axle casing, and the rear axle assembly

completed, in reverse to the dismantling.

1. If new gears or a new crown wheel and pinion have been fitted, a running-in lubricant must be used for the first 300 miles of running, this being drained away after 300 miles. Do not leave this in the axle since it will contain tiny particles of metal removed during the running-in process.

CHAPTER NINE

BRAKING SYSTEM

CONTENTS

SPECIFICATION

Type ... ... Hydraulically operated drum brakes on all four wheels
Handbrake ... ... Mechanical on rear wheels
Brake drum diameter (all models)
    Front and rear ... ... 8 in (20.3 cm)

Brake lining dimensions
    997 cc:
        Front and rear ... ... 7.68 x 1.25 in (19.51 x 3.18 cm)
    1198 cc:
        Front ... ... 6.26 x 1.75 in (15.88 x 4.45 cm)
        Rear ... ... 6.26 x 1.5 in (15.88 x 3.8 cm)
Minimum lining thickness (above rivets) ... ... $1/32$ in (1.0 mm)

Wheel cylinder bore
    997 cc Saloon ... ... 0.70 in (1.778 cm)
    997 cc Van, Estate and all 1198 cc ... ... 0.75 in (1.905 cm)

Master cylinder bore ... ... 0.625 in (1.58 cm)

GENERAL DESCRIPTION

The four wheel drum brakes fitted are of the internal expanding type and are operated by means of a pendant brake pedal, which is coupled to the brake master cylinder and hydraulic fluid reservoir.

The front brakes are of the two leading shoe type, with a separate cylinder for each shoe. The ends of each shoe are able to slide laterally in small grooves in the ends of the brake cylinders, so ensuring automatic centralisation when the brakes are applied.

The rear brakes are of the single leading shoe type, with one brake cylinder per wheel for both shoes. Attached to each of the rear wheel operating cylinders is a mechanical expander operated by the handbrake lever through a bowden cable which runs from the brake lever to a compensator mounted on the underside of the rear axle. Transverse rods run from the compensator to the backplate brake levers. This provides an independent means of rear brake application.

Drum brakes have to be adjusted periodically to compensate for wear in the linings. It is unusual to have to adjust the handbrake system as the efficiency of this system is largely dependent on the condition of the brake linings and the adjustment of the brake shoes. The handbrake can, however, be adjusted separately

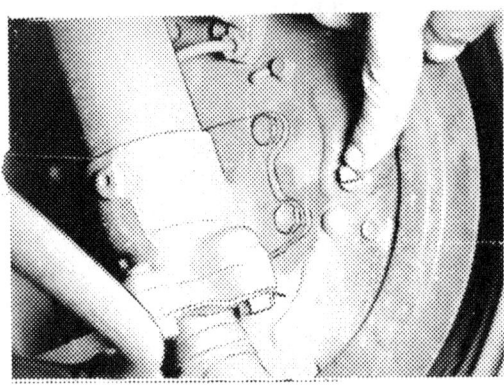

Fig. 9:1 The square-headed adjuster on one of the front brake back-plates. This should be turned in a clockwise direction to adjust the brake shoes.

to the footbrake operated hydraulic system.

The hydraulic brake system functions in the following manner: On application of the brake pedal, hydraulic fluid under pressure is pushed from the master cylinder to the brake operating cylinders at each wheel, by means of a five-way union and steel pipe lines and flexible hoses.

The hydraulic fluid moves the pistons out so pushing the brake shoes into contact with the brake drums. This provides an equal degree of retardation on all four wheels in direct proportion to the pressure applied to the brake pedal. Return springs between each pair of brake shoes draw the shoes together when the brake pedal is released.

2. DRUM BRAKES - MAINTENANCE

1. Every 1,000 miles, carefully clean the top of the brake master cylinder reservoir, remove the cap and check that the level of the fluid is not more than 1/4 in. below the bottom of the filler neck. Check that the breathing hole in the cap is clear.

2. If topping up becomes frequent then check the metal piping and flexible hosing for leaks, and check for worn brake or master cylinder seals which will also cause loss of fluid.

3. At intervals of 5,000 miles, or more frequently if pedal travel becomes excessive, adjust the brake shoes to compensate for wear of the brake linings.

4. At the same time, lubricate all joints in the handbrake mechanism with an oil can filled with Castrolite or similar.

3. FRONT BRAKE ADJUSTMENT

1. Each front brake shoe is adjusted individually, by turning the square headed snail-cam adjusters on the back-plate clockwise

when viewed from the plate, in order to expand the shoes and take up wear in the brake linings.

2. Raise the wheels clear of the ground, and turn the adjuster of one shoe in the anti-clockwise direction to bring the lining away from the drum. Now turn the other adjuster in the clockwise direction until the drum is locked, and then slacken back until the wheel is just sufficiently free to rotate without binding.

3. Rotate the other adjuster until the drum is locked, and then slacken back just enough to prevent any binding.

4. It is essential to obtain the minimum of clearance without binding in order to reduce the pedal travel to a minimum.

4. REAR BRAKE ADJUSTMENT

1. To adjust the rear brakes, raise the wheels clear of the ground and then turn the square-headed wedge adjuster which will be found above the rear axle housing clockwise until both shoes are firmly against the drum. Ease back the square-headed snail cam adjuster in the clockwise direction, until the cam can be felt to touch the shoe. Now slacken back the square-headed threaded adjuster by two clicks, and then slacken back the snail cam adjuster one twelfth of a turn (1/12).

2. If the shoe is binding at this point, ease back the snail cam adjuster just enough to free the shoe. If this had no effect, return the snail cam to its original location, and slacken back the wedge adjuster just enough to free the brake shoe.

5. HANDBRAKE LINKAGE ADJUSTMENT

1. First check the handbrake cable for damage and possible sharp bends, and then check the operating levers and brake plates for signs of rusting and stiffness.

2. Then check that each rear brake expander is free to slide in the brake plate slots, and examine the clevis pins, renewing as required.

3. Check the condition of the flexible mounting for the equaliser, and then adjust the handbrake rod which connects the equaliser to the right-hand brake so that the distance between the centre of the right-hand clevis and the inside face of the equaliser is between 31 7/8 in. and 32 1/32 in.

4. Fully release the handbrake lever, and then tighten the square-headed threaded adjuster on each back plate which will be

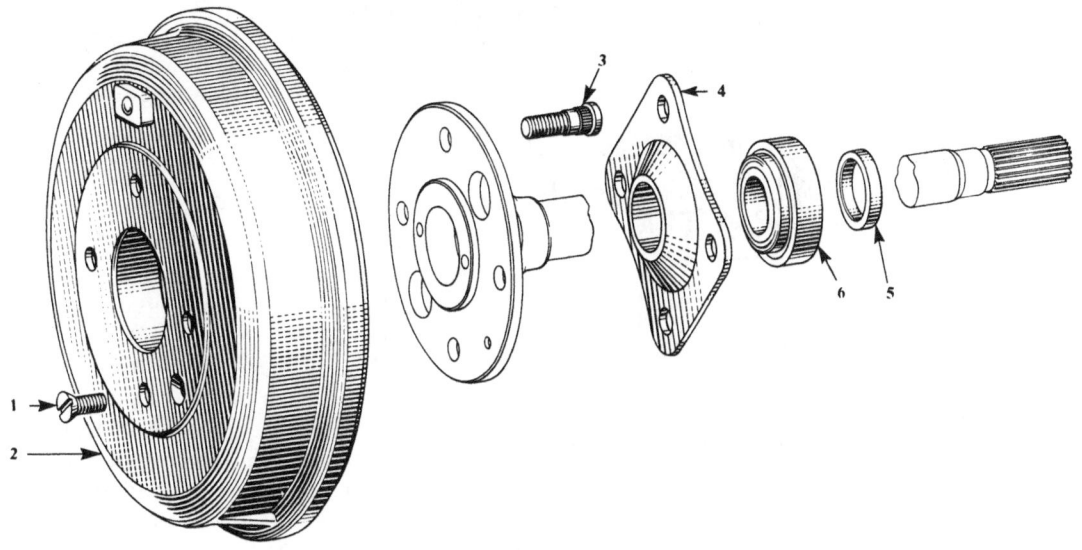

Fig. 9:2 EXPLODED VIEW OF THE REAR HUB AND BRAKE DRUM. 1 Securing screw. 2 Brake drum. 3 Wheel bolt. 4 Flange. 5 Seal. 6 Bearing.

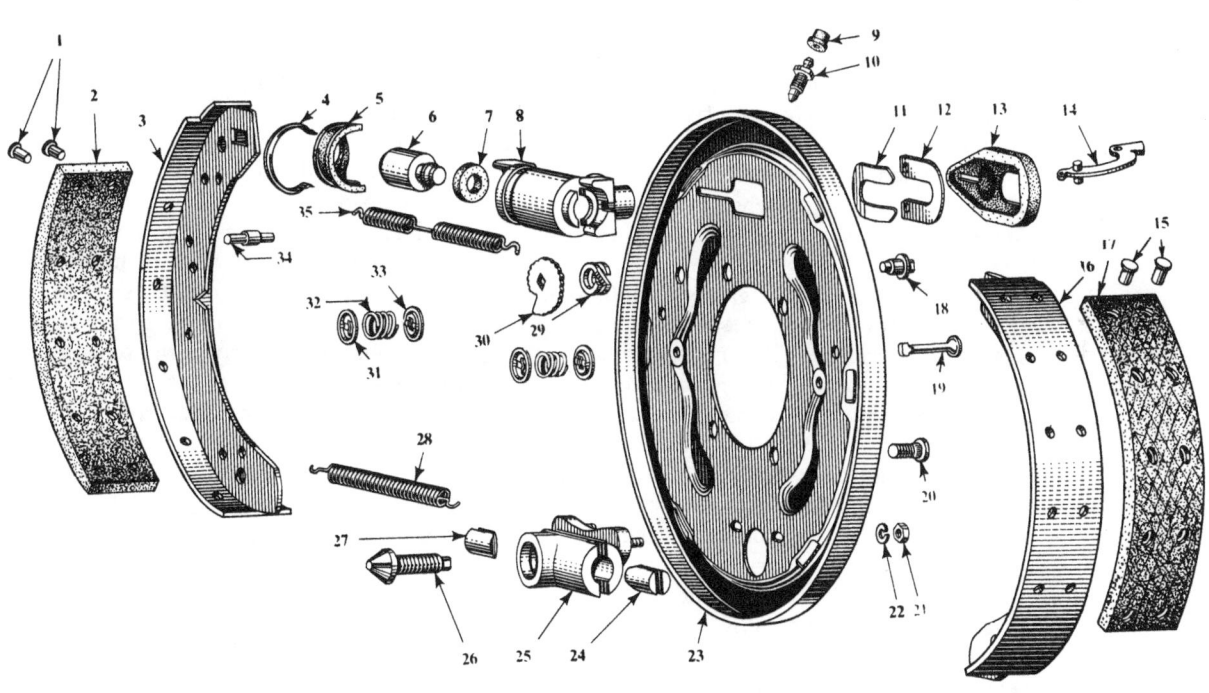

Fig. 9:3 EXPLODED VIEW OF THE REAR BRAKES.
1 Brake shoe rivets.   2 Brake lining.   3 Brake shoe.   4 Rubber boot retainer.   5 Rubber boot.   6 Piston.   7 Rubber sealing ring.   8 Piston.   9 Bleed valve cap.   10 Bleed valve.   11 Wheel cylinder retaining spring.   12 Wheel cylinder retaining plate. 13 Rubber boot.   14 Parking brake pivot lever.   15 Rivets.   16 Brake shoe.   17 Brake lining.   18 Brake shoe adjuster.   19 Pin. 20 Backplate to rear axle bolt.   21 Nut.   22 Spring washer.   23 Brake drum backplate.   24 Rear brake adjuster tappet.   25 Rear brake adjuster.   26 Brake adjuster wedge.   27 Tappet.   28 Pull off spring.   29 Adjusting spring.   30 Brake adjusting cam. 31 Hold down cup.   32 Hold down spring.   33 Hold down cup.   34 Pivot post.   35 Pull off spring.

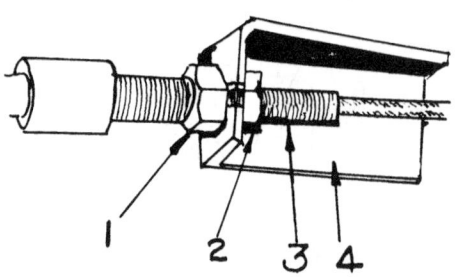

Fig. 9:4 The handbrake cable adjustment. 1 Adjusting nut. 2 Lock nut. 3 Adjusting sleeve. 4 Support bracket.

found just forward of the rear axle housing, until the brake is locked. Repeat on the opposite brake.

5. Now slacken the locknut on the adjuster sleeve which is located in the drive shaft tunnel, and tighten the adjusting nut until all play is removed from the handbrake cable. Tighten the locknut securely.

6. Now slacken the square headed threaded brake adjusters as described in the brake adjustments given earlier.

7. Check the handbrake lever operation which should move through four or five notches in order to lock both back wheels.

8. Note that when the handbrake is applied, the flexible mounting attached to the equaliser should be parallel to the centre line of the car.

9. To remove the handbrake cable when this requires renewal, disconnect the brake cable at the handbrake, unscrew the lock-nut securing the brake cable conduit to the bracket, and pull the conduit adjusting sleeve to the rear so the inner cable will slide free of the bracket.

10. Remove the nut, washer and bolt securing the equaliser to its flexible mounting and then disconnect the brake inner cable or rod at the slotted hole on each brake plate clevis, and remove the cable.

11. If the handbrake lever has to be removed, first unscrew the eight self-tapping screws holding the gaiter in position and then un-screw the two bolts holding the lever assembly to the floor.

6. BLEEDING THE HYDRAULIC SYSTEM

1. Removal of all the air from the hydraulic system is essential to the working of the braking system, and before undertaking this examine the fluid reservoir cap to ensure that both vent holes, one on top and the second underneath but not in line, are clear: check the level of fluid and top up if required.

2. Check all brake line unions and connections for possible seepage, and at the same time check the condition of the rubber hoses, which may be perished.

3. If the condition of the wheel cylinders is in doubt, check for possible signs of fluid leakage.

4. If there is any possibility of incorrect fluid having been put into the system, drain all the fluid out and flush through with methylated spirits. Renew all piston seals and cups since these will be affected and could possibly fail under pressure.

5. Gather together a clean jam jar, a 9 in. length of tubing which fits tightly over the bleed nipples, and a tin of the correct brake fluid. (To Ford specification ME 3833E).

6. To bleed the system clean the areas around the bleed valves, and start on the rear brakes first by removing the rubber cup over the bleed valve and fitting a rubber tube in position.

7. Place the end of the tube in a clean glass jar containing sufficient fluid to keep the end of the tube underneath during the operation.

8. Open the bleed valve with a spanner and quickly press down the brake pedal. After slowly releasing the pedal, pause for a moment to allow the fluid to recoup in the master cylinder and then depress again. This will force air from the system, and should continue until no more air bubbles can be seen coming from the tube. At intervals make certain that the reservoir is kept topped up, otherwise air will enter at this point again.

9. Repeat this operation on all four brakes, and when completed, check the level of the fluid in the reservoir and then check the feel of the brake pedal, which should be firm and free from any 'spongy' action, which is normally associated with air in the system.

7. FITTING NEW BRAKE LININGS

1. When the brake linings have become worn, the braking will no longer be effective, and application of brakes may be accompanied by squealing from one or more of the brakes.

2. Each lining is secured to the shoe with ten rivets, and when new linings have been fitted there should be no clearance between the lining and the shoe, and the leading edge

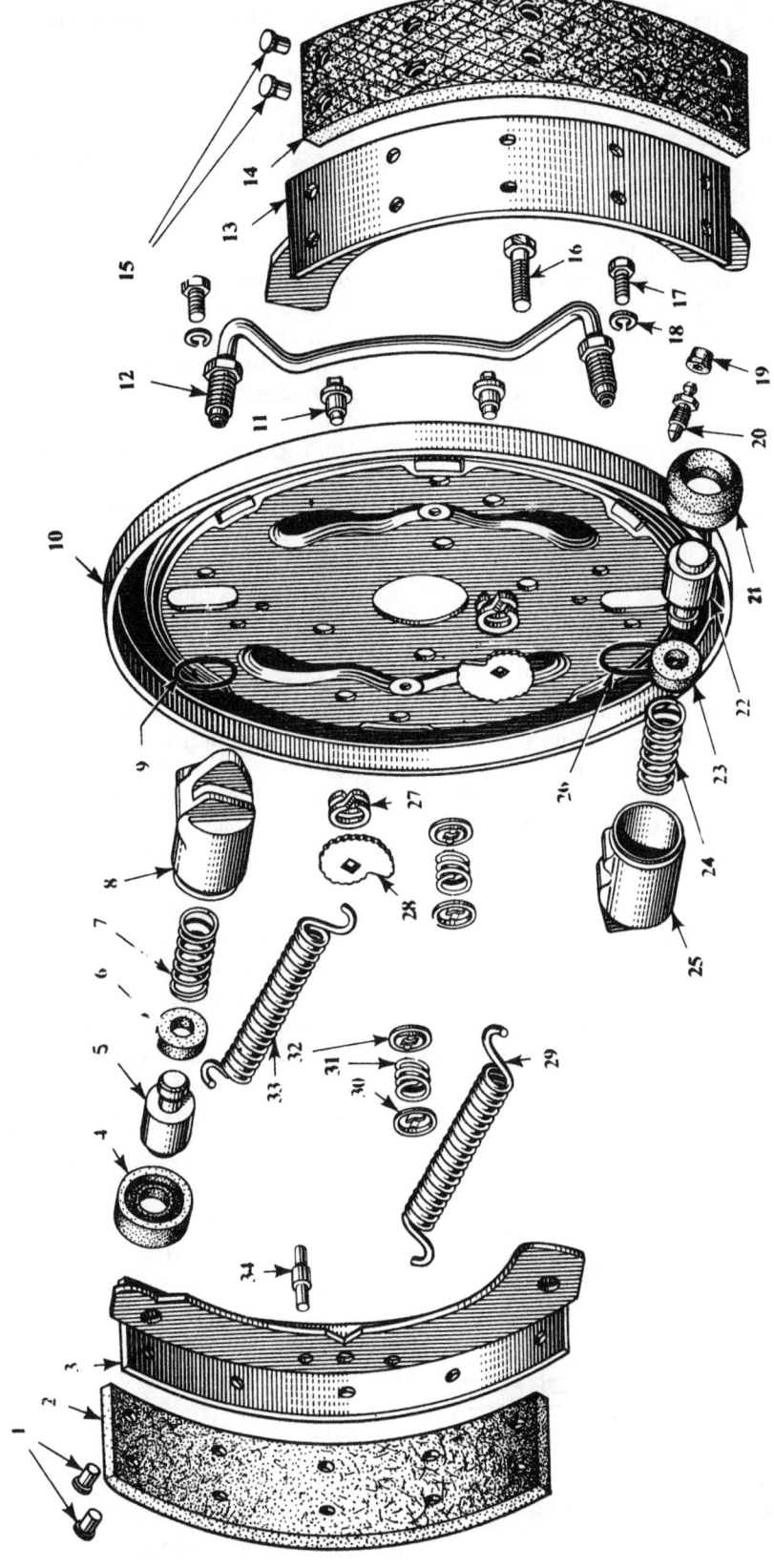

Fig. 9:5 EXPLODED VIEW OF THE FRONT BRAKES.

1 Brake shoe rivets.   2 Brake lining.   3 Brake shoe.   4 Rubber boot.   5 Piston.   6 Rubber piston seal.   7 Spring.   8 Wheel cylinder.   9 Cylinder to back-plate sealing ring.   10 Backplate.   11 Square headed brake adjuster.   12 Connecting pipe.   13 Brake shoe.   14 Brake lining.   15 Rivets.   16 Bolt.   17 Bolt.   18 Spring washer.   19 Bleed nipple cap.   20 Bleed nipple.   21 Rubber boot.   22 Piston.   23 Rubber piston seal.   24 Spring.   25 Wheel cylinder.   26 Cylinder to backplate sealing ring.   27 Brake shoe adjusting ring.   28 Adjusting cam.   29 Pull off spring.   30 Hold down cup.   31 Hold down spring.   32 Hold down cup.   33 Pull off spring.   34 Pivot post.

119

of the linings should be slightly chamfered with a file.

8. FRONT BRAKE SHOES - REMOVAL & REPLACEMENT

1. Jack up the front of the car and remove the road wheel. Remove the split pin, unscrew the centre nut and lift out the thrust washer. Pull the brake drum from the spindle taking care not to drop the outer wheel bearing.

2. Remove the brake shoe holding down spindle and the two dished washers which need to be rotated through 90° and then withdrawn. Remove the spring and then pull the tapered end of one shoe away from its position and disengage the other end from the slot in the back of the other cylinder and remove the retracting spring. Note the position of each shoe as it is removed so that it is replaced in the correct position when reassembled.

3. Apply a suitable high melting point grease to the brake shoe contact pads on the backplate.

4. When tightening the centre nut, tighten to a torque of 30 lb/ft. while rotating the hub in the same direction. Then back off the nut by two and not more than two and a half castellations in order that a split pin can be entered.

9. REAR BRAKE SHOES - REMOVAL & REPLACEMENT

1. Jack up the rear of the car, remove the rear wheel, make certain that the handbrake is in the fully off position, and then remove the single screw retaining the brake drum to the hub, and draw off the drum.

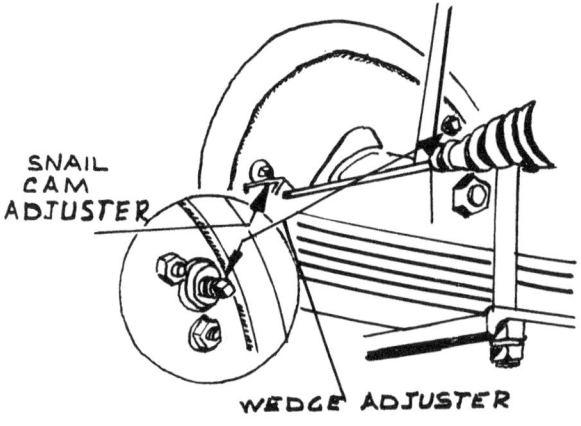

Fig. 9:6 The snail cam adjuster fitted to each rear brake backplate, together with the shoe wedge adjuster.

2. Remove the brake shoe holding down spindle, spring and two dished washers from each shoe, and withdraw the split pin from the handbrake mechanism.

3. Remove the shoes and the return springs, noting that these springs are of different lengths, the spring with the two sets of coils fitting to the expander housing, while the shorter spring fits adjacent to the adjuster housing. Reassembly of new shoes is the reverse to removal.

4. With all new shoes refitted, and the brake drums fitted, adjust all brakes as previously described.

10. FRONT BRAKE ASSEMBLY - REMOVAL & REPLACEMENT

1. When it becomes necessary to remove the front brake assembly, jack up the front end and remove the brake drum and shoes as described earlier, then disconnect the flexible hose at the upper wheel cylinder using a blanking plug in the end of the hose to prevent loss of fluid.

2. Unscrew the four self-locking nuts retaining the backplate to the suspension unit and remove the backplate.

3. With the unit on the bench; to dismantle, first disconnect the short pipe at the rear of the brake plate and then unscrew the two bolts and spring washers securing each operating cylinder to the plate.

4. To clean the parts of the brake operating gear before inspection use only methylated spirits or commercial alchohol. If petrol, paraffin, carbon tetrachloride or similar solvents are used they will affect the rubber parts, and the slightest trace of mineral oil will render these parts useless.

5. If wheel cylinders are suspect, it is normal practice to replace them with new factory assembled units.

6. NOTE that the snail cam adjusters are rivetted in position on the backplate, and if it is necessary to renew these, the rivet must first be filed down so that the stud can be removed from the backplate. NOTE the way in which the parts are removed in order that they may be reassembled in reverse.

11. REAR BRAKE ASSEMBLY - REMOVAL & REPLACEMENT

1. To remove the rear brake assembly first remove the shoes as detailed above and then rotate the axle shaft flange so that the two holes are vertical to give access to the retaining nuts securing the drive

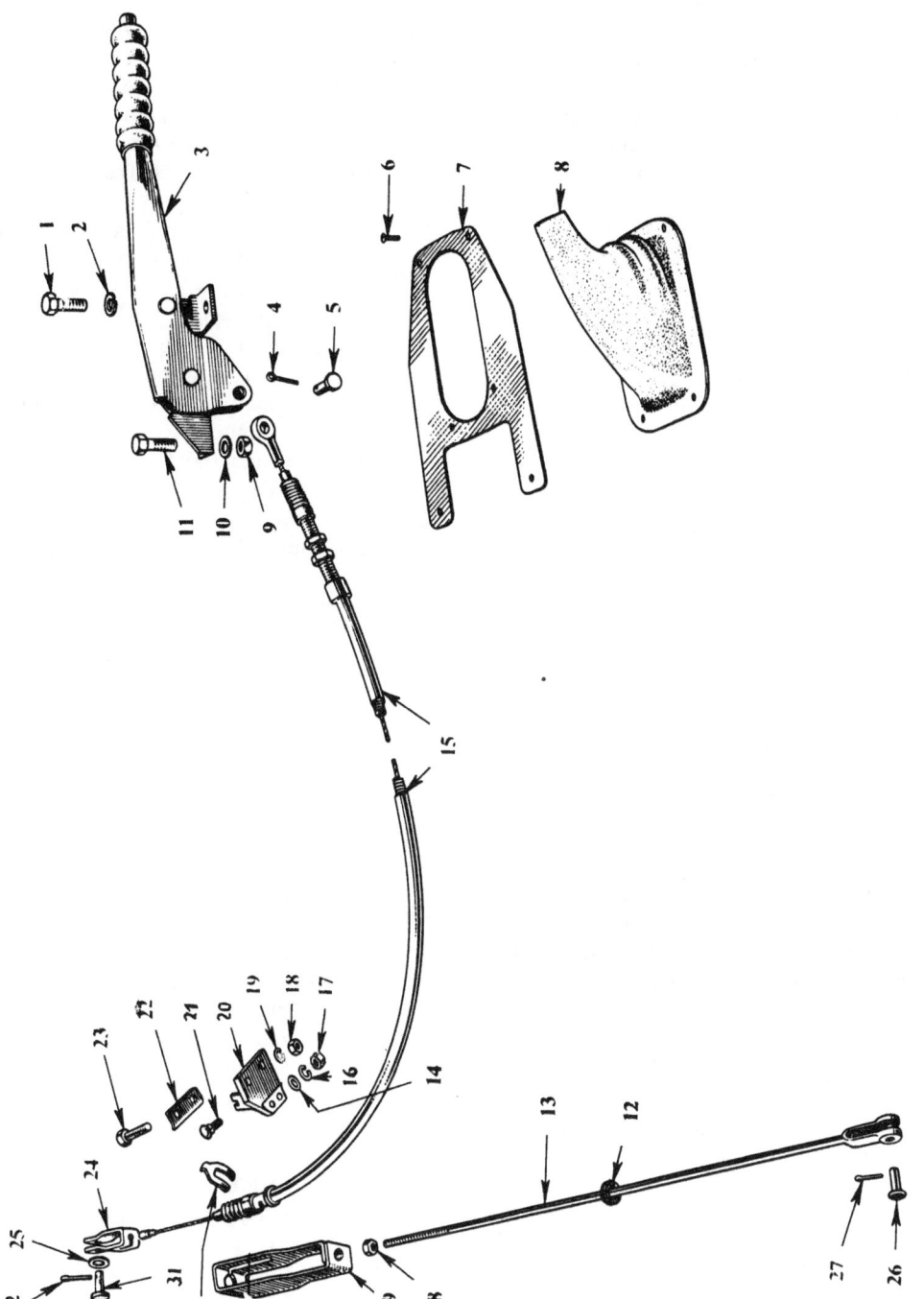

Fig. 9:7 EXPLODED VIEW OF THE HANDBRAKE.

1 Bolt. 2 Spring washer. 3 Handbrake lever. 4 Split pin. 5 Pin — brake lever to brake cable clevis. 6 Screw. 7 Plate. 8 Handbrake lever shroud. 9 Nut.
10 Washer. 11 Bolt. 12 Grommet. 13 Brake rod. 14 Washer. 15 Brake cable. 16 Spring washer. 17 Nut. 18 Nut. 19 Spring washer. 20 Rear axle
flexible mounting. 21 Bolt. 22 Bracket. 23 Clevis. 24 Washer. 25 Clevis pin. 26 Split pin. 27 Nut. 28 Adjuster bracket. 29 Retainer. 30 Clevis
pin. 31 Split pin.

shaft retaining flange and the backplate to the axle casing. Rotate the shaft through 90° and remove the other two nuts.

2. The axle shaft is removed using tool number P 3072-2 with the main tool.

3. Disconnect the brakepipe from the expander housing using a plug to prevent loss of fluid. Remove the split pin and clevis connecting the handbrake cable to the operating link. The backplate can now be lifted away.

4. To remove the expander cylinder, detach the rubber boot over the cylinder, and lift out the piston and seal as an assembly. The expander housing is removed from the backplate by extracting the retainer and retainer spring. As with the front brakes, where wheel cylinders are suspect, these can be replaced as a unit.

5. Reassembly is the reverse of dismantling, and it is important to stress that all brake parts should be kept away from oil, to prevent possible contamination in the hydraulic system.

12. BRAKE PEDAL ASSEMBLY - REMOVAL & REPLACEMENT

1. The brake pedal is of the pendant type employing the same bracket assembly as the clutch pedal, this bracket being bolted to the hull bulkhead beneath the instrument panel.

2. On cars built up to engine number 13000 adjustment for the height of brake and clutch pedals is provided by each master cylinder pushrod being attached to the pedal lever with an eccentric adjuster bolt. When this bolt is turned the length of the pushrod is varied, and this means that when the pedal is in its fully returned position there must be a clearance between the pushrod and the piston in the master cylinder.

3. On cars built after engine number 13000 a concentric bolt is fitted and no adjustment is provided.

4. To remove the assembly, unscrew the four bolts holding the bracket and master cylinders to the bulkhead. Remove the accelerator pedal by unscrewing the clamp bolt and return spring.

5. Disconnect the linkage from the carburettor and from the bulkhead so that this can be moved away to the left and out of engagement with the bush in the pedal assembly bracket.

6. Unscrew the nuts and remove the bolts holding the pushrods to the pedals, remove the bolt from each side of the upper face

of the bracket, and once these are clear move the pedal assembly downwards and draw out.

13. HYDRAULIC MASTER CYLINDER - DISMANTLING, INSPECTION & REASSEMBLY

1. When attention is needed and the master cylinder has to be removed, first detach the fluid line, using a blanking plug in the pipe to prevent dirt from entering the system.

2. Note that when a replacement cylinder is to be fitted, the working surfaces are protected, and it is essential to lubricate the seals before fitting.

3. Remove the blanking plugs from the pipe line, together with the pushrod dust cover so that clean brake fluid can be injected at these locations. By operating the piston several times the fluid will spread over the surfaces.

4. If the master cylinder is to be dismantled after removal, first pull back the pushrod cover and remove the circlip so that the pushrod and a dished washer can be pulled out. This will expose the plunger with a seal attached, and this must be removed as a unit. The assembly is separated by lifting the thimble leaf over the shouldered end of the plunger. The seal is then eased off.

5. Depress the plunger return spring allowing the valve stem to slide through the keyhole in the thimble, thus releasing the tension in the spring.

6. Detach the valve spacer taking care of the spacer spring washer which will be found located under the valve head.

7. Examine the bore of the cylinder carefully for any scores or ridges, and if this is found to be smooth all over, new seals can be fitted. If there is any doubt of the condition of the bore, then a new cylinder must be fitted.

8. If examination of the seals shows them to be apparently oversize, or very loose on the plunger, suspect oil contamination in the system. Oil will swell these rubber seals, and if one is found to be swollen, it is reasonable to assume that all seals in the braking system will need attention.

9. To reassemble the master cylinder, replace the old valve seal as shown, and then replace the spring washer with its domed side against the underside of the valve head.

10. Replace the plunger return spring centrally on the spacer, insert the thimble into the

spring and depress until the valve stem engaged in the keyhole of the thimble.

11. Check that the spring is central on the spacer before refitting a new plunger seal onto the plunger with the flat face against the face of the plunger, and a new back seal if required.

12. Insert the reduced end of the plunger into the thimble until the thimble engages under

the shoulder of the plunger and press home the thimble leaf as shown.

13. Make sure that the bore is clean, smear the plunger with brake fluid and insert the assembly into the bore valve end first, easing the lips of the plunger seal carefully into the bore.

14. Replace the pushrod and refit the circlip into the groove in the cylinder body, and replace the rubber cover.

Cause	Trouble	Remedy
SYMPTOM:	BRAKES TEND TO BIND, DRAG, OR LOCK-ON	
Incorrect adjustment	Brake shoes adjusted too tightly Handbrake cable over-tightened Master cylinder push rod out of adjust- ment giving too little brake pedal free movement	Slacken off brake shoe adjusters two clicks. Slacken off handbrake cable adjustment. Reset to manufacturer's specifications.
Wear or dirt in hydraulic system or incorrect fluid	Reservoir vent hole in cap blocked with dirt Master cylinder by-pass port restricted – brakes seize in 'on' position Wheel cylinder seizes in 'on' position	Clean and blow through hole. Dismantle, clean, and overhaul master cylinder. Bleed brakes. Dismantle, clean, and overhaul wheel cylinder. Bleed brakes.
Mechanical wear	Brake shoe pull off springs broken, stretched or loose	Examine springs and replace if worn or loose.
Incorrect brake assembly	Brake shoe pull off springs fitted wrong way round, omitted, or wrong type used	Examine, and rectify as appropriate.
Neglect	Handbrake system rusted or seized in the 'on' position	Apply 'Plus Gas' to free, clean and lubricate.

FAULT FINDING CHART

Cause	Trouble	Remedy
SYMPTOM:	PEDAL TRAVELS ALMOST TO FLOORBOARDS BEFORE BRAKES OPERATE	
Leaks and air bubbles in hydraulic system	Brake fluid level too low	Top up master cylinder reservoir. Check for leaks.
	Wheel cylinder leaking	Dismantle wheel cylinder, clean, fit new rubbers and bleed brakes.
	Master cylinder leaking (Bubbles in master cylinder fluid)	Dismantle master cylinder, clean, and fit new rubbers. Bleed brakes.
	Brake flexible hose leaking	Examine and fit new hose if old hose leaking. Bleed brakes.
	Brake line fractured	Replace with new brake pipe. Bleed brakes.
	Brake system unions loose	Check all unions in brake system and tighten as necessary. Bleed brakes.
Normal wear	Linings over 75% worn	Fit replacement shoes and brake linings.
Incorrect adjustment	Brakes badly out of adjustment	Jack up car and adjust brakes.
	Master cylinder push rod out or adjustment causing too much pedal free movement	Reset to manufacturer's specification.
SYMPTOM:	BRAKE PEDAL FEELS SPRINGY	
Brake lining renewal	New linings not yet bedded-in	Use brakes gently until springy pedal feeling leaves.
Excessive wear or damage	Brake drums badly worn and weak or cracked	Fit new brake drums.
Lack of maintenance	Master cylinder securing nuts loose	Tighten master cylinder securing nuts. Ensure spring washers are fitted.
SYMPTOM:	BRAKE PEDAL FEELS SPONGY & SOGGY	
Leaks or bubbles in hydraulic system	Wheel cylinder leaking	Dismantle wheel cylinder, clean, fit new rubbers, and bleed brakes.
	Master cylinder leaking (Bubbles in master cylinder reservoir)	Dismantle master cylinder, clean, and fit new rubbers and bleed brakes. Replace cylinder if internal walls scored.
	Brake pipe line or flexible hose leaking	Fit new pipeline or hose.
	Unions in brake system loose	Examine for leaks, tighten as necessary.
SYMPTOM:	EXCESSIVE EFFORT REQUIRED TO BRAKE CAR	
Lining type or condition	Linings badly worn	Fit replacement brake shoes and linings.
	New linings recently fitted - not yet bedded-in	Use brakes gently until braking effort normal.
	Harder linings fitted than standard causing increase in pedal pressure	Remove linings and replace with normal units.
Oil or grease leaks	Linings and brake drums contaminated with oil, grease, or hydraulic fluid	Rectify source of leak, clean brake drums, fit new linings.
SYMPTOM:	BRAKES UNEVEN & PULLING TO ONE SIDE	
Oil or grease leaks	Linings and brake drums contaminated with oil, grease, or hydraulic fluid	Ascertain and rectify source of leak, clean brake drums, fit new linings.
Lack of maintenance	Tyre pressures unequal	Check and inflate as necessary.
	Radial ply tyres fitted at one end of car only	Fit radial ply tyres of the same make to all four wheels.
	Brake backplate loose	Tighten backplate securing nuts and bolts.
	Brake shoes fitted incorrectly	Remove and fit shoes correct way round.
	Different type of linings fitted at each wheel	Fit the linings specified by the manufacturers all round.
	Anchorages for front suspension or rear axle loose	Tighten front and rear suspension pick-up points including spring anchorage.
	Brake drums badly worn, cracked or distorted	Fit new brake drums.

CHAPTER TEN

ELECTRICAL SYSTEM

CONTENTS

SPECIFICATIONS

Battery	12 volt Lead/acid
Earthed terminal	Positive
Capacity at 20 hr. rate	38 amp/hr.
Electrolyte	4.8 pints (2.73 litres)
Level above separators	0.25 in.
Dynamo	12 volt
Maximum output	20 amps.
No. of brushes	2
Length of brushes (new)	0.718 in. (18.233 mm.)
Renewal length of brushes	5/16 in. or less
Starter Motor	12 volt 4 brush
Control Box	5 terminal type
Cut in voltage	12.7 to 13.3 volts
Drop off voltage	8.5 to 11 volts
Windscreen Wiper	Lucas or Autolite

Bulbs	Volts.	Watts.
2 Headlamp	12	50/40
2 Side & Front Indicators	12	21/6
2 Rear & Stop Lights	12	21/6
2 Rear Indicators	12	21
1 Interior	12	3
1 Rear Number Plate Illumination	12	6
1 Instrument Panel	12	2.2
2 Indicator Warning Lights	12	2.2
1 Generator Warning Light	12	2.2
1 Oil Pressure Warning Light	12	2.2
1 Headlamp Main Beam Warning Light	12	2.2

1. GENERAL DESCRIPTION

The electrical system is of the 12-volt type and the major components comprise: A 12-volt 38 amp/hour battery with the positive terminal earthed: A voltage regulator and cut-out; A 12-volt two brush dynamo driven by the fan belt and the starter motor.

The 12-volt battery positioned on the right hand side of the engine compartment supplies a steady supply of current for the ignition, lighting, and other electrical circuits, and provides a reserve of electricity when the current consumed by the electrical equipment exceeds that being produced by the dynamo.

The dynamo is of the two brush type and works in conjunction with the voltage regulator and cut-out. The dynamo is cooled by a multi-bladed fan mounted behind the dynamo pulley, and blows air through cooling holes in the dynamo end brackets. The output from the dynamo is controlled by the voltage regulator which ensures a high output if the battery is in a low state of charge or the demands from the electrical equipment high, and a low output if the battery is fully charged and there is little demand from the electrical equipment.

2. BATTERY - REMOVAL & REPLACEMENT

1. Disconnect the positive and then the negative leads from the battery terminals by slackening the retaining nuts and bolts, or by unscrewing the retaining screws if these are fitted.

2. Remove the battery clamp and carefully lift the battery out of its compartment. Hold the battery vertical to ensure that none of the electrolyte is spilled.

3. Replacement is a direct reversal of this procedure. NOTE. Replace the negative lead before the earth (positive) lead and smear the terminals with petroleum jelly (vaseline) to prevent corrosion. NEVER use an ordinary grease as applied to other parts of the car.

3. BATTERY MAINTENANCE & INSPECTION

1. Normal weekly battery maintenance consists of checking the electrolyte level of each cell to ensure that the separators are covered by $\frac{1}{4}$ in. of electrolyte. If the level has fallen, top up the battery using distilled water only. Do not overfill. If the battery is overfilled or any electrolyte spilled, immediately wipe away the excess as electrolyte attacks and corrodes any metal it comes into contact with very rapidly.

2. As well as keeping the terminals clean and covered with petroleum jelly, the top of the battery, and especially the top of the cells, should be kept clean and dry. This helps prevent corrosion and ensures that the battery does not become partially discharged by leakage through dampness and dirt.

3. Once every three months remove the battery and inspect the battery securing bolts, the battery clamp plate, tray, and battery leads for corrosion (white fluffy deposits on the metal which are brittle to touch). If any corrosion is found, clean off the deposits with ammonia and paint over the clean metal with an anti-rust/anti-acid paint.

4. At the same time inspect the battery case for cracks. If a crack is found, clean and plug it with one of the proprietary compounds marketed by firms such as 'Holts' for this purpose. If leakage through the crack has been excessive then it will be necessary to refill the appropriate cell with fresh electrolyte as detailed later. Cracks are frequently caused to the top of the battery cases by pouring in distilled water in the middle of winter AFTER instead of BEFORE a run. This gives the water no chance to mix with the electrolyte and so the former freezes and splits the battery case.

5. If topping up the battery becomes excessive and the case has been inspected for cracks that could cause leakage, but none are found, the battery is being overcharg-

ELECTRICAL SYSTEM

ed and the voltage regulator will have to be checked and reset.

6. With the battery on the bench at the three monthly interval check, measure its specific gravity with a hydrometer to determine its state of charge and the condition of the electrolyte. There should be very little variation between the different cells and if a variation in excess of 0.025 is present it will be due to either:

 a) Loss of electrolyte from the battery at some time caused by spillage or a leak resulting in a drop in the specific gravity of the electrolyte, when the deficiency was replaced with distilled water instead of fresh electrolyte.

 b) An internal short circuit caused by buckling of the plates or a similar malady pointing to the likelihood of total battery failure in the near future.

7. The specific gravity for the electrolyte for fully charged conditions at the electrolyte temperature indicated, is listed in Table 1. The specific gravity of a fully discharged battery at different temperatures of the electrolyte is given in Table 2.

TABLE 1.

Specific Gravity - Battery fully charged

1.268 at 100°F or 38°C electrolyte temperature
1.272 at 90°F or 32°C   "   "
1.276 at 80°F or 27°C   "   "
1.280 at 70°F or 21°C   "   "
1.284 at 60°F or 16°C   "   "
1.288 at 50°F or 10°C   "   "
1.292 at 40°F or 4°C   "   "
1.296 at 30°F or -1.5°C   "   "

TABLE 2.

Specific Gravity - Battery fully discharged

1.098 at 100°F or 38°C electrolyte temperature
1.102 at 90°F or 32°C   "   "
1.106 at 80°F or 27°C   "   "
1.110 at 70°F or 21°C   "   "
1.114 at 60°F or 16°C   "   "
1.118 at 50°F or 10°C   "   "
1.122 at 40°F or 4°C   "   "
1.126 at 30°F or -1.5°C   "   "

4. ELECTROLYTE REPLENISHMENT

1. If the battery is in a fully charged state and one of the cells maintains a specific gravity reading which is 0.025 or more lower than the others, and a check of each cell has been made with a voltage meter to check for short circuits (a four to seven second test should give a steady reading of between 1.2 to 1.8 volts), then it is likely that electrolyte has been lost from the cell with the low reading at some time.

2. Top the cell up with a solution of 1 part sulphuric acid to 2.5 parts of water. If the cell is already fully topped up draw some electrolyte out of it with a pipette. When mixing the sulphuric acid and water NEVER ADD WATER TO SULPHURIC ACID - always pour the acid slowly onto the water in a glass container. IF WATER IS ADDED TO SULPHURIC ACID IT WILL EXPLODE. Continue to top up the cell with the freshly made electrolyte and then recharge the battery and check the hydrometer readings.

5. BATTERY CHARGING

1. In winter time when heavy demand is placed upon the battery, such as when starting from cold, and much electrical equipment is continually in use, it is a good idea to occasionally have the battery fully charged from an external source at the rate of 3.5 to 4 amps. Continue to charge the battery at this rate until no further rise in specific gravity is noted over a four hour period. Alternatively a trickle charger charging at the rate of 1.5 amps can be safely used overnight. Specially rapid 'boost' charges which are claimed to restore the power of the battery in 1 to 2 hours are dangerous as they can cause serious damage to the battery plates through overheating. While charging the battery note that the temperature of the electrolyte should never exceed 100°F.

6. DYNAMO - ROUTINE MAINTENANCE

1. Routine maintenance consists of checking the tension of the fan belt, and lubricating the dynamo rear bearing once every 5,000 miles.

2. The fan belt should be tight enough to ensure no slip between the belt and the dynamo pulley. If a shrieking noise comes from the engine when the unit is accelerated rapidly, it is likely that it is the fan belt slipping. On the other hand, the belt must not be too taut or the bearings will wear rapidly and cause dynamo failure or bearing seizure. Ideally $\frac{1}{2}$ in. of total free movement should be available at the fan belt midway between the fan and the dynamo pulley. To adjust the fan belt tension slightly slacken the three dynamo retaining bolts, and swing the dynamo on the upper two bolts outwards to increase the tension, and inwards to lower it. It is best to leave the bolts fairly tight so that considerable effort has to be used

127

to move the dynamo; otherwise it is difficult to get the correct setting. If the dynamo is being moved outwards to increase the tension and the bolts have only been slackened a little, a long spanner acting as a lever placed behind the dynamo with the lower end resting against the block works very well in moving the dynamo outwards. Retighten the dynamo bolts and check that the dynamo pulley is correctly aligned with the fan belt.

3. Lubrication on the dynamo consists of inserting three drops of S.A.E. 30 engine oil in the small oil hole in the centre of the commutator end bracket. This lubricates the rear bearing. The front bearing is prepacked with grease and requires no attention.

7. DYNAMO - TESTING IN POSITION

1. If, with the engine running no charge comes from the dynamo, or the charge is very low, first check that the fan belt is in place and is not slipping. Then check that the leads from the control box to the dynamo are firmly attached and that one has not come loose from its terminal. The lead from the 'D' terminal on the dynamo should be connected to the 'D' terminal on the control box, and similarly the 'F' terminals on the dynamo and control box should also be connected together.

2. Disconnect the leads from the terminals 'D' and 'F' on the dynamo and then join the terminals together with a short length of wire. Attach to the centre of this length of wire the negative clip of a 0-30 volts voltmeter and run the other clip to earth. Start the engine and allow it to idle at approximately 1000r.p.m. At this speed the dynamo should give a reading of about 15 volts on the voltmeter. There is no point in raising the engine speed above a fast idle as the reading will then be inaccurate.

3. If no reading is recorded then check the brushes and brush connections. If a very low reading of approximately 1 volt is observed then the field winding may be suspect.

4. If the voltmeter shows a good reading then with the temporary link still in position connect both leads from the control box to 'D' and 'F' on the dynamo ('D' to 'D' and 'F' to 'F'). Release the lead from the 'D' terminal at the control box end and clip one lead from the voltmeter to the end of the cable, and the other lead to a good earth. With the engine running at the same speed

as previously, an identical voltage to that recorded at the dynamo should be noted on the voltmeter. If no voltage is recorded then there is a break in the wire. If the voltage is the same as recorded at the dynamo then check the 'F' lead in similar fashion. If both readings are the same as at the dynamo then it will be necessary to test the control box. See 10/17 to 20.

8. DYNAMO - REMOVAL & REPLACEMENT

1. Slacken the two dynamo retaining bolts, and the nut on the sliding link, and move the dynamo in towards the engine so that the fan belt can be removed.

2. Disconnect the two leads from the dynamo terminals.

3. Remove the nut from the sliding link bolt, and remove the two upper bolts. The dynamo is then free to be lifted away from the engine.

4. Replacement is a reversal of the above procedure. Do not finally tighten the retaining bolts and the nut on the sliding link until the fan belt has been tensioned correctly. See 10/6.2 for details.

9. DYNAMO - DISMANTLING & INSPECTION

1. Mount the dynamo in a vice and unscrew and remove the two through bolts from the commutator end bracket.

9.1

9.2

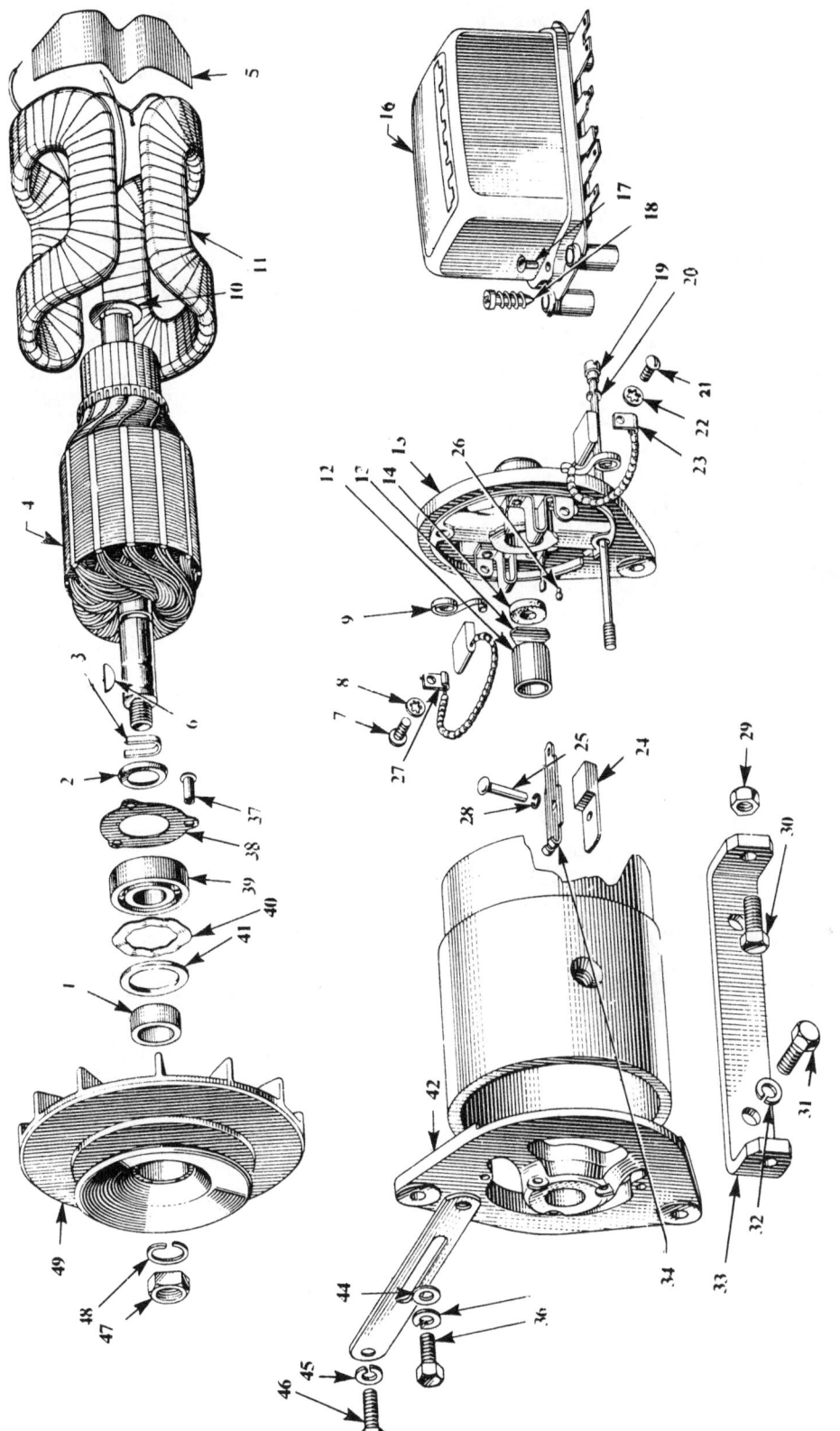

Fig. 10:1 THE DYNAMO REGULATOR AND CUT-OUT.

1 Pulley spacer. 2 Bearing ring retainer. 3 Bearing locating ring. 4 Armature. 5 Field coil insulator. 6 Woodruff key. 7 Screw. 8 Lockwasher. 9 Brush retaining spring. 10 Distance washer. 11 Coil. 12 End bearing bush. 13 Retainer. 14 Oil retaining felt. 15 End bracket. 16 Regulator and cut-out. 17 Screw. 18 Holding down screw. 19 Through bolt. 20 Spring washer. 21 Screw. 22 Star washer. 23 Brush and lead. 24 Field terminal insulator. 25 Rivet. 26 End plate dowel. 27 Brush and lead. 28 Spring washer. 29 Nut. 30 Bolt. 31 Bolt. 32 Spring washer. 33 Mounting bracket. 34 Field terminal. 35 Springwasher. 36 Bolt. 37 Rivet. 38 Bearing retainer plate. 39 Bearing. 40 Corrugated washer. 41 Oil retaining felt. 42 End bearing assembly. 43 Adjusting strap. 44 Washer. 45 Spring washer. 46 Bolt. 47 Pulley securing nut. 48 Spring washer. 49 Pulley and fan wheel.

129

2. Mark the commutator end bracket and the dynamo casing so the end bracket can be replaced in its original position. Pull the end bracket off the armature shaft. NOTE Some versions of the dynamo may have a raised pip on the end bracket which locates in a recess on the edge of the casing. If so marking the end bracket and casing is not necessary. A pip may also be found on the drive end bracket at the opposite end of the casing.

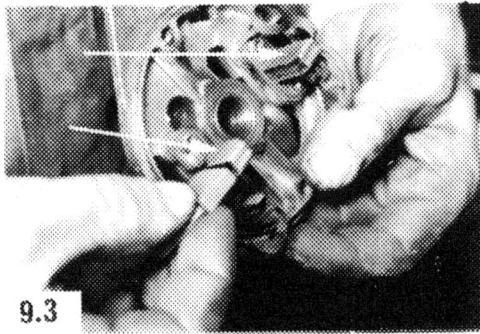

Photo 9:3

3. Lift the two brush springs and draw the brushes out of the brush holders (arrowed).

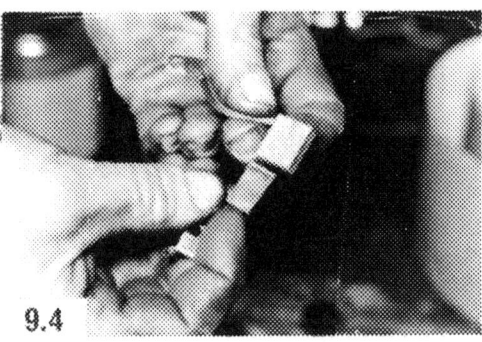

Photo 9:4

4. Measure the brushes and if worn down to 5/16 in. or less unscrew the screws holding the brush leads to the end bracket. Take off the brushes complete with leads. Old and new brushes are compared in the photograph.

5. If no locating pip can be found, mark the drive end bracket and the dynamo casing so the drive end bracket can be replaced in its original position. Then pull the drive end bracket complete with armature out of the casing.

6. Check the condition of the ball bearing in the drive end plate by firmly holding the plate and noting if there is visible side movement of the armature shaft in relation to the endplate. If play is present the armature assembly must be separated from the endplate. If the bearing is sound there is

no need to carry out the work described in the following two paragraphs.

7. Hold the armature in one hand (mount it carefully in a vice if preferred) and undo the nut holding the combined plastic pulley wheel and fan in place. Pull off the pulley wheel fan assembly taking care not to break it.

8. Next remove the woodruff key (arrowed) from its slot in the armature shaft and also the bearing locating ring.

9. Place the drive end bracket across the open jaws of a vice with the armature downwards and gently tap the armature shaft from the bearing in the end plate with the aid of a suitable drift.

10. Carefully inspect the armature and check it for open or short circuited windings. It is a good indication of an open circuited armature when the commutator segments are burnt. If the armature has short circuited the commutator segments will be very badly burnt, and the overheated armature windings badly discoloured. If open or short circuits are suspected then test by substituting the suspect armature for a new one.

11. Check the resistance of the field coils. To do this, connect an ohmmeter between the field terminal and the yoke and note the reading on the ohmmeter which should be about 6 ohms. If the ohmmeter reading is infinity this indicates an open circuit in the field winding. If the ohmmeter reading is below 5 ohms this indicates that one of the field coils is faulty and must be replaced.

12. Field coil replacement involves the use of a wheel operated screwdriver, a soldering iron, caulking and riveting and this operation is considered to be beyond the scope of most owners. Therefore, if the field coils are at fault either purchase a rebuilt dynamo, or take the casing to a Ford dealer or electrical engineering works for new field coils to be fitted.

13. Next check the condition of the commutator (arrowed). If it is dirty and blackened as shown clean it with a petrol damped rag. If the commutator is in good condition the surface will be smooth and quite free from pits or burnt areas, and the insulated segments clearly defined.

14. If, after the commutator has been cleaned pits and burnt spots are still present, wrap a strip of glass paper round the commutator taking great care to move the commutator ¼ of a turn every ten rubs till it is thoroughly clean.

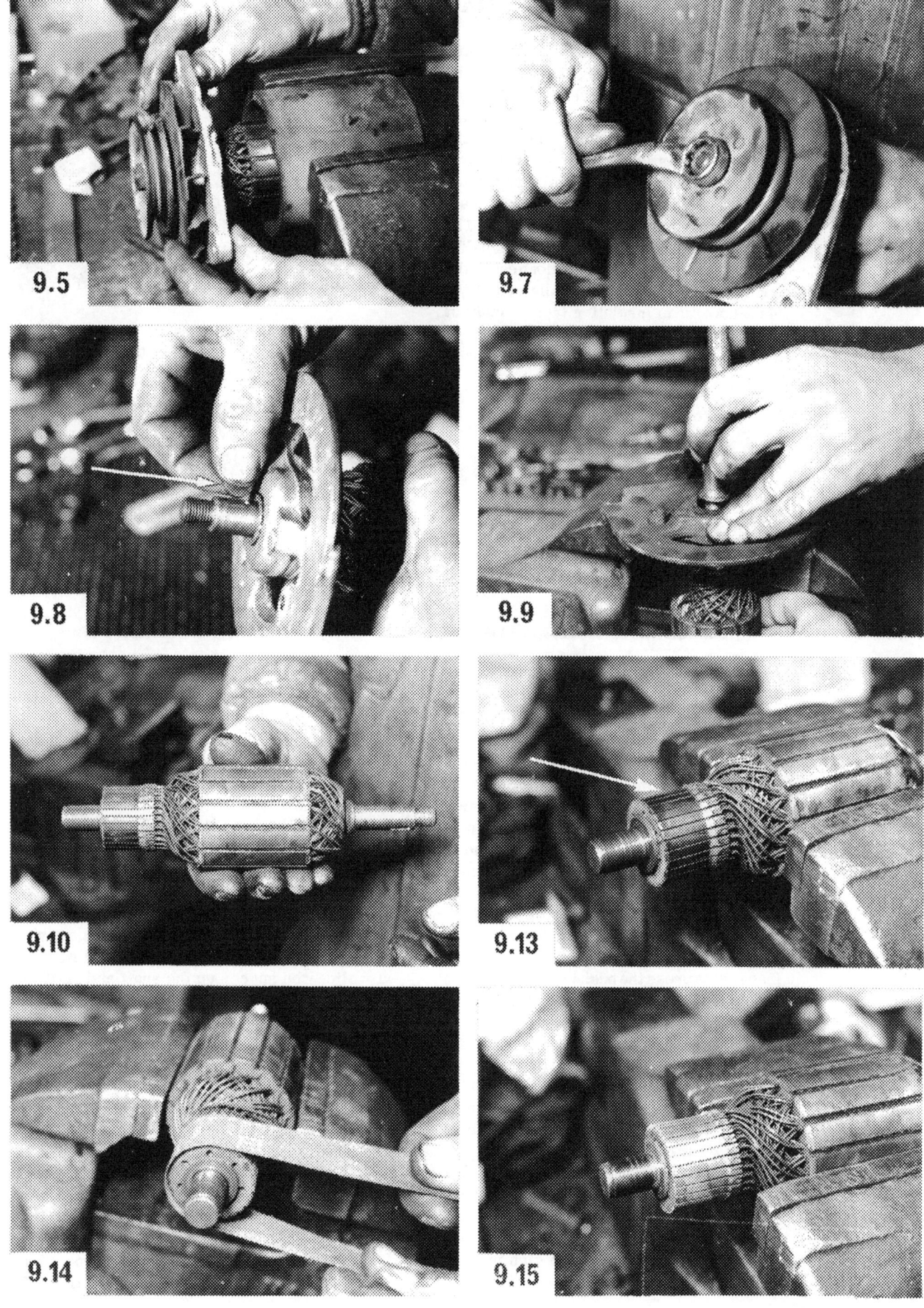

9.5

9.7

9.8

9.9

9.10

9.13

9.14

9.15

15. In extreme cases of wear the commutator can be mounted in a lathe and with the lathe turning at high speed, a very fine cut may be taken off the commutator. Then polish the commutator with glass paper. If the commutator has worn so that the insulators between the segments are level with the top of the segments, then undercut the insulators to a depth of 1/32 in. (.8mm.). The best tool to use for this purpose is half a hacksaw blade ground to the thickness of the insulator, and with the handle end of the blade covered in insulating tape to make it comfortable to hold. This is the sort of finish the surface of the commutator should have when finished.

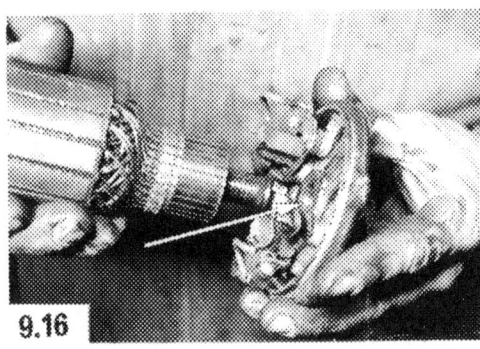

9.16

16. Check the bush bearing (arrowed) in the commutator end bracket for wear by noting if the armature spindle rocks when placed in it. If worn it must be renewed.
17. With a suitable extractor pull out the old bush from the commutator end bracket.
18. NOTE when fitting the new bush bearing that it is of the porous bronze type, and it is essential that it is allowed to stand in S.A.E. 30 engine oil for at least 24 hours before fitment.
19. Carefully fit the new bush into the end plate, pressing it in until the end of the bearing is flush with the inner side of the end plate. If available press the bush in with a smooth shouldered mandrel the same diameter as the armature shaft.

10. DYNAMO - REPAIR & REASSEMBLY

1. To renew the ball bearing fitted to the drive end bracket drill out the rivets which hold the bearing retainer plate to the end bracket and lift off the plate.
2. Press out the bearing from the end bracket and remove the corrugated and felt washers from the bearing housing.
3. Thoroughly clean the bearing housing, and the new bearing and pack with high melting-point grease.

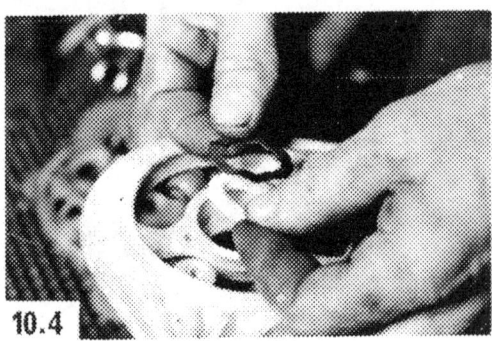

10.4

4. Place the felt washer and corrugated washer in that order in the end bracket bearing housing.

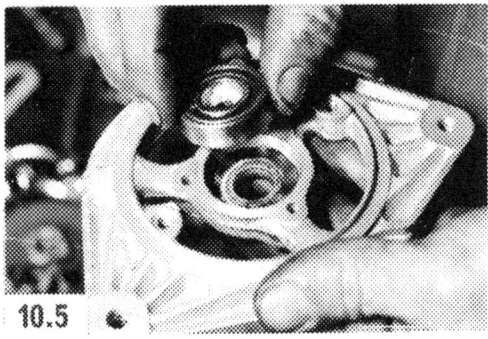

10.5

5. Then fit the new bearing as shown.
6. Gently tap the bearing into place with the aid of a suitable drift.
7. Replace the bearing plate and fit three new rivets.
8. Open up the rivets with the aid of a suitable cold chisel.
9. Finally peen over the open end of the rivets with the aid of a ball hammer as illustrated.
10. Refit the drive end bracket to the armature shaft. Do not try and force the bracket on but with the aid of a suitable socket abuting the bearing tap the bearing on gently so pulling the end bracket down with it.
11. Slide the spacer up the shaft and refit the bearing ring retainer and its locating ring, and the woodruff key.
12. Replace the combined fan and pulley wheel and then fit the spring washer and nut and tighten the latter. The drive bracket end of the dynamo is now fully assembled as shown.
13. If the brushes are little worn and are to be used again then ensure that they are placed in the same holders from which they were removed. When refitting brushes, either new or old, check that they move freely in their holders. If either brush sticks, clean with a petrol moistened rag and if still stiff,

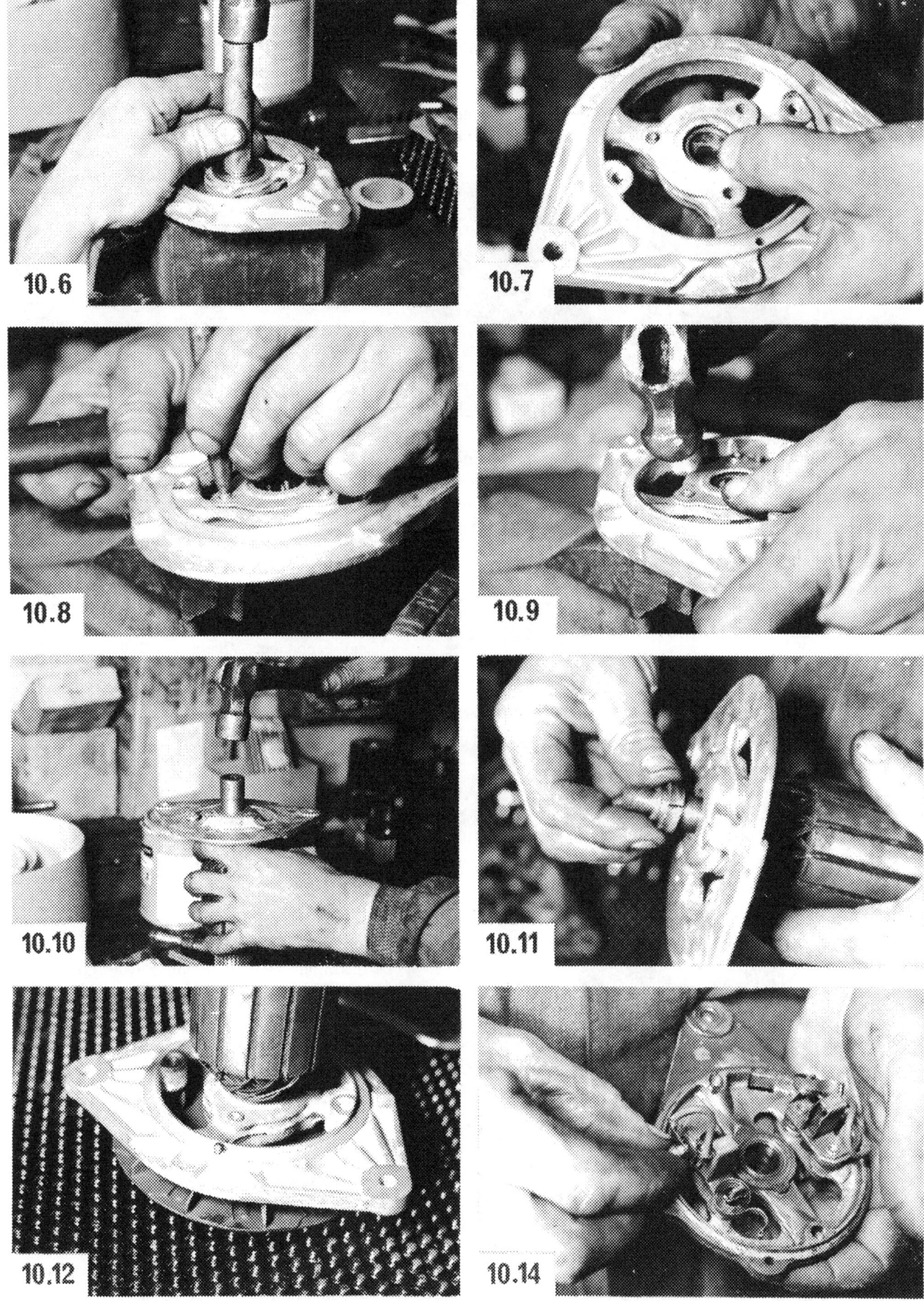

10.6

10.7

10.8

10.9

10.10

10.11

10.12

10.14

lightly polish the sides of the brush with a very fine file until the brush moves quite freely in its holder.

14. Tighten the two retaining screws and washers which hold the wire leads to the brushes in place.

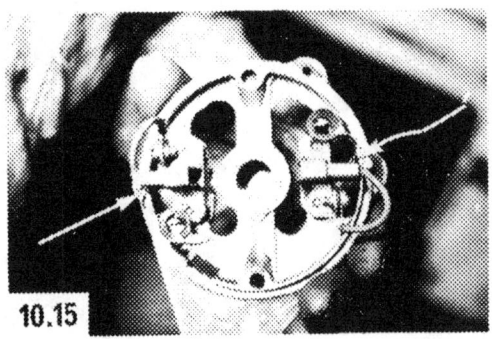

10.15

15. It is far easier to slip the endplate with brushes over the commutator if the brushes are raised in their holders as shown and held in this position by the pressure of the springs resting against their flanks (arrowed).

10.16

16. Refit the armature to the casing and then the commutator endplate and screw up the two through bolts.

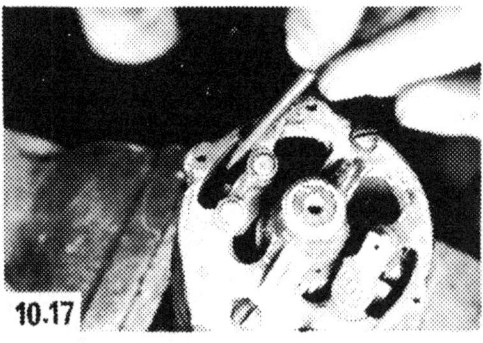

10.17

17. Finally, hook the ends of the two springs off the flanks of the brushes and onto their heads so the brushes are forced down into contact with the armature.

11. STARTER MOTOR - GENERAL DESCRIPTION

The starter motor is held in position by two bolts which also clamp the bellhousing flange.

The motor is of the four field coil, four pole piece type, and utilises four spring-loaded commutator brushes. Two of these brushes are earthed, and the other two are insulated and attached to the field coil ends.

12. STARTER MOTOR - TESTING ON ENGINE

1. If the starter motor fails to operate then check the condition of the battery by turning on the headlamps. If they glow brightly for several seconds and then gradually dim, the battery is in an uncharged condition.

2. If the headlamps glow brightly and it is obvious that the battery is in good condition, then check the tightness of the battery wiring connections (and in particular the earth lead from the battery terminal to its connection on the bodyframe). If the positive terminal on the battery becomes hot when an attempt is made to work the starter, this is a sure sign of a poor connection on the battery terminal. To rectify remove the terminal, clean the inside of the cap and the terminal post thoroughly and reconnect. Check the tightness of the connections at the relay switch and at the starter motor. Check the wiring with a voltmeter for breaks or shorts.

3. If the wiring is in order then check that the starter motor is operating. To do this, press the rubber covered button in the centre of the solenoid under the bonnet. If it is working the starter motor will be heard to 'click' as it tries to rotate. Alternatively check it with a voltmeter.

If the battery is fully charged, the wiring in order, and the switch working and the starter motor fails to operate, then it will have to be removed from the car for examination. Before this is done, however, ensure that the starter pinion has not jammed in mesh with the flywheel. Check by turning the square end of the armature shaft with a spanner. This will free the pinion if it is stuck in engagement with the flywheel teeth. On some models the square on the end of the shaft will be covered by a metal cap.

13. STARTER MOTOR - REMOVAL & REPLACEMENT

1. Disconnect the battery earth lead from the positive terminal.

2. Disconnect the starter motor cable from the terminal on the starter motor end plate.

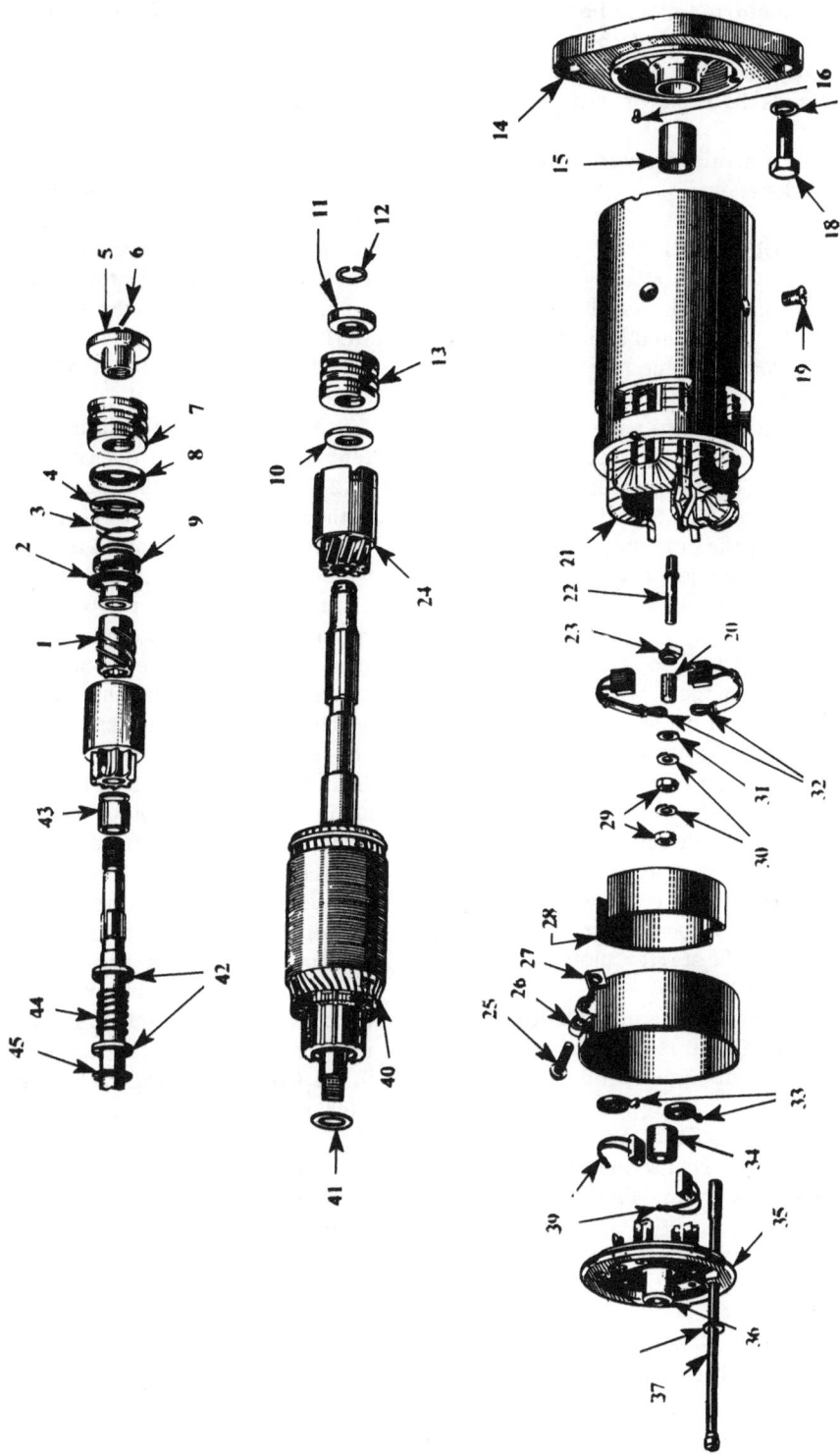

Fig. 10:2 EXPLODED VIEW OF THE STARTER MOTOR AND DRIVE GEAR.

1 Run off spring sleeve. 2 Spring retaining plate. 3 Spring. 4 Spring buffer washer. 5 Cup. 6 Split pin. 7 Drive main spring. 8 Run off spring support cup. 9 Alternative plate. 10 Washer. 11 Main drive spring cup. 12 Circlip. 13 Drive main spring. 14 End plate. 15 End plate bush. 16 End plate locating dowel. 17 Spring washer. 18 Bolt. 19 Screw. 20 Field terminal insulating spacer. 21 Field coil. 22 Field coil terminal post. 23 Field terminal insulating bush. 24 Pinion drive and nut assembly. 25 Screw. 26 Band. 27 Nut. 28 Field coil insulator. 29 Field terminal nuts. 30 Spring washers. 31 Flat washer. 32 Starter brushes. 33 Brush springs. 34 End plate bush. 35 End plate. 36 Bush housing. 37 Through bolts. 38 Spring washer. 39 Brushes. 40 Armature. 41 Washer. 42 Return spring cups. 43 Distance collar. 44 Spring. 45 Washer.

CHAPTER TEN

3. Unscrew the two starter motor bolts.

4. Lift the starter motor out of engagement with the teeth on the flywheel ring and pull it forward towards the radiator until it can be lifted clear.

5. Replacement is a straight reversal of the removal procedure.

14. STARTER MOTOR - DISMANTLING & REASSEMBLY

1. With the starter motor on the bench, loosen the screw on the cover band and slip the cover band off. With a piece of wire bent into the shape of a hook, lift back each of the brush springs in turn and check the movement of the brushes in their holders by pulling on the flexible connectors. If the brushes are so worn that their faces do not rest against the commutator, or if the ends of the brush leads are exposed on their working face, they must be renewed.

2. If any of the brushes tend to stick in their holders then wash them with a petrol moistened cloth and, if necessary, lightly polish the sides of the brush with a very fine file, until the brushes move quite freely in their holders.

3. If the surface of the commutator is dirty or blackened, clean it with a petrol dampened rag. Secure the starter motor in a vice and check it by connecting a heavy gauge cable between the starter motor terminal and a 12-volt battery.

4. Connect the cable from the other battery terminal to earth in the starter motor body. If the motor turns at high speed it is in good order.

5. If the starter motor still fails to function or if it is wished to renew the brushes, then it is necessary to further dismantle the motor.

6. Lift the brush springs with the wire hook and lift all four brushes out of their holders one at a time.

7. Remove the terminal nuts and washers from the terminal post on the commutator end bracket.

8. Unscrew the two through bolts which hold the end plates together and pull off the commutator end bracket. Also remove the driving end bracket which will come away complete with the armature.
At this stage, if the brushes are to be renewed, their flexible connectors must be unsoldered and the connectors of new brushes soldered in their place. Check that the new brushes move freely in their

holders as detailed above. If cleaning the commutator with petrol fails to remove all the burnt areas and spots, then wrap a piece of glass paper round the commutator and rotate the armature. If the commutator is very badly worn, remove the drive gear as detailed in the following section. Then mount the armature in a lathe and with the lathe turning at high speed, take a very fine cut out of the commutator and finish the surface by polishing with glass paper. DO NOT UNDERCUT THE MICA INSULATORS BETWEEN THE COMMUTATOR SEGMENTS.

10. With the starter motor dismantled, test the four field coils for an open circuit. Connect a 12-volt battery with a 12-volt bulb in one of the leads between the field terminal post and the tapping point of the field coils to which the brushes are connected. An open circuit is proved by the bulb not lighting.

11. If the bulb lights, it does not necessarily mean that the field coils are in order, as there is a possibility that one of the coils will be earthing to the starter yoke or pole shoes. To check this, remove the lead from the brush connector and place it against a clean portion of the starter yoke If the bulb lights the field coils are earthing. Replacement of the field coils calls for the use of a wheel operated screwdriver, a soldering iron, caulking and riveting operations and is beyond the scope of the majority of owners. The starter yoke should be taken to a reputable electrical engineering works for new field coils to be fitted. Alternatively, purchase an exchange starter motor.

12. If the armature is damaged this will be evident after visual inspection. Look for signs of burning, discolouration, and for conductors that have lifted away from the commutator. Reassembly is a straight reversal of the dismantling procedure.

15. STARTER MOTOR DRIVE - GENERAL DESCRIPTION

1. The starter motor drive is of the outboard type. When the starter motor is operated the pinion moves into contact with the flywheel gear ring by moving in towards the starter motor.

2. If the engine kicks back, or the pinion fails to engage with the flywheel gear ring when the starter motor is actuated no undue strain is placed on the armature shaft, as the pinion sleeve disengages from the pinion and turns independently.

136

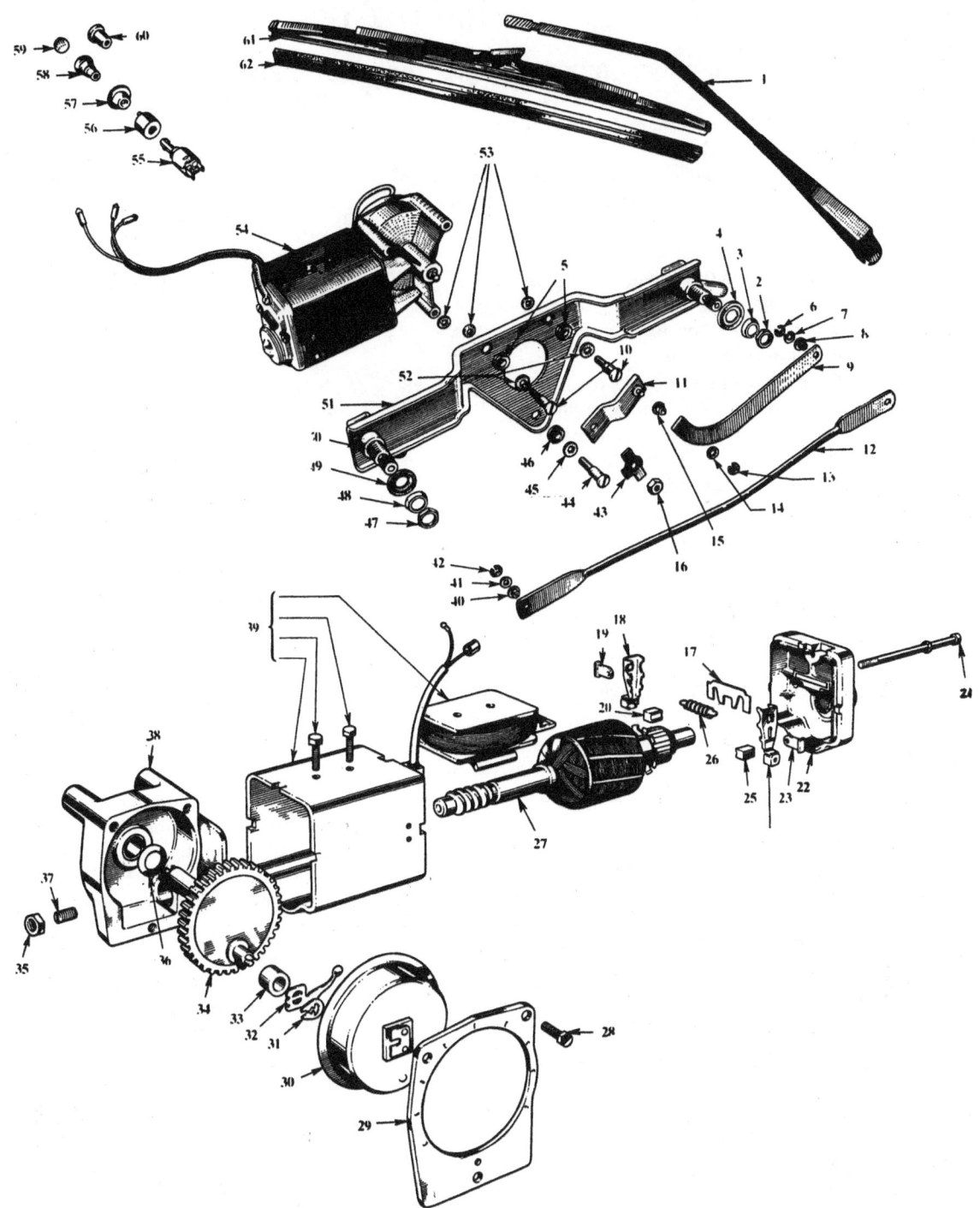

Fig. 10:3 EXPLODED VIEW OF THE WINDSCREEN WIPER MOTOR AND ASSOCIATED COMPONENTS USED UP TO SEPT. 1964.
1 Windscreen wiper arm. 2 Nut. 3 Grommet cover. 4 Grommet. 5 Wiper motor to bracket grommets. 6 Link clip. 7 Washer.
8 Drive to rotory link bush. 9 Wiper link. 10 Fixing screws. 11 Link. 12 Wiper arms connecting link. 13 Link clip.
14 Washer. 15 Link bush. 16 Nut. 17 Brush holder retainer. 18 Brush holder. 19 Insulator. 20 Brush. 21 Through bolt.
22 Commutator end plate. 23 Insulator. 24 Brush holder. 25 Brush. 26 Brush holder tension spring. 27 Armature and commutator assembly. 28 Bolt. 29 Gearbox cover plate. 30 Parking limit switch. 31 Clip. 32 Parking switch contact. 33 Gear
crank pin bush. 34 Gearwheel. 35 Nut. 36 Washer. 37 End float adjusting screw. 38 Gearbox housing. 39 Yoke, field coil
and thermostat assembly. 40 Link bush. 41 Washer. 42 Clip. 43 Tab washer. 44 Securing screw. 45 Washer. 46 Grommet.
47 Nut. 48 Grommet cover. 49 Grommet. 50 Inner spacer. 51 Mounting bracket. 52 Washers. 53 Washers. 54 Wiper
motor and gearbox assembly. 55 Wiper switch. 56 Spacer. 57 Bezel. 58 De Luxe switch knob. 59 Insert. 60 Plain knob.

137

CHAPTER TEN

16. STARTER MOTOR DRIVE - REMOVAL & RE-PLACEMENT

1. When the starter motor is removed the drive should be well washed in petrol or paraffin to remove any grease or oil which may be the cause of a sticking pinion. Under no circumstances should these parts be lubricated.
2. To dismantle the drive, compress the drive spring and cup employing a press for this purpose, and then extract the locking device, pin or circlip.
3. Ease the press and remove the drive spring cup, spring and retaining washer. Pull the drive pinion barrel assembly from the armature shaft. If the pinion is badly worn or broken, this must be replaced as an assembly. When refitting the pinion barrel assembly must be fitted with the pinion teeth toward the armature windings.

17. CONTROL BOX - GENERAL DESCRIPTION

The control box comprises the voltage regulator and the cut-out. The voltage regulator controls the output from the dynamo depending on the state of the battery and the demands of the electrical equipment, and ensures that the battery is not overcharged. The cut-out is really an automatic switch and connects the dynamo to the battery when the dynamo is turning fast enough to produce a charge. Similarly it disconnects the battery from the dynamo when the engine is idling or stationary so that the battery does not discharge through the dynamo.

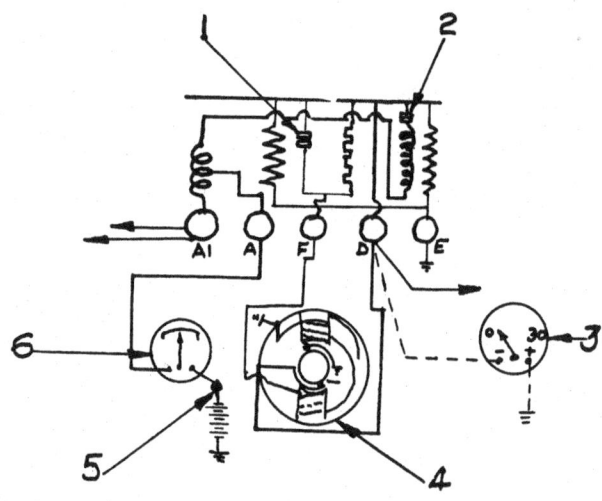

Fig. 10:4 The regulator wiring circuit. 1 Voltage regulator points 2 Cut-out points. 3 Test volt meter. 4 Generator. 5 Starter switch terminal. 6 Test ammeter.

18. VOLTAGE REGULATOR ADJUSTMENT

1. The regulator requires very little attention during its service life, and should there be any reason to suspect its correct functioning, tests of all circuits should be made to ensure that they are not the reason for the trouble.
2. These checks include the tension of the fan belt, to make sure that it is not slipping and so providing only a very low charge rate. The battery should be carefully checked for possible low charge rate due to a faulty cell, or corroded battery connections.
3. The leads from the generator may have been crossed during replacement, and if this is the case then the regulator points will have stuck together as soon as the generator starts to charge. Check for loose or broken leads from the generator to the regulator.
4. If after a thorough check it is considered advisable to test the regulator, this should only be carried out by an electrician who is well acquainted with the correct method, using test bench equipment.
5. Check the regulator setting by removing and joining together the cables from the control box terminals A1 and A, after slipping a thin piece of card between the cut out contacts. Then connect the negative lead of a 20-volt voltmeter to the 'D' terminal on the regulator and the positive lead to a good earth. Start the engine and increase its speed until the voltmeter needle flicks and then steadies. This should occur at about 1,500 r.p.m. If the voltage at which the needle steadies is outside the limits listed below, then remove the control box cover and turn the adjusting screw clockwise, a quarter of a turn at a time to raise the setting, and a similar amount, anti-clockwise, to lower it.

Air Temperature	Open circuit voltage
10°C or 50°F	15.7 to 16.1
20°C or 68°F	15.6 to 16.0
30°C or 86°F	15.5 to 15.9
40°C or 104°F	15.4 to 15.8

It is vital the adjustments be completed within 30 seconds of starting the engine as otherwise the heat from the shunt coil will affect the readings.

19. CUT-OUT & REGULATOR CONTACTS MAINTENANCE

1. Every 12,000 miles check the cut-out and regulator contacts. If they are dirty or

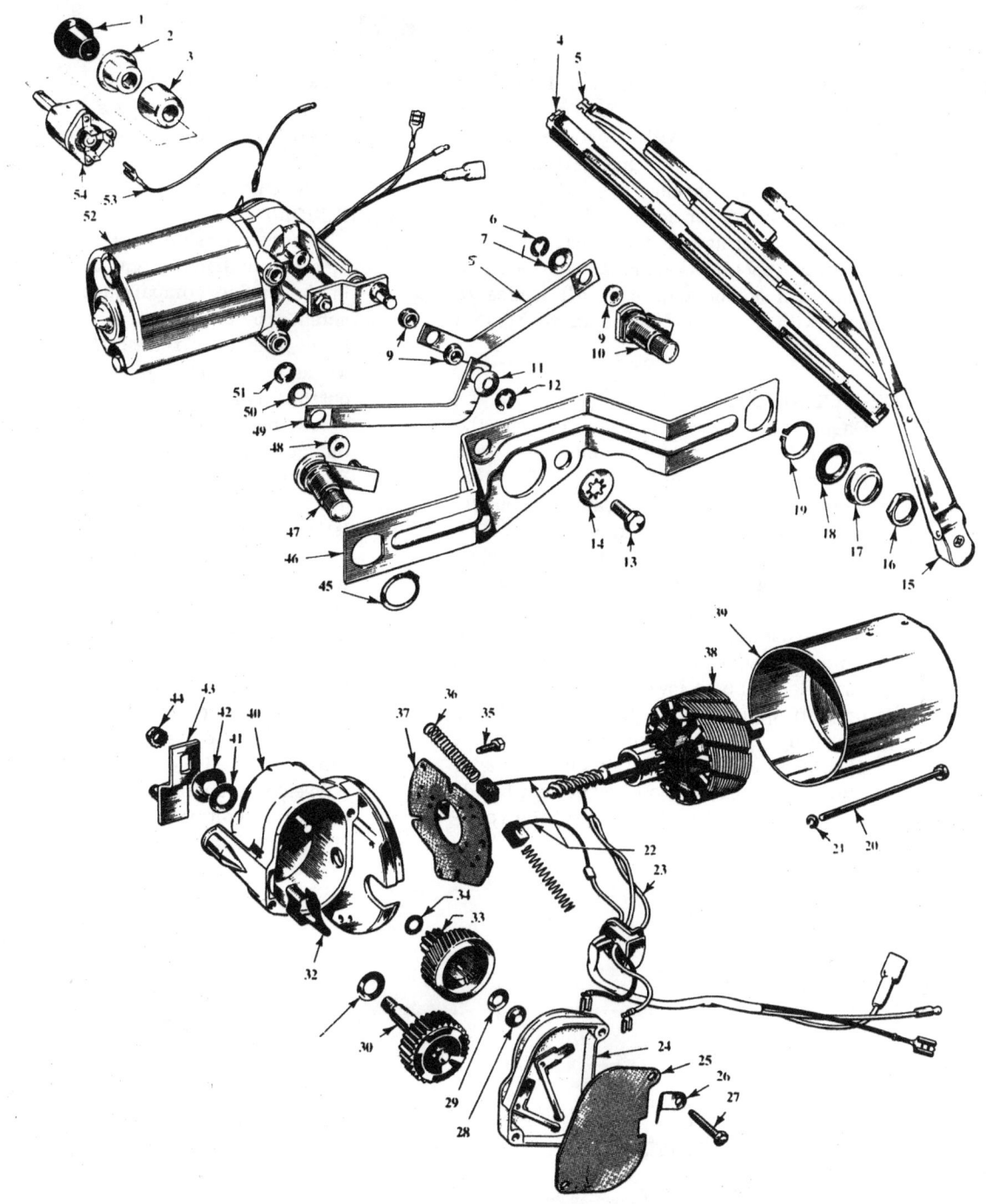

Fig. 10:5 EXPLODED VIEW OF THE AUTOLITE WINDSCREEN WIPER MOTOR AND ASSOCIATED COMPONENTS — SEPT. 1964 ON.
1 Windscreen wiper knob. 2 Windscreen wiper switch bezel. 3 Spacer. 4 Rubber blade. 5 Metal blade. 6 Link clip. 7 Washer.
8 Wiper link.   9 Grommets.   10 Windscreen wiper arm mounting pivot. 11 Washer. 12 Circlip.   13 Bolt.   14 Star washer.
15 Wiper blade arm.   16 Nut.   17 Grommet cover.   18 Grommet.   19 Circlip.   20 Through bolt.   21 Spring washer.   22 Brushes.
23 Brush wires.   24 Limit switch and cover.   25 Switch housing cover.   26 Clip.   27 Bolt.   28 Gear to housing nut.   29 Washer.
30 Shaft and gearwheel.   31 Washer.   32 Limit stop.   33 Gear and pinion.   34 Washer.   35 Bolt.   36 Brush spring.   37 Brush
holder plate.   38 Armature and commutator assembly.   39 Armature cover and magnet assembly.   40 Gear housing.   41 Washer.
42 Washer.   43 Wiper output arm.   44 Locknut.   45 Circlip.   46 Bracket.   47 Windscreen wiper arm mounting pivot.   48 Grommet.
49 Wiper link.   50 Washer.   51 Link clip.   52 Wiper motor and gear assembly.   53 Wire to switch.   54 Wiper motor switch.

rough or burnt place a piece of fine glass paper (DO NOT USE EMERY PAPER OR CARBORUNDUM PAPER) between the cut-out contacts, close them manually and draw the glass paper through several times.

2. Clean the regulator contacts in exactly the same way, but use emery or carborundum paper and not glass paper. Carefully clean both sets of contacts from all traces of dust with a rag moistened in methylated spirits.

20. CUT-OUT ADJUSTMENT

1. Check the voltage required to operate the cut-out by connecting a voltmeter between the control box terminals 'D' and 'E'. Remove the control box cover, start the engine and gradually increase its speed until the cut-outs close. This should occur when the reading is between 12.7 to 13.3 volts. If the reading is outside these limits turn the cut-out adjusting screw a fraction at a time clockwise to raise the voltage, and anti-clockwise to lower it. To adjust the drop off voltage bend the fixed contact blade carefully. The adjustment to the cut-out should be completed within 30 seconds of starting the engine as otherwise heat build-up from the shunt coil will affect the readings.

2. If the cut-out fails to work, clean the contacts, and, if there is still no response, renew the cut-out and regulator unit.

FLASHER CIRCUIT - FAULT TRACING & RECTIFICATION

1. The actual flasher unit is enclosed in a small cylindrical metal container located in the engine compartment. The unit is actuated by the direction indicator switch.

2. If the flasher circuit fails to operate, or works very slowly or very rapidly, check out the flasher indicator circuit as detailed below, before assuming there is a fault in the unit itself.

3. Examine the direction indicator bulbs front and rear for broken filaments.

4. If the external flashers are working but the internal flasher warning light has ceased to function check the filament of the warning bulb and replace as necessary.

5. With the aid of the wiring diagram check all the flasher circuit connections if a flasher bulb is sound but does not work.

6. In the event of total direction indicator failure, check the fuse.

7. With the ignition turned on check that current is reaching the flasher unit by connecting a voltmeter between the 'plus' or 'B' terminal and earth. If this test is pos-

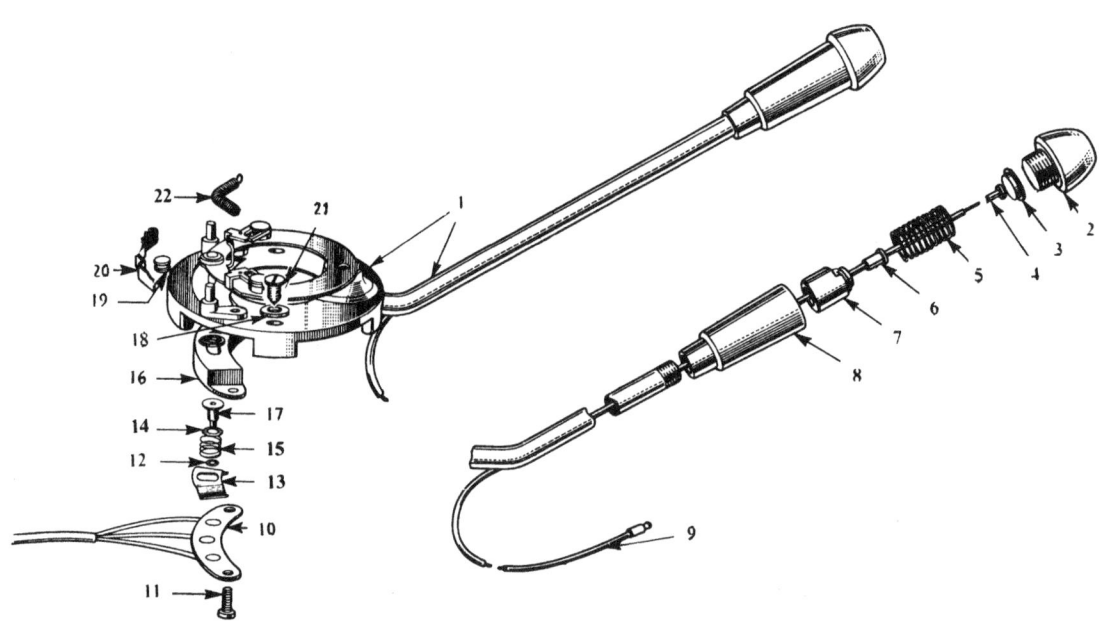

Fig. 10:6 EXPLODED VIEW OF THE DIRECTION INDICATOR & HORN BUTTON.
1 Direction indicator and horn switch body and arm. 2 Horn switch cap. 3 Horn moving contact. 4 Horn fixed contact. 5 Spring.
6 Horn switch insulator. 7 Retaining nut. 8 Arm. 9 Horn wire. 10 Direction indicator contact and wire assembly. 11 Screw.
12 Washer. 13 Indicator switch contact plate. 14 Washer. 15 Spring. 16 Indicator switch top cover. 17 Contact. 18 Washer.
19 Indicator switch roller. 20 Indicator switch cam. 21 Screw. 22 Spring.

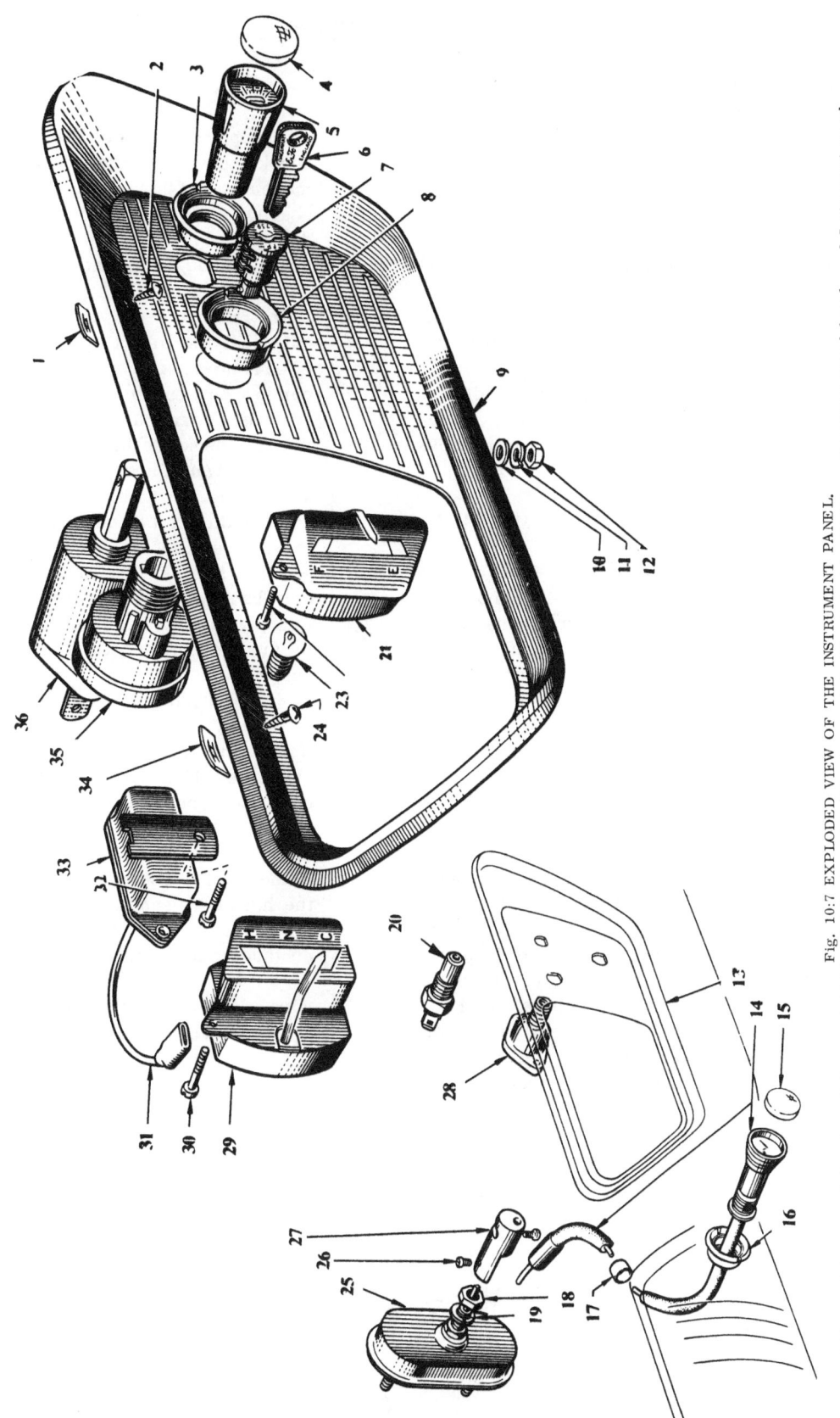

Fig. 10:7 EXPLODED VIEW OF THE INSTRUMENT PANEL.

1 Nut. 2 Screw. 3 Bezel. 4 Cap. 5 Light switch knob. 6 Ignition key. 7 Ignition lock and cylinder. 8 Ignition switch bezel. 9 Instrument panel. 10 Washer. 11 Lockwasher. 12 Nut. 13 De Luxe instrument panel. 14 Van starter control. 15 Cap. 16 Bezel. 17 Grommet. 18 Nut. 19 Starter unit washer. 20 Temperature gauge sender assembly. 21 Fuel tank contents gauge. 22 Bolt. 23 Bulb. 24 Screw. 25 Starter relay switch. 26 Grub screw. 27 Connector. 28 Ignition switch — less cylinder. 29 Nut. 30 Securing screw. 31 Lead. 32 Securing screw. 33 Instrument voltage regulator assembly. 34 Nut. 35 Ignition switch — less cylinder and key. 36 Turn/Pull light switch.

141

itive connect the 'plus' or 'B' terminal and the 'L' terminal and operate the flasher switch. If the flasher bulb lights up the flasher unit itself is defective and must be replaced as it is not possible to dismantle and repair it.

22. WINDSCREEN WIPER MECHANISM - MAINTENANCE

Renew the windscreen wiper blades at intervals of 12,000 miles, or more frequently if necessary.

The washer round the wheelbase spindle can be lubricated with several drops of glycerine every 6,000 miles. The windscreen wiper links can be lightly oiled at the same time.

23. WINDSCREEN WIPER MECHANISM - FAULT DIAGNOSIS & RECTIFICATION
1. Either a Lucas or Autolite windscreen wiper mechanism may be fitted depending on the year of manufacture. The components are arranged as shown in Figs. 10.3 and 10.5 and both units are sufficiently different in shape to make identification easy.
2. Should the windscreen wipers fail, or work very slowly, then check the terminals for loose connections, and make sure the insulation of the external wiring is not cracked or broken. If this is in order then check the current the motor is taking by connecting up a 1-20 volt voltmeter in the circuit and turning on the wiper switch. Consumption should be between 2.3 to 3.1 amps.
3. If no current is passing through check the fuse. If the fuse has blown replace it after having checked the wiring of the motor and other electrical circuits serviced by this fuse for short circuits. If the

fuse is in good condition check the wiper switch.
4. If the wiper motor takes a very high current check the wiper blades for freedom of movement. If this is satisfactory check the gearbox cover and gear assembly for damage and measure the armature end float which should be between .009 to .012 in. (.20 to .30 mm.).
5. If the motor takes a very low current ensure that the battery is fully charged. Check the brush gear after removing the commutator end bracket and ensure that the brushes are bearing on the commutator. If not, check the brushes for freedom of movement and if necessary, renew the tension spring. If the brushes are very worn they should be replaced with new ones. The brush levers should be quite free on their pivots. If stiff, loosen them by moving them backwards and forwards by hand and by applying a little thin machine oil. Check the armature by substitution if this unit is suspected.

24. HORN - FAULT TRACING & RECTIFICATION

1. If the horn works badly or fails completely, check the wiring leading to it for short circuits and loose connections. Check that the horn is firmly secured and that there is nothing lying on the horn body.
2. If the fault is not an external one remove the horn cover and check the leads inside the horn. If these are sound, check the contact breaker contacts. If these are burnt or dirty, clean them with a fine file and wipe all traces of dirt and dust away with a petrol moistened rag. Test the current consumption of the horn which should be between 3 and $3\frac{1}{2}$ amps.

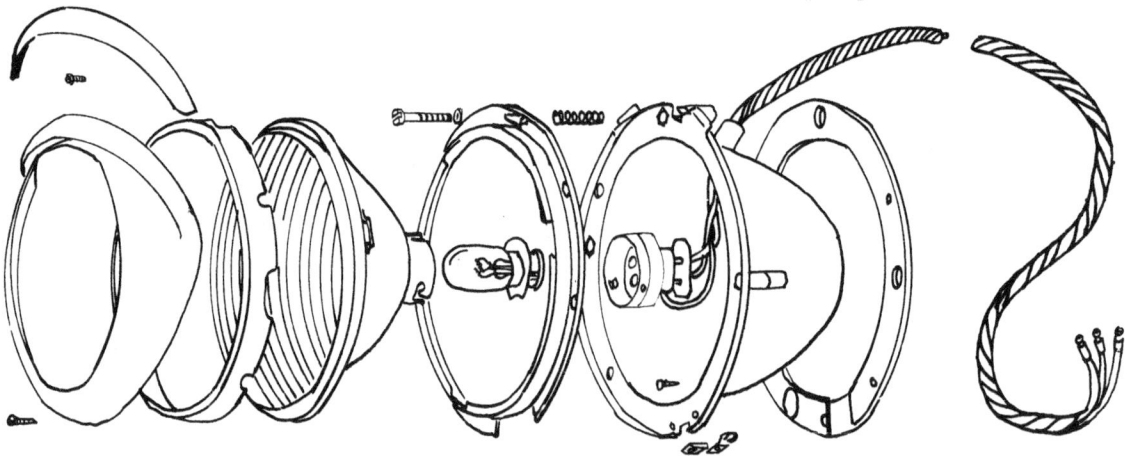

Fig. 10:8 EXPLODED VIEW OF A FRONT HEADLIGHT ASSEMBLY.

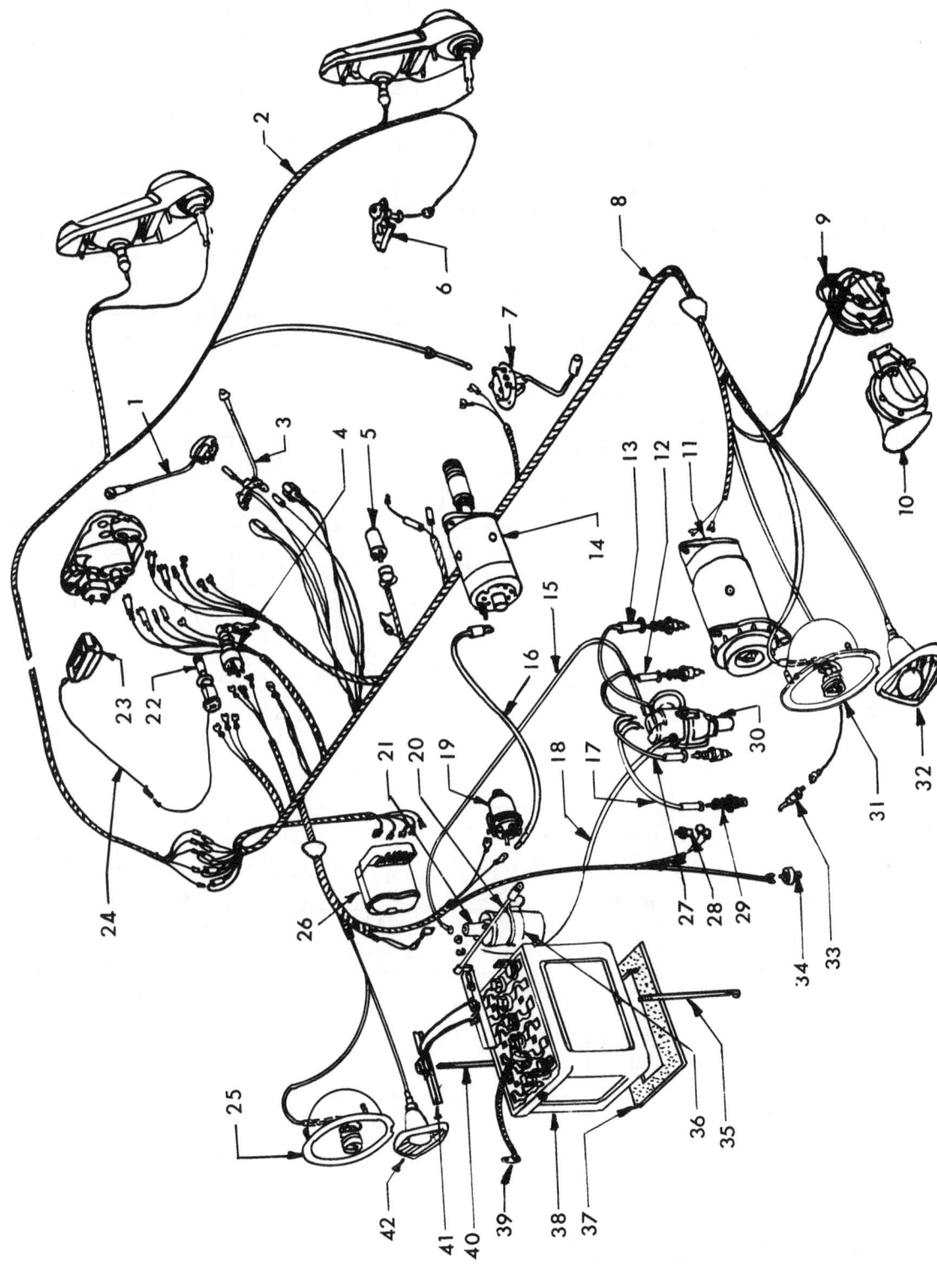

FIG. 10:9 GENERAL VIEW OF THE LAYOUT OF THE IGNITION AND ELECTRICAL SYSTEM.

1 Direction indicator and horn button.   2 Cable to rear light.   3 Alternative type of direction indicator.   4 Ignition switch.   5 Indicator flasher unit.   6 Rear number plate light.   7 Fuel tank sender unit.   8 Main cable.   9 Normal horn.   10 Windtone horn.   11 Dynamo.   12 No. 3 H.T. lead.   13 No. 4 H.T. lead. 14 Starter motor.   15 Coil H.T. lead.   16 Starter motor lead.   17 No. 1 H.T. lead.   18 Distributor L.T. lead.   19 Starter solenoid.   20 Lead from battery to solenoid.   21 Coil.   22 Switch.   23 Interior light.   24 Cable to interior light.   25 Right headlight.   26 Regulator and cut out.   27 No. 2 H.T. lead.   28 Oil warning sender unit.   29 Sparking plug.   30 Distributor.   31 Left headlight.   32 Side light.   33 Temperature warning sender unit.   34 Oil warning sender unit. 35 Battery fixing bolt.   36 Coil support.   37 Battery tray.   38 Battery.   39 Earth battery lead.   40 Battery fixing bolt.   41 Battery securing strap.   42 Front light.

143

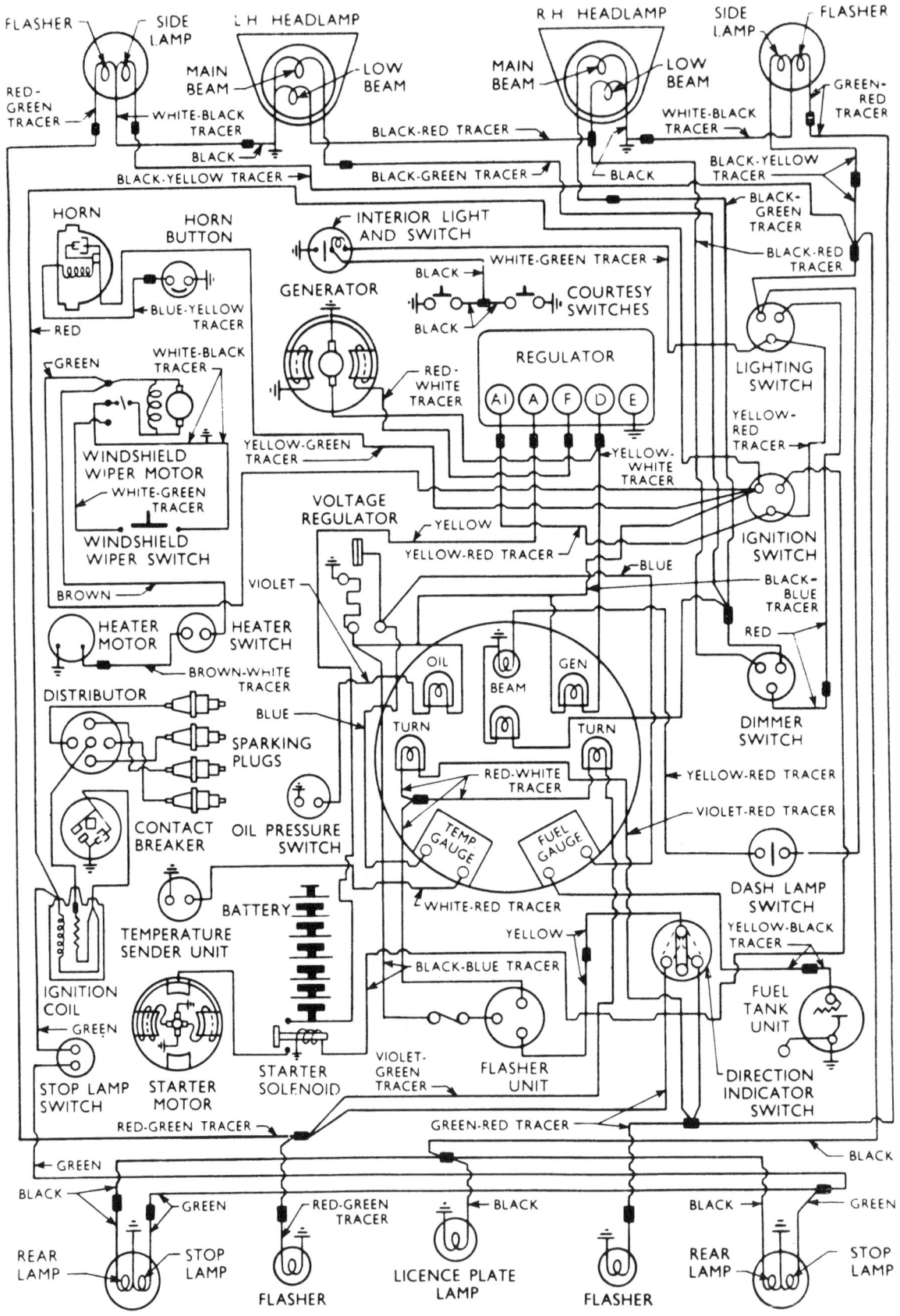

WIRING DIAGRAM

Cause	Trouble	Remedy
SYMPTOM:	STARTER MOTOR FAILS TO TURN ENGINE	
No electricity at starter motor	Battery discharged	Charge battery.
	Battery defective internally	Fit new battery.
	Battery terminal leads loose or earth lead not securely attached to body	Check and tighten leads.
	Loose or broken connections in starter motor circuit	Check all connections and tighten any that are loose.
	Starter motor switch or solenoid faulty	Test and replace faulty components with new.
Electricity at starter motor: faulty motor	Starter motor pinion jammed in mesh with flywheel gear ring	Disengage pinion by turning squared end of armature shaft.
	Starter brushes badly worn, sticking, or brush wires loose	Examine brushes, replace as necessary, tighten down brush wires.
	Commutator dirty, worn, or burnt	Clean commutator, recut if badly burnt.
	Starter motor armature faulty	Overhaul starter motor, fit new armature.
	Field coils earthed	Overhaul starter motor.
SYMPTOM:	STARTER MOTOR TURNS ENGINE VERY SLOWLY	
Electrical defects	Battery in discharged condition	Charge battery.
	Starter brushes badly worn, sticking, or brush wires loose	Examine brushes, replace as necessary, tighten down brush wires.
	Loose wires in starter motor circuit	Check wiring and tighten as necessary.
SYMPTOM:	STARTER MOTOR OPERATES WITHOUT TURNING ENGINE	
Dirt or oil on drive gear	Starter motor pinion sticking on the screwed sleeve	Remove starter motor, clean starter motor drive.
Mechanical damage	Pinion or flywheel gear teeth broken or worn	Fit new gear ring to flywheel, and new pinion to starter motor drive.
SYMPTOMS:	STARTER MOTOR NOISY OR EXCESSIVELY ROUGH ENGAGEMENT	
Lack of attention or mechanical damage	Pinion or flywheel gear teeth broken or worn	Fit new gear teeth to flywheel, or new pinion to starter motor drive.
	Starter drive main spring broken	Dismantle and fit new main spring
	Starter motor retaining bolts loose	Tighten starter motor securing bolts. Fit new spring washer if necessary.
SYMPTOM:	BATTERY WILL NOT HOLD CHARGE FOR MORE THAN A FEW DAYS	
Wear or damage	Battery defective internally	Remove and fit new battery.
	Electrolyte level too low or electrolyte too weak due to leakage	Top up electrolyte level to just above plates
	Plate separators no longer fully effective	Remove and fit new battery.
	Battery plates severely sulphated	Remove and fit new battery.
Insufficient current flow to keep battery charged	Fan/dynamo belt slipping	Check belt for wear, replace if necessary, and tighten.
	Battery terminal connections loose or corroded	Check terminals for tightness, and remove all corrosion.
	Dynamo not charging properly	Remove and overhaul dynamo.
	Short in lighting circuit causing continual battery drain	Trace and rectify.
	Regulator unit not working correctly	Check setting, clean, and replace if defective.
SYMPTOM:	IGNITION LIGHT FAILS TO GO OUT, BATTERY RUNS FLAT IN A FEW DAYS	
Dynamo not charging	Fan belt loose and slipping, or broken	Check, replace, and tighten as necessary.
	Brushes worn, sticking, broken, or dirty	Examine, clean, or replace brushes as necessary.
	Brush springs weak or broken	Examine and test. Replace as necessary.
	Commutator dirty, greasy, worn, or burnt	Clean commutator and undercut segment separators.

	Armature badly worn or armature shaft bent	Fit new or reconditioned armature.
	Commutator bars shorting	Undercut segment separations.
	Dynamo bearings badly worn	Overhaul dynamo, fit new bearings.
	Dynamo field coils burnt, open, or shorted.	Remove and fit rebuilt dynamo.
	Commutator no longer circular	Recut commutator and undercut segment separators.
	Pole pieces very loose	Strip and overhaul dynamo. Tighten pole pieces.
Regulator or cut-out fails to work correctly	Regulator incorrectly set	Adjust regulator correctly.
	Cut-out incorrectly set	Adjust cut-out correctly.
	Open circuit in wiring of cut-out and regulator unit	Remove, examine, and renew as necessary.

Failure of individual electrical equipment to function correctly is dealt with alphabetically, item by item, under the headings listed below:

FUEL GAUGE

Fuel gauge gives no reading	Fuel tank empty!	Fill fuel tank.
	Electric cable between tank sender unit and gauge earthed or loose	Check cable for earthing and joints for tightness.
	Fuel gauge case not earthed	Ensure case is well earthed.
	Fuel gauge supply cable interrupted	Check and replace cable if necessary.
	Fuel gauge unit broken	Replace fuel gauge.
Fuel gauge registers full all the time	Electric cable between tank unit and gauge broken or disconnected	Check over cable and repair as necessary.

HORN

Horn operates all the time	Horn push either earthed or stuck down	Disconnect battery earth. Check and rectify source of trouble.
	Horn cable to horn push earthed	Disconnect battery earth. Check and rectify source of trouble.
Horn fails to operate	Blown fuse	Check and renew if broken. Ascertain cause.
	Cable or cable connection loose, broken or disconnected	Check all connections for tightness and cables for breaks.
	Horn has an internal fault	Remove and overhaul horn.
Horn emits intermittent or unsatisfactory noise	Cable connections loose	Check and tighten all connections.
	Horn incorrectly adjusted	Adjust horn until best note obtained.

LIGHTS

Lights do not come on	If engine not running, battery discharged	Push-start car, charge battery.
	Light bulb filament burnt out or bulbs broken	Test bulbs in live bulb holder.
	Wire connections loose, disconnected or broken	Check all connections for tightness and wire cable for breaks.
	Light switch shorting or otherwise faulty	By-pass light switch to ascertain if fault is in switch and fit new switch as appropriate.
Lights come on but fade out	If engine not running battery discharged	Push-start car, and charge battery.
Lights give very poor illumination	Lamp glasses dirty	Clean glasses.
	Reflector tarnished or dirty	Fit new reflectors.
	Lamps badly out of adjustment	Adjust lamps correctly.
	Incorrect bulb with too low wattage fitted	Remove bulb and replace with correct grade
	Existing bulbs old and badly discoloured	Renew bulb units.
	Electrical wiring too thin not allowing full current to pass	Rewire lighting system.

ELECTRICAL SYSTEM

Cause	Trouble	Remedy
Lights work erratically - flashing on and off, especially over bumps	Battery terminals or earth connection loose Lights not earthing properly Contacts in light switch faulty	Tighten battery terminals and earth connection. Examine and rectify. By-pass light switch to ascertain if fault is in switch and fit new switch as appropriate.
WIPERS		
Wiper motor fails to work	Blown fuse Wire connections loose, disconnected, or broken Brushes badly worn Armature worn or faulty Field coils faulty	Check and replace fuse if necessary. Check wiper wiring. Tighten loose connections. Remove and fit new brushes. If electricity at wiper motor remove and overhaul and fit replacement armature. Purchase reconditioned wiper motor.
Wiper motor works very slowly and takes excessive current	Commutator dirty, greasy, or burnt Drive to wheelboxes too bent or un-lubricated Wheelbox spindle binding or damaged Armature bearings dry or unaligned Armature badly worn or faulty	Clean commutator thoroughly. Examine drive and straighten out severe curvature. Lubricate. Remove, overhaul, or fit replacement. Replace with new bearings correctly aligned. Remove, overhaul, or fit replacement armature.
Wiper motor works slowly and takes little current	Brushes badly worn Commutator dirty, greasy, or burnt Armature badly worn or faulty	Remove and fit new brushes. Clean commutator thoroughly. Remove and overhaul armature or fit replacement.
Wiper motor works but wiper blades remain static	Driving cable rack disengaged or faulty Wheelbox gear and spindle damaged or worn Wiper motor gearbox parts badly worn	Examine and if faulty, replace. Examine and if faulty, replace. Overhaul or fit new gearbox.

CHAPTER ELEVEN

SUSPENSION – DAMPERS – STEERING

CONTENTS

SPECIFICATIONS

FRONT SUSPENSION

Type	Independent by coil spring/vertical struts
Spring: Free length	14.06 in. (35.71 cm.)
Fitted length	7.66 in. (19.46 cm.)
Diameter of coil wire	0.417 in. (1.06 cm.)
Caster Angle	$1^\circ 30'$ to $3^\circ 0'$) Static
Camber Angle	$0^\circ 30'$ to $2^\circ 0'$) Unladen
King Pin Inclination	$4^\circ 45'$ to $6^\circ 15'$) Condition
Toe In	1/8 in. to 3/16 in. (3.17 to 4.76 mm.)
Dampers	Hydraulic in vertical struts
Damper Fluid	M 100502 - E (Ford Part No.)

REAR SUSPENSION

Type	Semi-elliptic underslung
Spring	Leaf
Dampers	Lever Hydraulic
Damper Fluid	M 100502 - E (Ford Part No.)

STEERING

Type	Worm and nut
Turning Circle	32 ft.
Ratio	14 to 1
Lubricant	S.A.E. 90 Hypoid Oil

CHAPTER ELEVEN

WHEELS
    Type ... ...   Disc - 4 stud fixing

TYRES
    Size : Saloon Cars ... ...   5. 20 by 13 4 ply
            Estate cars & Vans ... ...   5. 60 by 13 6 ply
    Tyre Pressure : Front ... ...   22 lb/sq. in.
    Tyre Pressure : Rear ... ...   22 lb/sq. in.

MAXIMUM TORQUE WRENCH SETTINGS
    Anti roll bar/Stabiliser mounting foot ... ...   27 lbs. ft.
    Anti roll bar/Stabiliser retaining nut ... ...   30 lbs. ft.
    Anti roll bar/Stabiliser 'U' bolts ... ...   18 lbs. ft.
    Idler arm bracket ... ...   30 lbs. ft.
    Piston rod gland cap... ... ...   31 lbs. ft.
    Steering ball joints nuts ... ...   22 lbs. ft.
    Steering spindle arm ... ...   35 lbs. ft.
    Suspension thrust bearing retaining nut ... ...   55 lbs. ft.
    Track control arm ball joint nut ... ...   45 lbs. ft.

1. GENERAL DESCRIPTION

Each of the independent front suspension units consists of a vertical strut enclosing a double acting damper s u r r o u n d e d by a coil spring. Half way down the strut is a seat in which the bottom of the spring rests.

At the upper end, a rubber-mounted thrust bearing is secured to each front mudguard; and the wheel spindle carrying the brake assembly and wheel hub is forged integrally with the suspension unit foot.

A track rod arm is connected to each unit, the inner end being mounted to the front cross-member in rubber bushes, while the outer end is connected to the steering arm.

A stabiliser bar is fitted between the outer ends of each track control arm and secured at the front to a mounting on the body side members.

When repairs are being carried out on any part of the front suspension unit it is essential that spring clips be fitted to the coil springs otherwise personal injury may result when dismantling the unit.

Whenever repairs have been carried out on a suspension unit it is essential to check the wheel alignment as the linkage could be altered which will a f f e c t the c o r r e c t front wheel settings.

Every time the car goes over a bump vertical m o v e m e n t of a front wheel pushes the damper body upwards a g a i n s t the combined resistance of the coil spring and the damper piston.

Hydraulic fluid in the damper is displaced and it is then forced through the compression valve into the space between the inner and outer cylinder. On the downward movement of the suspension, the road spring forces the damper body downward against the pressure of the hydraulic fluid which is forced back again through the rebound valve. In this way the natural oscillations of the spring are damped out and a comfortable ride is obtained.

The steering gear on the Anglia is of the worm and nut type with recirculatory balls running inside the nut. The steering box is fixed to the right hand cross frame member and an idler arm is fitted in a corresponding position on the opposite side of the frame member.

Inside the steering box a rocker shaft running in bushes has its splined bottom end fixed to the drop arm, and its top end connected to the nut.

Turning the steering wheel turns the shaft which, because the nut cannot turn screws it up or down. As the nut is connected to the rocker shaft this rotates so turning the drop arm.

On the front uprights it is worth noting that there is a shroud inside the coil spring which protects the machined surface of the piston rod from road dirt.

The upper mounting assembly consists of a steel sleeve with a rubber bush bonded to it. Two ball thrust races are fitted in the mounting the inner races being bonded to the rubber bush.

The bearings can be renewed when necessary, but the mounting must be replaced as a complete assembly.

Two adjustments are provided for the steering:-
    a) steering s h a f t bearing adjustment and
    b) rocker shaft end-float adjustment.

Only the rocker shaft end-float adjustment can be carried out with the steering box in position, and when it is evident that such adjustment is required, this will also indicate that the box needs a complete overhaul, and should be removed from the vehicle.

At the rear the axle is held by two inverted 'U' bolts at each end of the casing to underslung semi elliptic springs which provide both lateral and longditudinal location.

Twin cylinder hydraulic dampers are fitted and work in principle in a similar way to those at the front but of course they are of a different design. On hitting a bump the damper arm moves the piston inside the larger cylinder so forcing hydraulic fluid past a valve to the second cylinder. As the wheel comes down bringing the arm with it the fluid is forced back into the first cylinder against the resistance of the valve so damping out the natural oscillation of the spring.

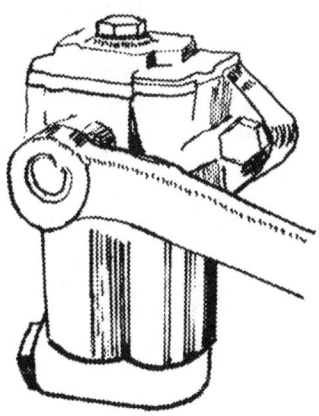

Fig. 11:2 Rear shock absorber, showing the filler plug at the top through which the fluid level is checked.

2. FRONT AND REAR SUSPENSION – MAINTENANCE

Every 2,500 miles grease the nipples on the front suspension as indicated in the lubrication chart on page 8. Clean the dirt off the rear springs and spray them with penetrating oil. With a spanner check the inverted 'U' bolts for tightness.

STEERING GEAR – MAINTENANCE

Every 2,500 miles remove the plug on the top of the steering box and add Castrol Hypoy Gear Oil until the level reaches the filler plug hole. Then replace the filler plug.

4. FRONT DAMPERS – MAINTENANCE

Every 5,000 miles the suspension unit needs to be topped up with genuine shock absorber fluid, (Part number M-100502-E) when the vehicle is standing on level ground.

To top up, remove the combined level and filler plug and add fluid until the level reaches the bottom of the filler hole. Replace the filler

Fig. 11:1 Close up of the rear spring U-bolts and securing nuts being checked for tightness.

plug securely. Note particularly that topping up must not be done when the vehicle is under more than normal standing weight, nor must the topping up be done with the wheel lifted from the ground.

5. REAR DAMPERS - MAINTENANCE

At intervals of 5,000 miles thoroughly clean the area in the vicinity of the damper filler plug; unscrew the plug; and check the level of the hydraulic fluid which should be just below the filler plug threads. Replenish the fluid level as necessary.

6. FRONT HUB BEARINGS - MAINTENANCE & ADJUSTMENT
1. Every 5,000 miles remove the hub and dust caps, clean out the old grease and repack with Castrolease LM.
2. To check the condition of the hub bearings, jack up the front end of the vehicle and grasp the road wheel at two opposite points to check for any rocking movement in the wheel hub. Watch carefully for any movement in the steering gear, which may otherwise be mistaken for hub movement.
3. If a front wheel hub has excessive movement, this is adjusted by removing the hub cap and then levering off the small dust cap covering the hub centre nut. Remove the split pin securing the centre castle nut and then while turning the wheel in its normal forward direction, tighten up the centre nut until just a slight drag can be felt. Then turn the nut back one castellation at a time until the wheel runs quite freely and there is just a perceptible end-float.
4. Note that the hub has two split pin holes set at 90 degrees to each other in order to provide alternative positions for the split pin. Having corrected the bearing movement, FIT A NEW SPLIT PIN TO SECURE THE CENTRE NUT.

7. FRONT SUSPENSION UNITS - REMOVAL
1. It is difficult to work on the front suspension of the Anglia without one or two special tools, the most important of which are a set of spring clips to hold the coil spring compressed. This latter tool is vital and no attempt should be made to remove or dismantle the units unless it is available.
2. Having jacked up the front of the vehicle securely, first fit the spring clips number P 5010 over as many coils of each spring as possible and connect with a safety strap. Remove the hub and dust caps, unscrew the centre castle nut after removing the split

pin; withdraw the washer and hub bearing and then remove the hub, brakedrum and wheel front centre spindle.
3. Remove the brake back plate assembly, and support the unit so that the rubber hose is not distorted or stretched. Bend back the tabs of the tab washer and unscrew the three bolts which secure the steering arm to the foot of the suspension unit.
4. Lift the bonnet and unscrew the three self-locking nuts which secure the upper mounting unit to the mudguard reinforcing plate, and lower the suspension unit from the vehicle.

8. FRONT SUSPENSION UNITS - DISMANTLING
1. Employ tool number P5025 to unscrew the self-locking nut retaining the upper thrust bearing and withdraw this bearing race and cage. Remove the upper mounting assembly, lift the lower thrust bearing off the inner bearing race and slide the race from the piston rod. This will allow the upper spring seat to be removed and the piston rod shroud can then be lifted off.
2. Leave the spring clips in position and draw the coil spring over the end of the suspension unit.
3. Remove the filler plug and drain out the fluid by moving the piston rod up and down, and then using tool number P 5017 unscrew the piston rod gland cup.
4. The cylinder body is staked over in the slot of the gland cup and this metal will have to

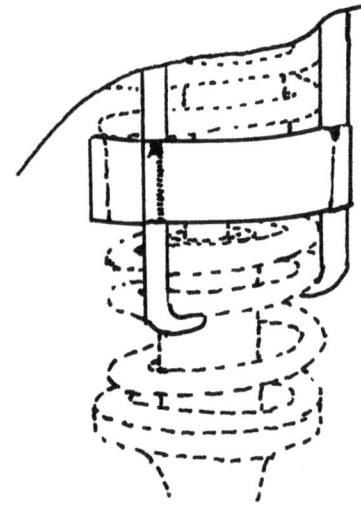

Fig. 11:3 The spring clip tool which is used to hold the coils together.

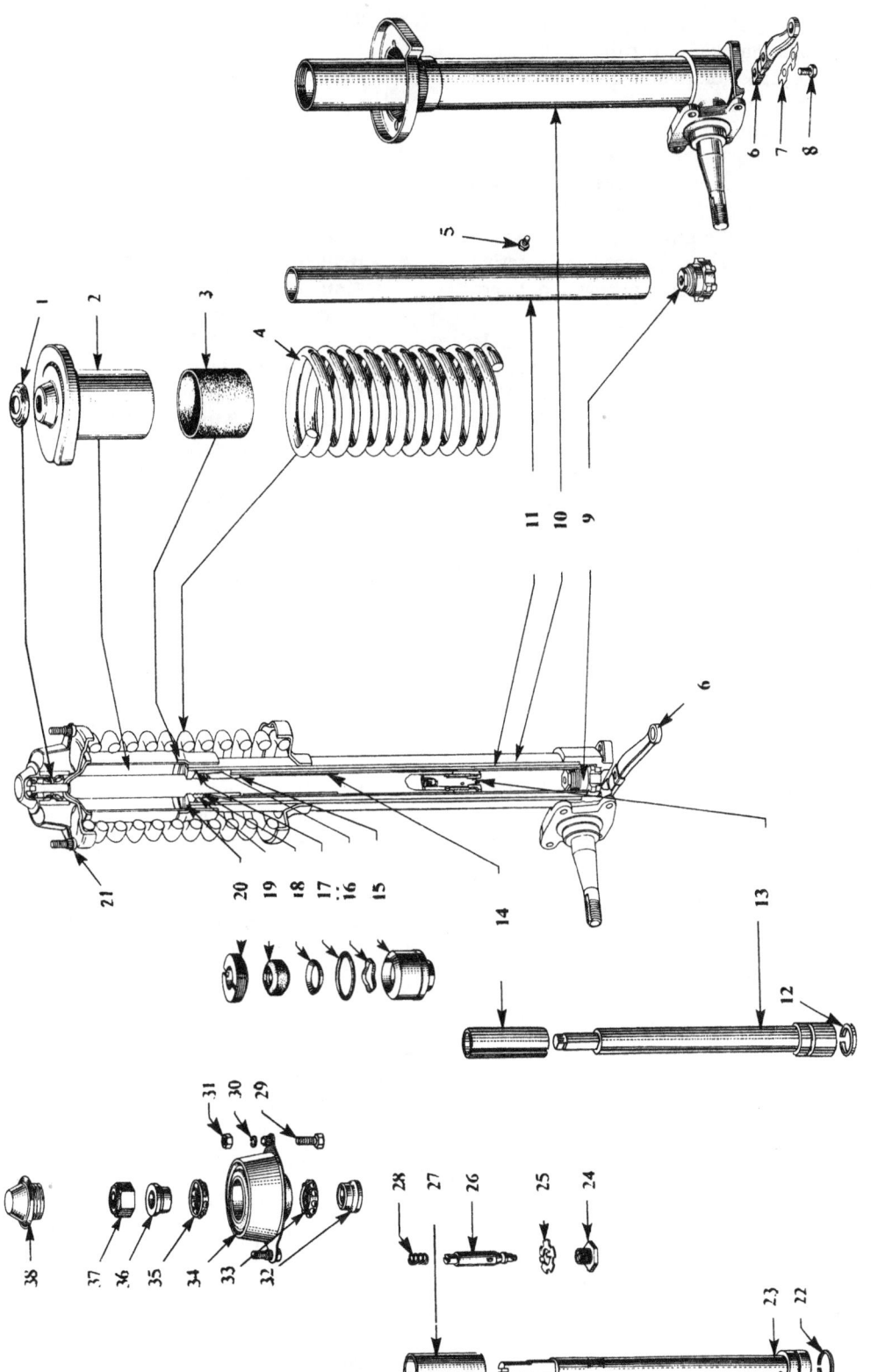

Fig. 11: EXPLODED VIEW OF THE FRONT SUSPENSION SPRING AND DAMPER STRUTS.

1 Upper seat spring reinforcement.   2 Top spring seat and shroud.   3 Piston rod shroud extension.   4 Front spring.   5 Damper filler plug.   6 Steering arm.
7 Tab lockwasher.   8 Bolt.   9 Compression unit base valve.   10 Suspension strut.   11 Suspension unit cylinder.   12 Suspension unit piston ring.   13 Rod and
piston damper assembly.   14 Piston rebound tube.   15 Piston rod guide.   16 Piston rod gland washer — waved.   17 Outer tube oil sealing ring.   18 Piston rod
gland cup.   19 Piston rod gland.   20 Cap.   21 Upper mounting items bracket fit here.   22 Suspension unit piston ring.   23 Rod and piston assembly.   24 Recup-
erating valve screw.   25 Washer.   26 Damper valve assembly.   27 Rebound tube.   28 Damper valve spring.   29 Upper mounting bolt.   30 Spring washer.
31 Nut.   32 Inner race.   33 Ball bearing and cage assembly.   34 Upper mounting assembly.   35 Ball bearing and cage assembly.   36 Inner race.   37 Nut.
38 Upper bearing dust cap.

153

be removed before fitting the tool. The gland cup is removed by turning in the anti-clockwise direction, and once this is away remove the rubber ring and then pull the piston and cylinder out of the unit.

5. When the compression and foot valve assembly have been extracted from the base of the cylinder in the end of the hexagonal nut will be found a small set screw which is in fact employed for setting the valve during production. This screw should not be interfered with.

6. The piston is next withdrawn from the cylinder, leaving the upper guide and gland in position in the top of the cylinder. Next lift the tabs of the lockwasher holding the piston valve nut in position and remove the valve nut from the piston assembly.

7. Extract the valve assembly and the valve spring, and note that the adjustment of the piston valve is sealed and should not be moved therefore.

8. Withdraw the piston rod gland from the upper guide and lift out the gland cup and the spring from the upper guide. The upper guide can then be removed, followed by the rebound stop tube, although normally this will not be necessary.

9. FRONT SUSPENSION UNITS - REASSEMBLY & REPLACEMENT

1. Having obtained all the required new parts, particular attention should be paid to the condition of the wheel spindle and the valves.

2. The fluid ports drilled in the piston rod must be inspected for possible dirt, and to ensure that the two leak grooves in the compression valve body are clear they should be well cleaned.

3. Check the condition of the piston rod for scratches and scores, particularly if the shroud has been dislodged in service so that dirt has been collecting on the rod.

4. Reassembly of the unit is the reverse to dismantling, with the following points to observe. When replacing the gland in position the words "This side down" must be towards the gland seat.

5. When tightening the gland cap use a torque of between 23 to 31 lbs. ft.

6. Swage the outer gland casing of the unit into the slot in the cap to prevent this from loosening in service.

7. Refill the unit with correct hydraulic shock absorber fluid, by placing the unit in a vice vertically with the piston rod in its lowest position.

8. Move the piston rod up and down over its full travel at least six times to enable the fluid to flow throughout the system, and then top up again with the piston rod in its lowest position. Refit the filler plug.

9. If it is necessary to fit a new coil spring, the clips should be removed by clamping the spring in the compressor tool number P 5008 to enable all the tension to be eased away slowly once the spring clips are removed. This tool is also required to compress a new spring in order to allow the clips to be fitted in position.

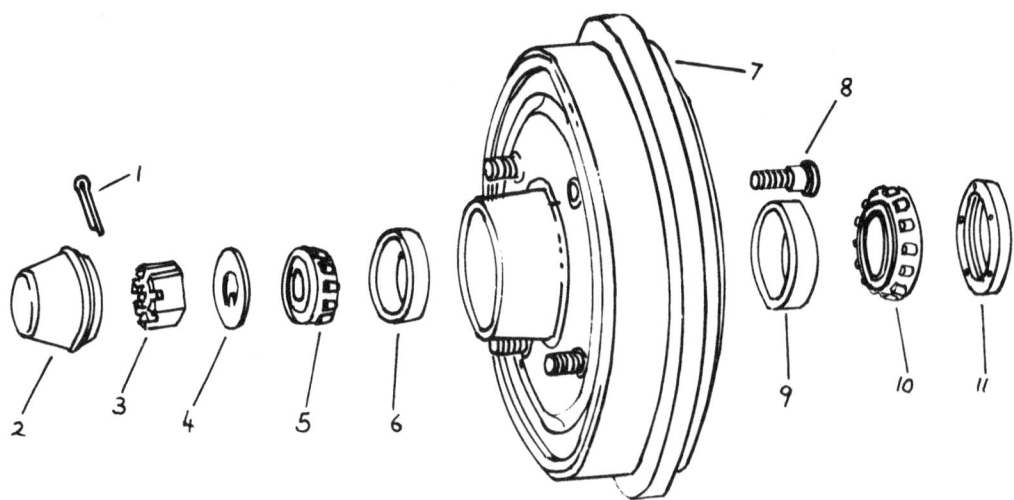

Fig. 11:5 Exploded view of the parts of the front hub in their order of assembly.

1 Split pin.   2 Grease cap.   3 Bearing adjusting nut.   4 Securing thrust washer.   5 Outer ball race.   6 Outer bearing cone.
7 Brake drum.   8 Wheel stud.   9 Inner bearing cone.   10 Inner bearing.   11 Seal.

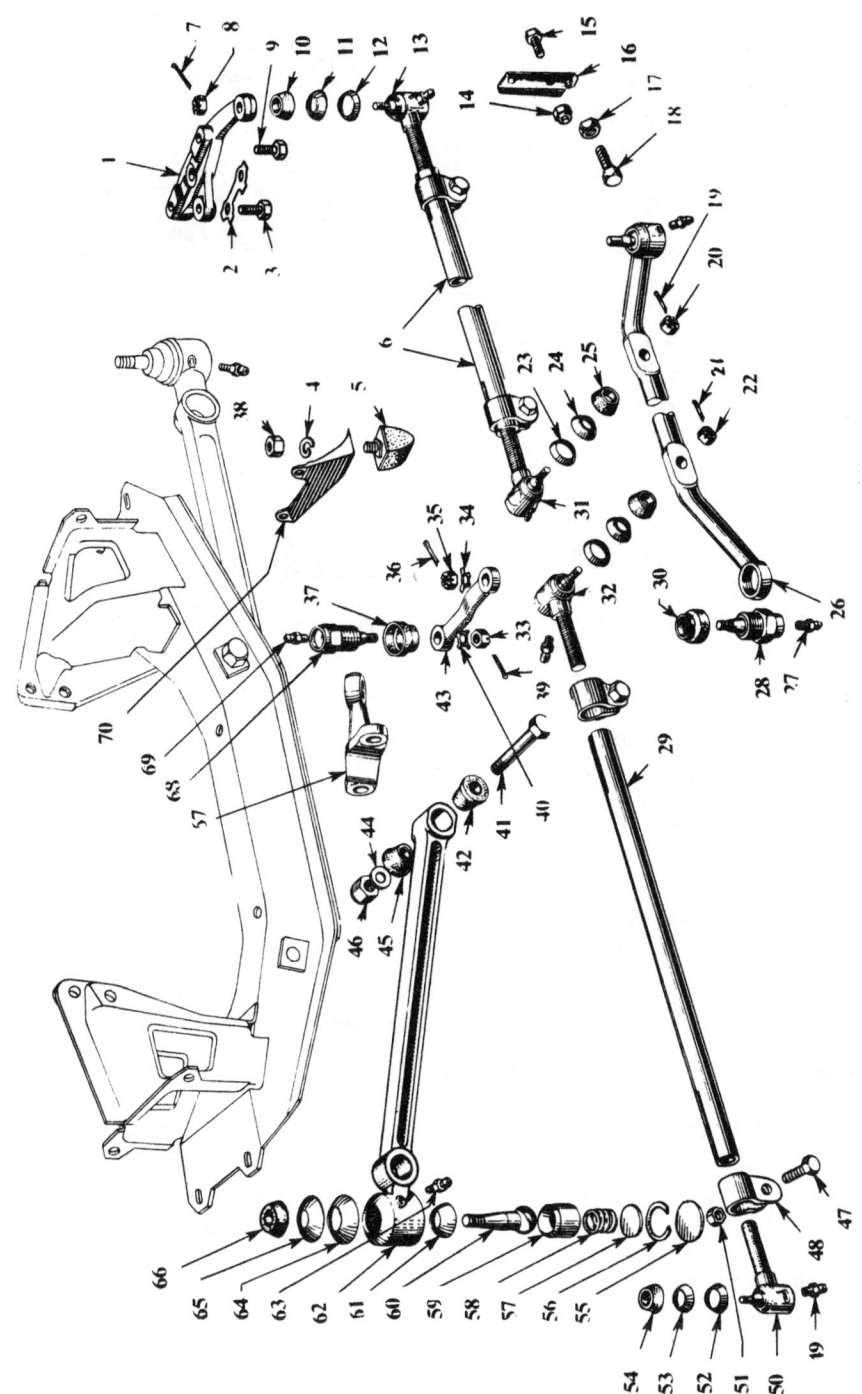

Fig. 11:7 EXPLODED VIEW OF THE FRONT SUSPENSION STEERING LAYOUT AND TRACK LINKS.

1 Steering arm. 2 Tab lockwasher. 3 Bolt. 4 Spring washer. 5 Bump stop — where fitted. 6 Track rod. 7 Splitpin. 8 Nut. 9 Bolt. 10 Dust seal. 11 Upper cap. 12 Lower cap. 13 Track rod ball joint assembly. 14 Self locking nut. 15 Nut. 16 Bracket. 17 Nut. 18 Bolt. 19 Split pin. 20 Castellated nut. 21 Split pin. 22 Castellated nut. 23 Ball joint dust seal. 24 Cap. 25 Inner cap. 26 Track rod ball joint assembly. 27 Steering drop arm to idler arm rod. 28 St d. 29 Track rod. 30 Seal. 31 Track rod end L. H. thread. 32 Track rod end R. H. thread. 33 Castellated nut. 34 Tab washer. 35 Castellated nut. 36 Split pin. 37 Seal. 38 Nut. 39 Split pin. 40 Tab washer. 41 Bolt. 42 Bush. 43 Steering idler arm. 44 Washer. 45 Bush. 46 Nut. 47 Bolt. 48 Track rod end clamp. 49 Grease nipple. 50 Track rod end ball joint assembly. 51 Nut. 52 Cap. 53 Upper cup. 54 Dust seal. 55 Plug. 56 Spring retaining ring. 57 Spring retaining plate. 58 Spring. 59 Ball joint seal. 60 Ball joint stud. 61 Ball joint stud bearing. 62 Track control arm assembly. 63 Grease nipple. 64 Lower cap. 65 Upper cap. 66 Seal. 67 Steering idler arm bracket. 68 Stud. 69 Grease nipple. 70 Reinforcement bracket.

10. The correct tightening torque for the thrust bearing retaining locknut at the top of the unit is 45 to 55 lbs. ft.

11. The suspension unit is refitted to the vehicle in the reverse order to dismantling, the nuts securing the top of the unit to the mudguard being tightened to a torque of 18 lbs. ft.

10. ANTI-ROLL BAR/STABILISER - REMOVAL & REPLACEMENT

1. When it is necessary to carry out repairs on the anti-roll bar and the bushes, the spring clips must first be fitted to the coil springs, and the car can then be lifted at the front.

2. Remove the bar U bolts, withdraw the split pins and unscrew the bar nuts.

3. Dismantle the conical rubber bushes from the track control arms, and then lift the stabiliser bar from the vehicle.

4. Remove the attachment mounting foot pivot bolt, nut and flat washer and slide the attachment from the side member.

5. When reassembling, position the mounting foot bushes in the foot, lubricate the flanges of the bushes with soapy water and enter the mounting foot between the flanges of the side member. Fit the pivot bolt, washer and self-locking nut but do not tighten at this stage.

6. Place new rubber bushes on each side of the bar with the flanges toward the flanges on the bar and refit the bar to the track control arms so that the sweep in the bar is upwards.

7. Push a new rubber bush on to the stabiliser bar at the other side of the control arm with the flange outwards; fit a flat washer and castle nut to each end of the bar, and tighten these nuts to a torque of 25 to 30 lbs. ft., locking up each nut with a split pin.

8. Fit the stabiliser bar in position with the U bolts, tightening the nuts to a torque of 15 to 18 lbs. ft.; and secure the nuts with the tabs on the locking plate.

9. Lower the vehicle to the ground, and tighten the stabiliser attachment foot pivot bolts and nuts to a torque of 22 to 27 lbs. ft.

11. STEERING GEAR - REMOVAL

1. To remove the steering gear from the vehicle, first disconnect and remove the battery from the vehicle.

2. Remove the four screws which hold together the two half housings of the steering column clamp and remove the housings.

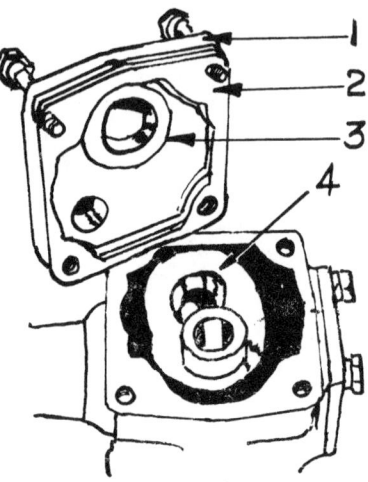

Fig. 11:8 Steering rocker shaft end-float adjustment. The top plate — 1 — is removed, together with the gaskets and shims — 2. 3 Rocker shaft support bush. 4 Rocker shaft.

3. From inside the vehicle, remove the centre ornament by prising it upwards from the centre of the steering wheel, bend back the locating tabs around the centre nut, unscrew the nut and remove it together with the tab washer.

4. Pull off the steering wheel with a puller tool and with this away unscrew the two screws securing the direction indicator and horn switch assembly to the steering column and remove the switch but leave the wiring connected.

5. Remove the two screws securing the dip switch to the column.

6. Unscrew the two screws securing the steering column bracket to the parcels tray and remove the bracket.

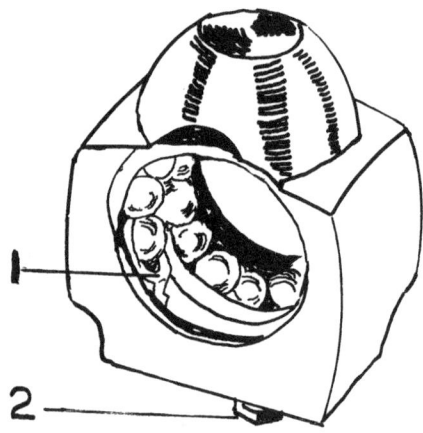

Fig. 11:9 The steering nut assembly showing the ball transfer tube — 1 — and the transfer tube clamp bolt at — 2.

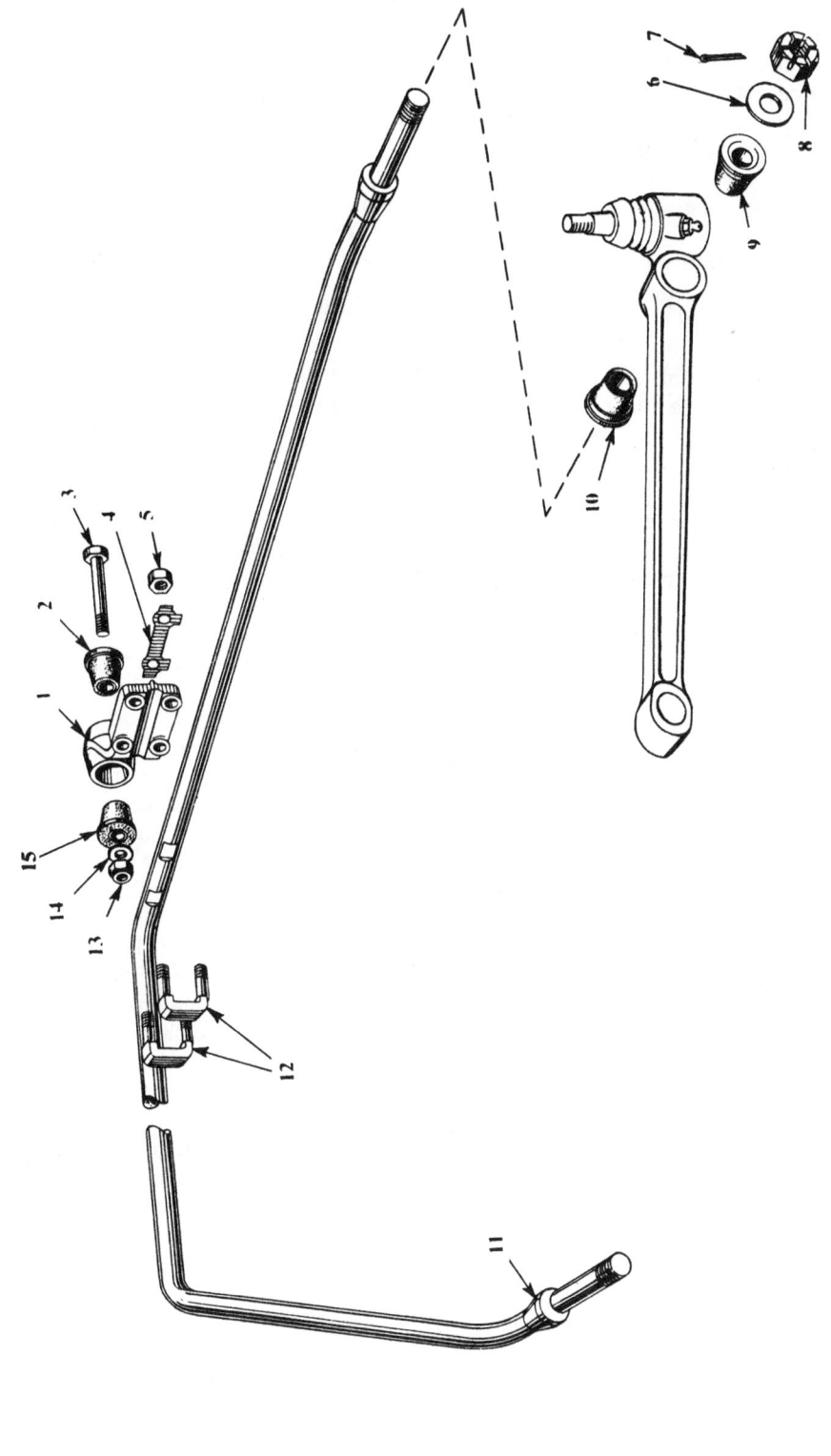

Fig. 11:10 THE COMPONENTS COMPRISING THE ANTI-ROLL BAR ASSEMBLY.

1 Anti-roll bar attachment foot.   2 Bush.   3 Bolt.   4 Tab lockwasher.   5 Nut.   6 Washer.   7 Split pin.   8 Castellated nut.   9 Bush.   10 Bush.   11 Anti-roll bar.   12 Attachment foot clips.   13 Nut.   14 Washer.   15 Bush.

157

7. Next remove the two screws which secure the column upper mounting to the fascia panel, and also the screws holding the cover plate and draught excluder to the floor.

8. The car should now be jacked up securely and then the drop idler arm is removed by taking out the split pin from the castle nut and by using the special tool to separate the joint.

9. The track rod is then disconnected from the drop arm, followed by the idler arm bracket which is removed from the underside of the body.

10. Next remove the track rod. In the case of major overhaul where the engine has already been lifted away, it is only necessary to disconnect the rod on the steering box side.

11. Remove the three bolts securing the steering box to the body member, noting that two of these bolts secure the top bracket in position, and then lift the steering gear away from underneath the vehicle.

12. STEERING GEAR - DISMANTLING

1. If the steering gear has been removed in order to overhaul and take up excessive play caused by worn parts, the method of dismantling is straightforward, but requires a number of special tools mainly to handle the bushes.

2. Remove the drop arm using a puller, and then remove the rubber filler plug and drain away the lubricating oil.

3. Unscrew the bolts securing the steering rocker shaft spring.

4. Unscrew the two set screws and the two bolts, nuts and spring washers from the cover plate and remove the plate together with the gaskets and shims, taking care to keep these all together.

5. By removing the four bolts securing the end plate on the steering box this can be lifted away together with gaskets and shims which again must be kept together.

6. Now withdraw the direction indicator cam from the steering shaft, and then partially remove the shaft from its housing by screwing it downwards through the nut in order to displace a spacing washer and the lower bearing assembly.

7. During this operation the ten balls in the upper bearing will be displaced, and as the lower cup from the bearing is eased away, a further ten ball bearings will fall out.

8. It is therefore necessary to spread rag around the area during this dismantling in order to keep the loose balls together.

9. The steering shaft is now completely removed by being screwed right through the steering nut, and it will be found that there are thirty balls inside the nut.

10. The rocker shaft can now be lifted away from the steering box together with the nut, and the shaft upper bearing cup.

11. In order to withdraw the rocker shaft bushes if these are worn and need replacement, it is necessary to use a puller tool after the oil seal has been levered out.

13. STEERING GEAR - REASSEMBLY & REPLACEMENT

1. Before starting reassembly the new steering shaft upper support bush which is made of felt should be well soaked in heavy grease for an hour or so, and then installed into the upper end of the steering tube close up to the retainer.

2. If the rocker bushes have been removed to make way for new ones, these should be installed, and the one fitted to the steering gear housing will need to be broached out, once it is firmly in position.

3. Once the flanged bush has been pushed squarely in position, it should be burred over slightly to retain its position, but as this bush is presized, it is important not to damage the working surface.

4. Once the bushes have been assembled the whole box must be well washed to remove any swarf and loose metal.

5. When the new oil seal is fitted in the housing the sharp edge of the seal must be towards the steering box.

6. The steering shaft upper bearing cup must be pressed home squarely, and then grease applied to the centre of the nut in order to hold the thirty balls in position.

7. The nut can be assembled either way round and to do this, pass the shaft through the steering box and rotate the shaft to accept the screw in the nut.

8. Now turn the assembly over and retain the shaft about half an inch above the upper bearing cup while the ten balls are fitted.

9. With these in position push the steering shaft home so that the upper bearing will be kept in place.

10. Now grease the lower bearing cup and locate the ten balls into this and then fit into the steering box with the thick spacing washer in its correct location against the lower bearing cup.

11. Now the steering shaft bearing adjustment detailed later and the adjustments to the rocker shaft end float can be carried out,

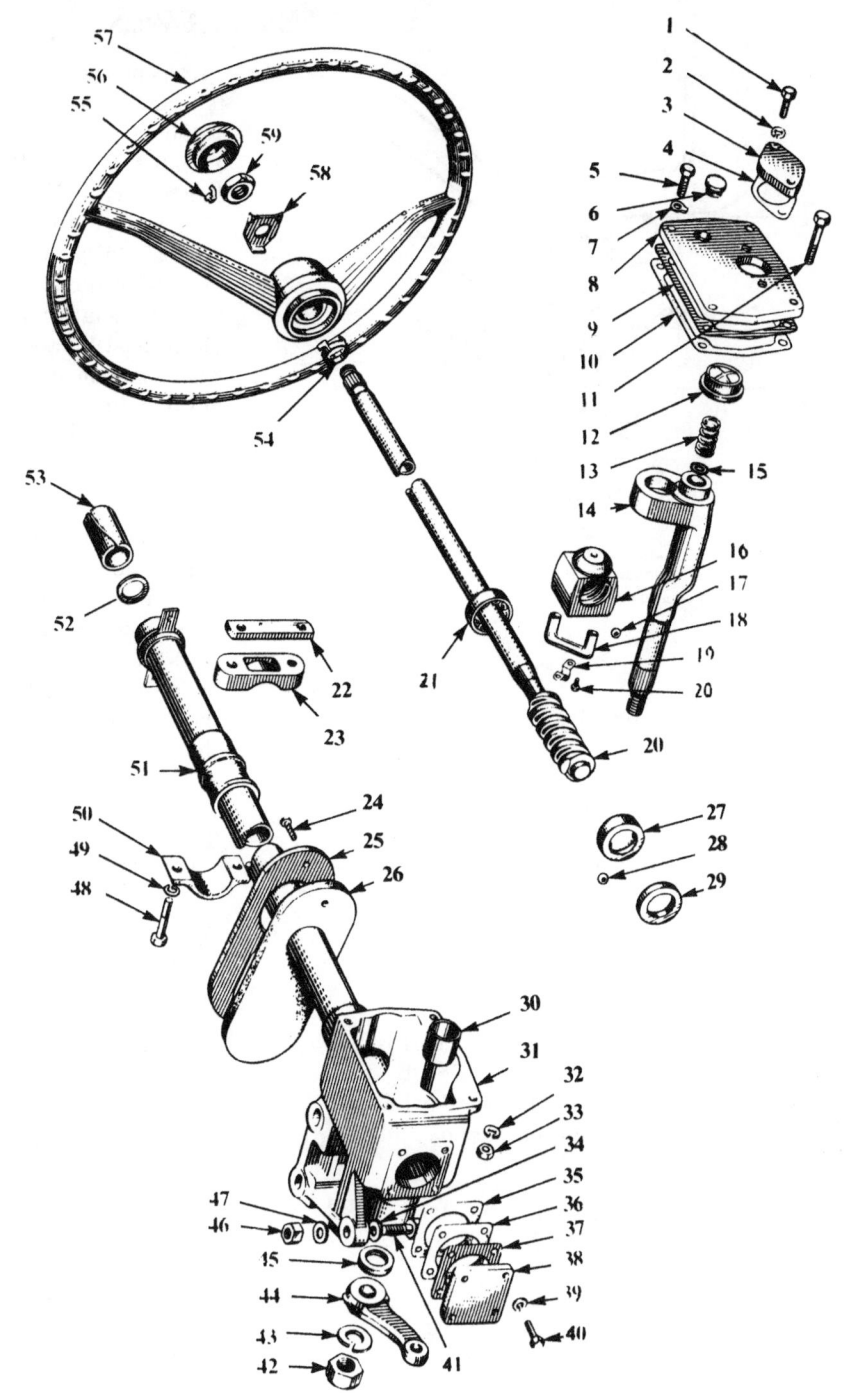

Fig. 11:11 EXPLODED VIEW OF THE WORM AND NUT STEERING GEAR.

1 Bolt.   2 Spring washer.   3 Top outer cover.   4 Gasket.   5 Bolt.   6 Oil filler plug.   7 Tab washer.   8 Steering gear cover.
9 Shim.   10 Gasket.   11 Bolt.   12 Rocker shaft upper bush.   13 Spring.   14 Rocker shaft.   15 Washer.   16 Steering nut.
17 Steering ball.   18 Ball transfer tube.   19 Transfer tube securing clip.   20 Clip screw.   20A Steering shaft worm.   21 Cup.
22 Steering column bracket plate.   23 Steering column mounting bracket.   24 Screw.   25 Steering cover opening, securing plate.
26 Pad.   27 Steering gear shaft bearing cup.   28 Ball bearing.   29 Washer.   30 Bush.   31 Steering box casing.   32 Spring washer.
33 Nut.   34 Washer.   35 End plate gasket.   36 End plate shim.   37 End plate gasket.   38 End plate.   39 Spring washer.
40 Bolt.   41 Steering box to sidemember bolt.   42 Nut.   43 Spring washer.   44 Steering drop arm.   45 Rocker shaft seal.
46 Nut.   47 Spring washer.   48 Column securing bolt.   49 Spring washer.   50 Column clamp.   51 Steering column mounting
bracket bush.   52 Bush retaining washer.   53 Steering gear shaft bush.   54 Direction indicator turn cam.   55 Emblem retaining
clip.   56 Emblem.   57 Steering wheel.   58 Steering wheel nut retaining washer.   59 Retaining nut.

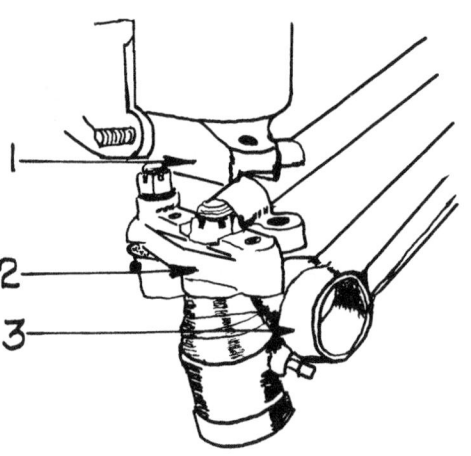

Fig. 11:12 The location of the steering arm at the base of the suspension unit foot.   1 Suspension unit foot.   2 Steering arm.   3 Track control arm.

thus completing the steering box assembly and adjustment.

12. Fit the drop arm to the rocker shaft, and then with the steering gear in the straight ahead position locate the drop arm on the shaft splines so that it is parallel with the steering shaft. Fit a spring washer and the large nut and tighten securely.

13. Replacement is a straight forward reversal of the removal sequence.

14. STEERING SHAFT BEARING ADJUSTMENT

1. This adjustment is controlled by the gaskets and shims located at the lower end of the steering box between the box and the end plate.

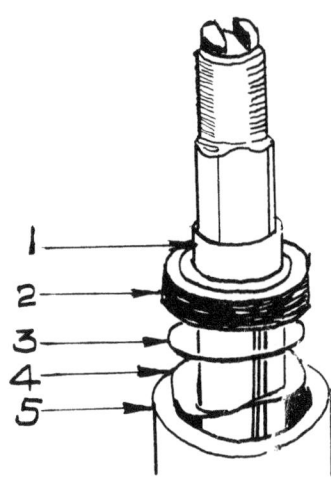

Fig. 11:13 Upper Gland Seal Assembly.   1 Piston rod.   2 Gland.   3 Gland seat.   4 Wave spring.   5 Upper guide.

2. Fit a paper gasket against the steering box face and locate the set of shims originally removed, and then fit a second gasket. Locate the end plate in its correct position loosely with the four bolts and rotate the shaft while at the same time tightening each bolt carefully and in such a manner that any binding of the shaft will be felt at once. If this happens it will indicate that a further shim must be added.

3. The shaft should be free to rotate without any end-float, and the trial of shims should continue until this condition is attained.

15. STEERING BOX - ROCKER SHAFT ADJUSTMENT

1. The amount of end-float will be set by varying the thickness of the gaskets and shims located between the steering gear housing and the top cover plate.

2. With the cover removed, turn the steering on either lock until the hole in the end of the rocker shaft and the hole in the cone on the nut are concentric. This is best checked with the aid of an indicator dial gauge which will indicate a minimum reading. The shaft end-float should be between 0.003" (0.076 mm.) and 0.006" (0.152 mm.)

3. If these figures cannot be obtained, adjustment of the shim thickness will give the correct float with the cover bolted down tightly.

4. Turn the steering wheel slowly from lock to lock in order to check that there is no binding at any point.

5. It will be found that the steering gear will be slightly tighter at the extreme of each lock than it is in the central position.

6. If this adjustment is being carried out when the steering gear has not been dismantled it is important to check the steering shaft bearing adjustment first before proceeding with the end-float adjustment.

7. Toe in should be between 1/16 to 1/8th. in.

16. REAR DAMPERS - REMOVAL & REPLACEMENT

1. It is not necessary to jack up the rear of the car for removal of the rear dampers if a pit or ramp is available. Otherwise jack up, and firmly support the rear of the car.

2. To remove a damper unscrew the nut and spring washer from the bolt which holds the damper arm to the link arm; remove the two nuts and spring washers from the damper securing bolts and remove the bolts; thread the lever over the link arm bolt and so remove the damper.

3. Keep the damper upright to prevent air getting into the operating chamber. Reassembly is a straight reversal of the removal procedure.

REAR SEMI-ELLIPTIC SPRINGS - REMOVAL & REPLACEMENT

1. Jack up the rear body of the car and support it on suitable stands. Then place a further jack underneath the differential to give support to the rear axle when the springs are removed. Do not raise the jack under the differential so that the springs are flattened, but raise the jack just sufficiently to take the full weight of the axle with the springs in the fully extended position.

2. The rear of each spring is supported by a shackle while the front is fixed to a hanger bracket. Remove the rear shackle nuts, pins, and plates, the front bracket through bolts and the check stop (where fitted). Undo the four nuts from each set of 2 'U' bolts at either end of the axle and lift away the springs. When refitting the rear springs make certain that the U bolts are in the correct position. See Chapter 8/2.10.

CHAPTER TWELVE

BODYWORK AND UNDERFRAME

CONTENTS

1. GENERAL DESCRIPTION

The combined body and underframe is of all steel welded construction. This makes a very strong and torsionaly rigid shell. Two doors are fitted with hinges at the front and door stops. Push button handles work rotary locks. On the passenger's side the door is locked from the inside and on the driver's from the outside. Forward hinging quarter lights are fitted at the front and are held shut by push button catches. The windows in the doors wind down completely.

The windscreen is of safety glass and is curved, and the rear window is flat with a reverse rake.

The standard Anglia has a small painted radiator grille with horizontal slats, while the Anglia De Luxe has a full width chromium plated mesh grille.

Other differences between the standard and De Luxe models are that on the latter the rear windows open. The tail light trims and windshield wiper arms are of bright metal. Padded arm rests are fitted to the doors which are covered in a two tone PVC trim as are the seats. The glove box is lockable and twin sun visors are fitted. In addition two ash trays are fitted at the rear.

Inside both models two bucket type seats are fitted at the front and a bench rear seat with PVC upholstery. Rubber mats are fitted front and rear and the PVC headlining is washable. A full width parcels shelf extends across the car under the facia.

2. MAINTENANCE - BODYWORK & UNDER — FRAME

1. The condition of your car's bodywork is of considerable importance as it is on this that the second hand value of the car will mainly depend. It is very much more difficult to repair neglected bodywork than to renew mechanical assemblies. The hidden portions of the body, such as the wheel arches and the underframe and the engine compartment are equally important, though obviously not requiring such frequent attention as the immediately visible paintwork.

2. Once a year or every 12,000 miles, it is a sound scheme to visit your local main agent and have the underside of the body steam cleaned. This will take about $1\frac{1}{2}$ hours and costs about £3. All traces of dirt and oil will be removed and the underside can then be inspected carefully for rust, damaged hydraulic pipes, frayed electrical wiring and similar maladies. The car should be greased on completion of this job.

3. At the same time the engine compartment should be cleaned in the same manner. If steam cleaning facilities are not available then brush 'Gunk' or a similar cleanser over the whole engine and engine compartment with a stiff paint brush, working it well in where there is an accumulation of oil and dirt. Do not paint the ignition system and protect it with oily rags when the 'Gunk' is washed off. As the 'Gunk' is

163

washed away it will take with it all traces of oil and dirt, leaving the engine looking clean and bright.

4. The wheel arches should be given particular attention as undersealing can easily come away here and stones and dirt thrown up from the road wheels can soon cause the paint to chip and flake, and so allow rust to set in. If rust is found, clean down to the bare metal with wet and dry paper, paint on an anti-corrosive coating such as 'Kurust', or if preferred, red lead, and renew the paintwork and undercoating.

5. The bodywork should be washed once a week or when dirty. Thoroughly wet the car to soften the dirt and then wash the car down with a soft sponge and plenty of clean water. If the surplus dirt is not washed off very gently, in time it will wear the paint down as surely as wet and dry paper. It is best to use a hose if this is available. Give the car a final washdown and then dry with a soft chamois leather to prevent the formation of spots.

6. Spots of tar and grease thrown up from the road can be removed with a rag moistened with petrol.

7. Once every six months, or every three months if wished, give the bodywork and chromium trim a thoroughly good wax polish. If a chromium cleaner is used to remove rust on any of the car's plated parts remember that the cleaner also removes part of the chromium, so use sparingly.

3. MAINTENANCE - UPHOLSTERY & CARPETS

Remove the carpets and thoroughly clean the interior of the car every three months, or more frequently if necessary. Beat out the carpets and vacuum clean them if they are very dirty. If the headlining or upholstery is soiled apply an upholstery cleaner with a damp sponge and wipe off with a clean dry cloth.

4. MINOR BODY REPAIRS

1. At some time during your ownership of your car it is likely that it will be bumped or scraped in a mild way, causing some slight damage to the body. Major damage must be repaired by your local Ford agent, but there is no reason why you cannot successfully beat out, repair, and respray minor damage yourself. The essential items which the owner should gather together to ensure a really professional job are:-
a) A plastic filler such as Holt's 'Cataloy'.
b) Paint whose colour matches exactly that of the bodywork, either in a can for application by a spray gun, or in an aerosol can.

c) Fine cutting paste.
d) Medium and fine grade wet and dry paper. Never use a metal hammer to knock out small dents as the blows tend to scratch and distort the metal. Knock out the dent with a mallet or rawhide hammer and press on the underside of the dented surface a metal dolly or smooth wooden block roughly contoured to the normal shape of the damaged area.

2. After the worst of the damaged area has been knocked out, rub down the dent and surrounding area with medium wet and dry paper and thoroughly clean away all traces of dirt.

3. The plastic filler comprises a paste and a hardener which must be thoroughly mixed together. Mix only a small portion at a time as the paste sets hard within five to fifteen minutes depending on the amount of hardener used.

4. Smooth on the filler with a knife or stiff plastic to the shape of the damaged portion and allow to thoroughly dry - a process which takes about six hours. After the filler has dried it is likely that it will have contracted slightly so spread on a second layer of filler if necessary.

5. Smooth down the filler with fine wet and dry paper wrapped round a suitable block of wood and continue until the whole area is perfectly smooth and it is impossible to feel where the filler joins the rest of the paintwork. Spray on from an aerosol can, or with a spray gun, an anti-rust undercoat, smooth down with wet and dry paper, and then spray on two coats of the final finishing using a circular motion. When thoroughly dry polish the whole area with a fine cutting paste to smooth the resprayed area into the remainder of the wing and to remove the small particles of spray paint which will have settled round the area. This will leave the wing looking perfect with not a trace of the previous unsightly dent.

5. MAJOR BODY REPAIRS

1. Because the body is built on the monocoque principle and is integral with the underframe, major damage must be repaired by competent mechanics with the necessary welding and hydraulic straightening equipment.

2. If the damage is serious it is vital that the bodyshell is in correct alignment, as otherwise the handling of the car will suffer and many other faults such as excessive tyre wear, and wear in the transmission and steering, may occur.

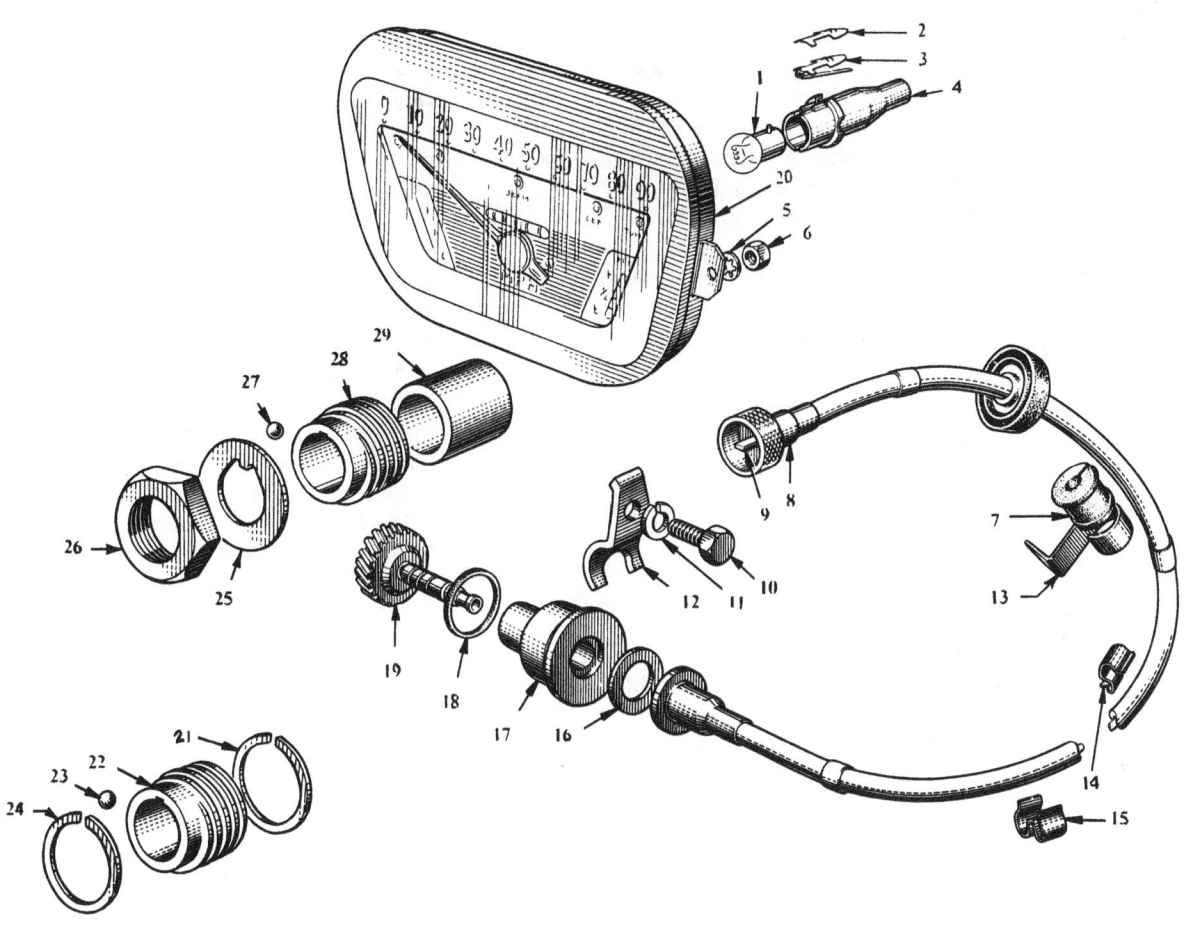

Fig. 12:1 EXPLODED VIEW OF THE SPEEDOMETER AND DRIVE COMPONENTS.

1 Bulb.   2 Lucas clip.   3 Lucas clip.   4 Bulb holder.   5 Star washer.   6 Nut.   7 Grommet.   8 Outer cable.   9 Inner cable.
10 Bolt.   11 Spring washer.   12 Clip.   13 Locating clip.   14 Clip.   15 Clip.   16 Washer.   17 Driven gear bearing.   18 Washer
seal.   19 Speedometer driven gear.   20 Speedometer head.   21 Circlip.   22 Worm gear.   23 Ball.   24 Circlip.   25 Washer
— alternative.   26 Nut — alternative.   27 Ball.   28 Worm gear.   29 Spacer.

6. MAINTENANCE - HINGES, LOCKS & DOORS

1. Once every six months or 5,000 miles the door, bonnet, and boot hinges should be oiled with a few drops of engine oil from an oil can. The door striker plates can be given a thin smear of grease to reduce wear and ensure free movement.

2. At the same mileage probe the drain holes in the bottom edge of each door to make certain there is nothing blocking them. If they become obstructed water will collect inside and will cause rust to begin, which in serious cases can eat right through the metal.

7. DOOR STRIKER PLATES - ADJUSTMENT, REMOVAL & REPLACEMENT

1. After high mileages wear on the door hinges, lock and striker plates may give rise to rattles and slight difficulty in opening and closing.

2. To check if the striker plates need adjustment close each door in turn and then push and pull on the handles. If there is any movement then the set screws, holding the plate in place, must be loosened slightly and the striker plate moved inwards.

3. Tighten the set screws and try closing the door. If there is still slight movement, move the striker plate in even further.

4. Conversely, if the door is very difficult to shut then move the striker plate slightly outwards.

5. If the striker plate becomes worn and it is wished to replace it, first mark its position on the door pillar so that the new plate can be fixed in the correct position. Unscrew the set screws holding the plate to the door pillar and lift the plate away. Replacement is a direct reversal of the removal process.

8. WINDSCREEN - REMOVAL & REPLACEMENT

1. If it is wished to renew the rubber seal round the windscreen or to fit a new windscreen glass first cover the bonnet with a thick blanket. Then lift the wiper blades off their splined spindles.

2. Carefully take off the two joint cover clips and then prise the bright metal mouldings from the groove in the rubber windscreen seal.

3. Unscrew the two Phillips screws holding the rear mirror in place and then run a blunt tool such as a screwdriver round the top half of the windscreen from inside the car, forcing the rubber lip outside the body

flange. When this has been done support the outside area of the glass and hit the inside top area of the glass smartly with the palm of your hand. The windscreen glass complete with rubber surround should come out easily when hit. If difficulty is experienced then free more of the rubber lip.

4. Replacement commences by fitting the windscreen glass to the inner channel of the weatherstrip. Start at one end of the glass and carefully work the weatherstrip into position.

5. The next step is to thread two pieces of string round the outer channel of the weatherstrip. The windscreen complete with weatherstrip, is fitted to the body from outside the car. Press the windscreen and weatherstrip against the windscreen body frame. Pull out the string from the inside of the weatherstrip, and then from the outside. As the string is pulled away the rubber weatherstrip will peel over the windscreen body flange, so holding the windscreen firmly to the body.

6. With the windscreen properly in position coat a suitable adhesive between the weatherstrip rubber and the windscreen, and the weatherstrip rubber and the body on the outside of the car. This will seal the windscreen and ensure no leaks develope.

9. DOOR TRIM PANELS & INTERIOR HANDLES - REMOVAL & REPLACEMENT

1. To remove the interior handles unscrew the single screw which holds the centre of each handle to the door handle shaft. Remove the handles and escutcheon plates.

2. Where fitted undo the two Phillips screws which hold the door pull to the door and then carefully lever the trim panel away.

3. Replacement is a straightforward reversal of the removal sequence. Remember to fit a shakeproof washer under the head of each of the handle securing screws.

10. DOOR LOCKS - REMOVAL & REPLACEMENT

1. Follow the instructions in Chapter 12/9. Then refit the lock remote control handle without inserting the securing screw and operate the handle. Free the control rod from the lock.

2. Free the door glass rear channel and then undo the screws which hold the lock assembly in place. The assembly can then be removed from the inner frame of the door.

3. Replacement is a straightforward reversal of the removal sequence.

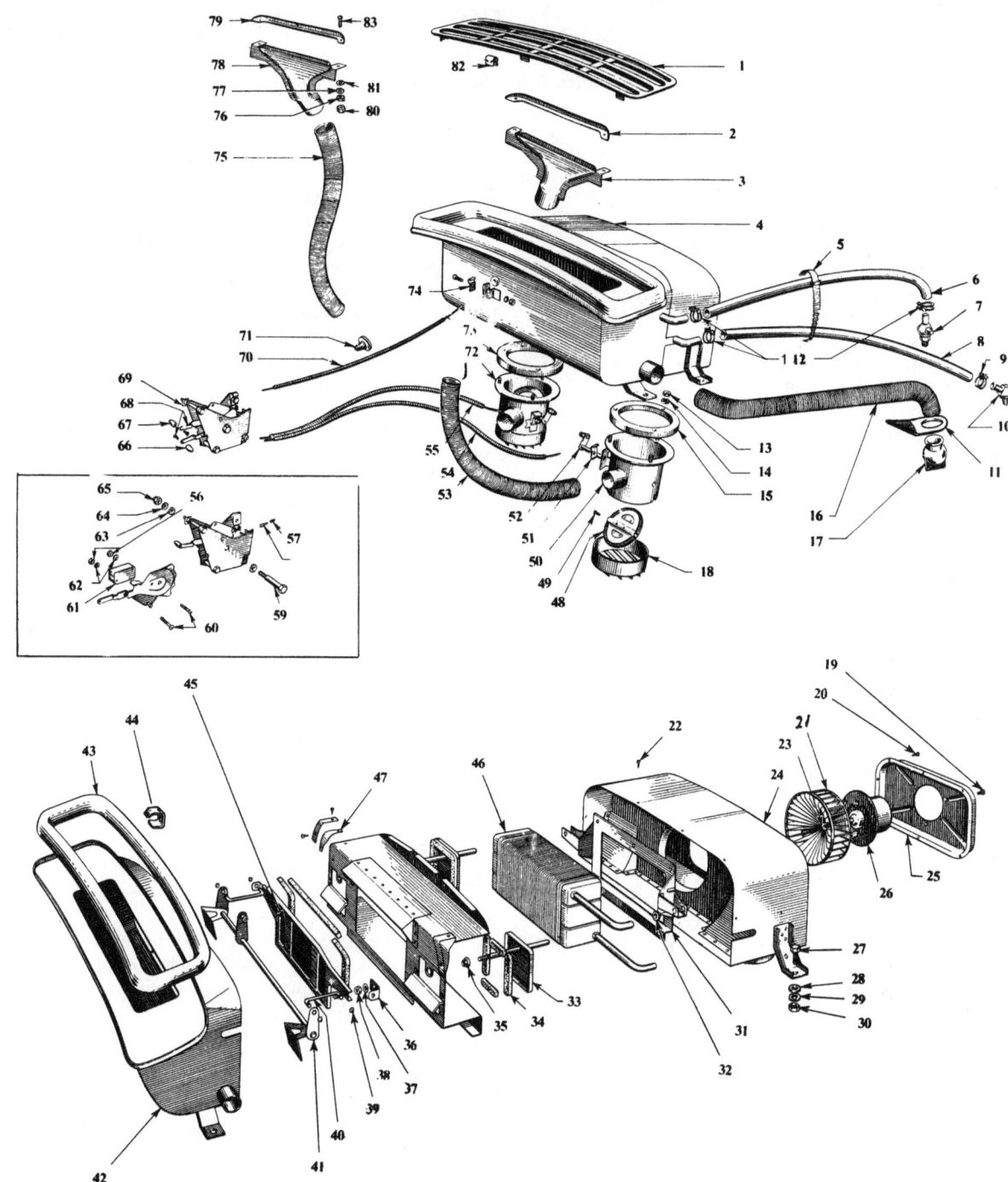

Fig. 12:2 EXPLODED VIEW OF THE HEATER AND HEATER CONTROLS.

1 Air intake grille.   2 Demister nozzle shroud.   3 Demister nozzle.   4 Heater unit assembly.   5 Clip.   6 Water hose.   7 Two way valve.   8 Heater hose pipe.   9 Hose clip.   10 Heater hose to water pump adaptor.   11 Bracket.   12 Hose clips.   13 Nut. 14 Spring washer.   15 Seal.   16 Tube.   17 Tube end cover.   18 Air deflector.   19 Screw.   20 Screw.   21 Heater motor fan. 22 Screw.   23 Spindle.   24 Heater unit case.   25 Heater motor mounting plate.   26 Heater motor.   27 Bolt.   28 Washer. 29 Spring washer.   30 Nut.   31 Radiator retaining plate.   32 Hot and cold air valve bush.   33 Cold air valve.   34 Cold air seal. 35 Hot and cold air valve bush.   36 Link bracket.   37 Washer.   38 Nut.   39 Lever to link retaining clip.   40 Link.   41 Air valve temperature lever.   42 Plenum chamber.   43 Seal.   44 Clip.   45 Hot air control valve.   46 Heater radiator.   47 Securing bracket.   48 valve.   49 Screw.   50 Air and Demister valve box.   51 Heater and fresh air duct cabler clamp.   52 Pivot.   53 Air tube.   54 Air and Demister valve control cable.   55 Air and Demister valve control cable.   56 Nut.   57 Control plunger spring. 58 Plunger.   59 Control panel pivot bolt.   60 Screws.   61 On/Off heater switch.   62 Lockwashers.   63 Double coil lockwashers. 64 Washer.   65 Nut.   66 Temperature control knob.   67 Temperature control knob.   68 Control levers.   69 Temperature control assembly.   70 Cable control.   71 Cable grommet.   72 Air and Demister valve box.   73 Seal.   74 Clip.   75 Air tube to demister.   76 Nut.   77 Washer.   78 Demister nozzle.   79 Demister nozzle shroud.   80 Nut.   81 Washer.   82 Clip.   83 Screw.

INDEX

INDEX

INDEX

Zeitfracht Medien GmbH
Ferdinand-Jühlke-Straße 7
99095 Erfurt, Deutschland
produktsicherheit@kolibri360.de